D1546433

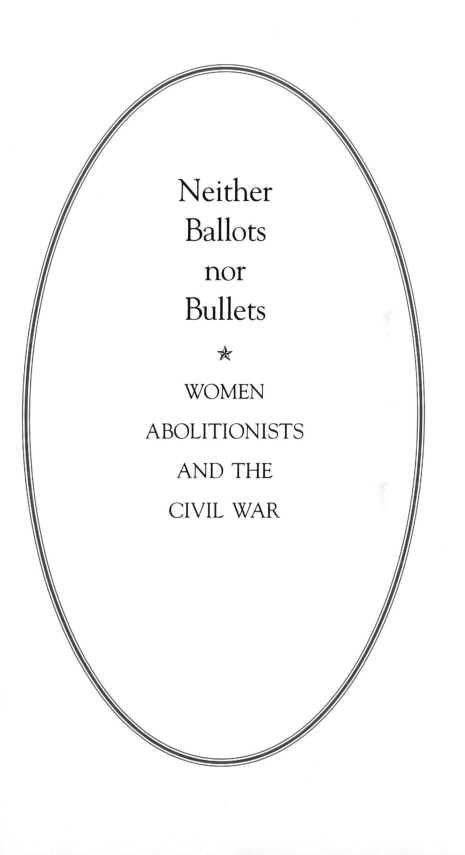

Neither Ballots nor Bullets

✸

WOMEN ABOLITIONISTS AND THE CIVIL WAR

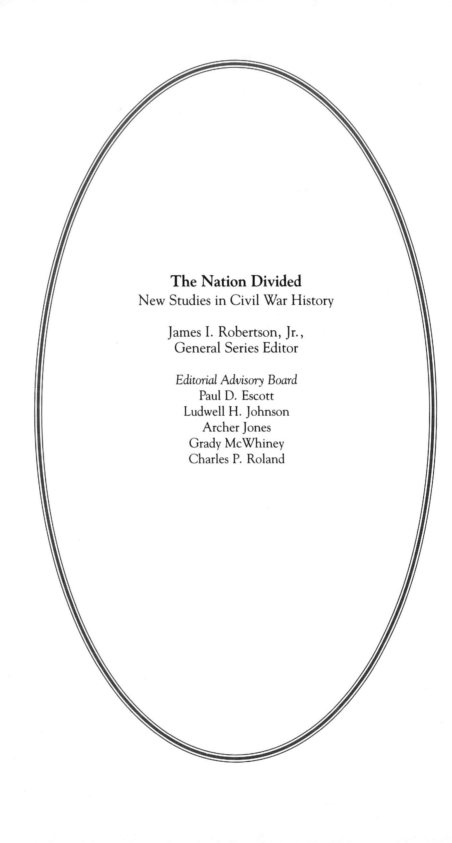

Neither
BALLOTS
nor
BULLETS

WOMEN ABOLITIONISTS
AND THE CIVIL WAR

WENDY HAMAND VENET

University Press of Virginia
Charlottesville & London

THE UNIVERSITY PRESS OF VIRGINIA
Copyright © 1991 by the Rector and Visitors
of the University of Virginia

First published 1991

Library of Congress Cataloging-in-Publication Data
Venet, Wendy Hamand.
    Neither ballots nor bullets : women abolitionists and the Civil
War / Wendy Hamand Venet.
        p.   cm. — (The Nation divided)
    Includes bibliographical references and index.
    ISBN 0-8139-1342-X (cloth)
    1. United States—History—Civil War, 1861–1865—Women.   2. Women
abolitionists—United States—History—19th century.   I. Title.
II. Series.
E628.V46   1991
973.7′15042—dc20   91-12421
                                                                                    CIP

Printed in the United States of America

For Allen

Contents

Illustrations

following page 56

Elizabeth Cady Stanton and her daughter Harriot
Susan B. Anthony
Anna Dickinson
One of Anna Dickinson's oratorical rivals
Hannah Tracy Cutler
Sarah Parker Remond
Harriet Beecher Stowe
Fanny Kemble
Lydia Maria Child
Julia Ward Howe
Ellen Wright and her brothers
Wendell Phillips
Charles Sumner
William Lloyd Garrison and his daughter Fanny Garrison Villard
Broadside of the Woman's National Loyal League

Preface

"The story of the [Civil] War will never be fully written if the achievements of women are left untold." Elizabeth Cady Stanton wrote these words in her autobiography, published in 1898. Women "do not figure in the official reports," Stanton continued; "they are not gazetted for gallant deeds; the names of thousands are unknown beyond the neighborhood where they lived, or the hospitals where they loved to labor." And yet, Stanton concluded, "there is no feature of our War more creditable to us as a nation, none from its positive newness so well worthy of record."

During Stanton's own lifetime, several writers published books extolling the virtues of women's patriotism. L. P. Brockett and Mary C. Vaughan wrote *Woman's Work in the Civil War: A Record of Heroism, Patriotism, and Patience*, in which they focused on charitable and nursing work and estimated there were ten thousand soldier's aid societies in the North during the Civil War. Twentieth-century scholars have written at length about women's relief work: local bandage-rolling groups, fund-raising fairs, even Dorothea Dix's legendary nurses.

The prewar antislavery movement has inspired dozens of authors to write books about the abolitionists' lives, goals, tactics, and philosophical differences. James M. McPherson's important work *The Struggle for Equality* carries the story through the Civil War, though its breadth of topic precludes a thorough analysis of women's role. *Crusade for Freedom* by Alma Lutz and *The Slavery of Sex* by Blanche Hersh provide valuable insights about women abolitionists but concern their Civil War activities only tangentially. Ellen Carol DuBois has investigated the interplay between the abolition and woman's rights movements in her pathbreaking book *Feminism and Suffrage*. DuBois's principal concern is the period 1865–69, and especially the chain of events that inspired women to sever their ties to antislavery and form an independent feminist movement.

By contrast, this monograph focuses on the Civil War and the activities of an important group of women who directed their efforts toward the political and constitutional struggle to end slavery. Most of these women were white and middle-class. While many black and white abolitionists devoted their wartime efforts to the vitally important work of feeding, housing, and schooling the freedmen—and in working together forged important interracial bonds—this book is not their story.

Politically active women worked for abolition by attempting to sway public opinion during the war. Their philosophical and tactical approaches varied greatly. Quaker teenager Anna Dickinson gave impassioned speeches, earning the title of abolition's Joan of Arc. Poet Julia Ward Howe wrote the most stirring verses of the war. Actress Fanny Kemble and novelist Harriet Beecher Stowe wrote manifestos designed to promote abolition in America and support for the Union cause in England. Collectively women founded the Woman's National Loyal League. By gathering signatures on a "mammoth petition," league members helped win public support for abolition and congressional support for constitutional emancipation. Their work also would have significant implications for the late nineteenth-century feminist movement. In focusing on these themes, I hope this book will fill a significant historiographical gap in the literature of the abolition movement, the Civil War, and nineteenth-century feminism.

Portions of this book have been published as articles. " 'No Voice from England': Mrs. Stowe, Mr. Lincoln, and the English in the Civil War," *New England Quarterly* 61 (March 1988): 3–24, is reprinted with the permission of the *New England Quarterly*. "The Woman's National Loyal League: Feminist Abolitionists and the Civil War," *Civil War History* 35 (March 1989): 39–58, is reprinted by permission of the Kent State University Press.

Many people have assisted me both in research and writing. Since this project began as a doctoral dissertation at the University of Illinois, Urbana-Champaign, my first thanks go to my dissertation adviser, Robert W. Johannsen, who taught me a great deal about the craft of history and the complexities of Abraham Lincoln and has continued to serve as a mentor and role model. Since accepting a teaching appointment at Eastern Illinois University, I have enjoyed the support of many wonderful colleagues and owe a special debt to the Council for Faculty Research at Eastern for supporting my work with two summer stipends. Several graduate students have helped me with library research: Peggy McGill, Delores Archaimbault, Jim Watson, and Tim Jaeger.

Dozens of librarians have assisted me over the years. My special thanks go to the reference and interlibrary loan departments of the University of Illinois and Eastern Illinois University libraries. Librarians at the Newberry Library in Chicago were most helpful in my research in the women's periodical press, and I am also grateful to the staff of the British Newspaper Library in Colindale, suburban London, for their helpfulness toward visiting scholars and their fondness for "Mrs. Beecher Stowe."

I would also like to offer my thanks to manuscript librarians of the American Antiquarian Society, the Boston Public Library, the Butler Library of Columbia University, the Chicago Historical Society, the Cornell University Library, the Essex Institute, the Historical Society of Pennsylvania, the Houghton Library at Harvard, the Henry E. Huntington Library, the Library of Congress, the Massachusetts Historical Society, the National Archives, the Rochester University Library, the Schlesinger Library at Radcliffe, the Sophia Smith Collection at Smith College, the Stowe-Day Library in Hartford, the University of Virginia Library, and the Vassar College Library. I am especially grateful to Marianne Roos of the Library of Congress, David Kepley of the National Archives, and Ellen Oldham of the Boston Public Library.

I received letters of encouragement and support from Rhoda Barney Jenkins, great-granddaughter of Elizabeth Cady Stanton, and David Lloyd Garrison, great-grandson of William Lloyd Garrison and grandson of Ellen Wright Garrison. I am grateful to each for granting me permission to quote from the speeches and correspondence of their famous ancestors.

Elizabeth Fox-Genovese read the entire manuscript and offered insightful comments. Her views helped to shape my thinking about women's sphere and political activism. This is a better book because of her efforts. Bud Robertson, editor of the series, reviewed the manuscript with a critical eye and helped to shape my thinking on military issues. Several friends and colleagues read all or part of the manuscript—a special thanks to Jeffrey Brown, Lynn Campbell, and Evelyn Boyd Bohac.

No author could ask for a greater degree of support than I have received from the staff of the University Press of Virginia. John McGuigan believed in this project from the beginning and told me so. Through missed deadlines and computer printer glitches, he has been a persistent and understanding editor.

Lastly, I want to thank my family, whose support has sustained me through the many years in which I worked on this project both as dissertation and book. My deepest appreciation goes to my parents, who first instilled in me a love of history and respect for the English language, and to my husband, who planned family vacations around research trips, listened to unending analyses and anecdotes about women abolitionists, and offered support and encouragement when I needed it most.

Neither
Ballots
nor
Bullets

WOMEN
ABOLITIONISTS
AND THE
CIVIL WAR

The Prewar Abolition Movement

Abolitionists are the people's conscience.
—Susan B. Anthony, 4th of July Address,
Framingham, Massachusetts, 1862

On 14 May 1863 a crowd of delegates gathered at the Church of the Puritans in New York City to inaugurate a new organization, the Woman's National Loyal League. Officers of this new organization represented the states of New York, New Jersey, Pennsylvania, Connecticut, Massachusetts, Maine, Wisconsin, and California. They included the most important feminist abolitionists in the nation: Elizabeth Cady Stanton, who helped to launch the feminist movement in 1848; Susan Anthony, whose dedication as a reformer was second to none; Lucy Stone, considered by some the most eloquent of women orators; Angelina Grimké Weld, the pioneering abolitionist and first woman ever to address a state legislature; Antoinette Brown Blackwell, one of the nation's first ordained female ministers; Ernestine Potowski Rose, a Polish Jewish immigrant of extraordinary intellect; Martha Coffin Wright, a veteran of the first woman's rights convention in Seneca Falls and a younger sister of Lucretia Coffin Mott; and Amy Kirby Post, an upstate New York activist.

Together they would inaugurate the most successful petition drive in the history of the abolition movement. Their efforts would add several hundred thousand voices to the congressional movement toward passage of a constitutional amendment to end slavery. Equally significant, their organization would be the first national feminist network, with members in all the Union states. Through their efforts as abolitionists, they would attempt to raise the feminist consciousness of all American women. They were unable to play a direct political or military role in the war, neither voting in elections nor fighting on the battlefield; the right of petition was one of the few tools through which they could express themselves in the public sphere. At the American Anti-Slavery Society's third decade meeting in 1863, Susan Anthony expressed the sentiments of activist women when she declared, "Women can neither take the ballot nor the bullet . . .

therefore to us, the right to petition is the one sacred right which we ought not to neglect."[1]

Their efforts would draw several hundred thousand women into the political realm as petition signers and a significant number as lecturers, organizers, and agitators. They would gain stature and confidence as public figures and would gain surprising public acceptance for their work. They would realize once and for all that the moral suasion which characterized antebellum reform must give way to political activism. They would learn, some of them more readily than others, that the alliances, tactics, and strategies of the antebellum years must give way to the new feminism of the postbellum era. The antislavery movement had given many of America's first-wave feminists their political beginnings. The Civil War marked both the pinnacle of women's abolitionist contributions and the end of a once fruitful relationship.

Women were involved in abolitionism from its earliest days as an organized movement. In the 1820s Elizabeth Chandler, an idealistic young Quaker, began contributing articles to Benjamin Lundy's colonizationist newspaper *The Genius of Universal Emancipation*. Impressed by Chandler's skill as a writer, Lundy appointed her editor of the "Ladies Repository" section of the paper. Elizabeth Chandler was so discreet that she did not allow her name to appear in print, but her importance as a role model for later women abolitionists has been recognized by several historians, including Alma Lutz and Blanche Hersh. Chandler's essays and poems were frequently recited in abolition meetings; through her "Ladies Repository" column she continually emphasized that women, as moral arbiters of the home, had a special place in the antislavery movement. Taken to task by a New England woman who argued that antislavery agitation was man's work, she replied that "to plead for the miserable . . . can never be unfeminine or unbefitting the delicacy of woman."[2]

In 1832, having emigrated to the Michigan Territory, Chandler organized an antislavery society which was probably the first such female group in the Old Northwest. Increasingly dissatisfied with Lundy's gradualist approach, she was drawn toward the philosophy of William Lloyd Garrison, a Lundy protégé who had founded a radical weekly newspaper, the *Liberator*, in 1831. More than any other figure, he was responsible for rejecting the once popular gradualist approach to antislavery, including compensation for slaveholders and colonization abroad. Garrison believed that slavery was a sin and must be abolished through moral suasion, not by participation in the morally corrupt American political system. After

Elizabeth Chandler's death in 1834 at the age of twenty-six, Garrison eulogized her as "the first American woman who devoted her time and talents to the cause of the slave."[3]

When Elizabeth Chandler defended her activities as befitting the "delicacy of woman," she was paying heed to widely held beliefs about women's appropriate sphere. The first half of the nineteenth century was an era of rapid industrial expansion, rampant materialism, and rising affluence for the urban middle class. As men's work carried them away from home production and into the marketplace, women began to reign supreme over day-to-day activities of the family. While emphasizing women's alleged physical and intellectual weaknesses, society labeled them as divinely gifted with the virtues of piety, purity, and domesticity. Although this "cult of true womanhood" or doctrine of separate spheres, as Barbara Welter, Linda Kerber, Nancy Cott, and others have revealed, was a limiting force for women's lives, it also gave them the freedom to act as the moral and religious teachers of the family.[4]

Abolitionism was one segment of a wider reform movement which swept the Northern states in the decades preceding the Civil War. Stimulated by growing economic prosperity, increasing political democracy, and a flowering of American culture, this reform movement was based on the millennial notion of the perfectibility of humankind. All barriers to human improvement must be removed. Women first became involved in reform societies that were church affiliated, forming groups to distribute religious tracts, promote missionary activities, and raise money for widows and orphans. Although evangelical religion for the most part reinforced ideas of female subordination, indirectly religious participation emboldened women by affording them a public outlet, as Lawrence Foster and others have pointed out.[5]

Women's involvement in such reform movements as peace, health, and temperance was important, but their antislavery contributions represented what Keith Melder has called "the climax of women's involvement in reform."[6] William Lloyd Garrison quickly realized women's potential importance to the movement. Hoping to recruit women to abolitionism, he included a "Ladies Department" in the *Liberator*, which pictured on its masthead a female slave in chains over the caption "Am I not a Woman and a Sister?" Garrison continually reminded his readers that slave women were subjected to violence, cruelty, and sexual abuse.[7]

The Garrisonian notion of immediate emancipation became the rallying cry for a series of new abolition societies. The first such organization was the New England Anti-Slavery Society, begun in Boston in 1832. The following year Garrison had enough followers to call a national convention in Philadelphia, from which the American Anti-Slavery Society was born. Although the society's membership rose steadily during the 1830s, public opinion as a whole was far from sympathetic. American Anti-Slavery Society lecturers were frequently greeted by violent mobs; petitions to Congress were unceremoniously tabled following passage of the notorious gag rule of 1836; and Elijah Lovejoy, an abolitionist editor, was murdered by Illinois vigilantes while trying to protect his press.[8]

Garrison's appeals to women in the *Liberator* evoked a strong response among a coterie of activist women. Maria Weston Chapman, her three sisters, and a few of their friends founded the Boston Female Anti-Slavery Society in 1832. Many members of the Boston group were married to male abolitionists, but it was considered socially improper for men and women to join the same organizations. Like the men, members of the Boston Female Anti-Slavery Society were dedicated, hardworking immediatists, but initially at least their role was primarily that of adjunct to the male societies. At weekly gatherings, they prayed for the slaves and planned ways to raise money and distribute petitions. In spite of their subordinate position, they attracted public criticism because their activism was perceived as both radical and unladylike.[9]

Maria Weston Chapman was one of Garrison's most devoted followers. Born in Weymouth, Massachusetts, she married Henry Grafton Chapman, a successful merchant and one of the few wealthy Bostonians who sympathized with Garrison. After her husband's death, she continued to work on behalf of the slave. Contemporaries often commented on her intellect, her strong will, and her physical beauty. Edmund Quincy described Chapman as "the most perfect creature morally, intellectually, physically that I ever knew." Harriet Martineau became a friend in the 1830s, and the two remained close until Martineau's death in 1876, when Chapman became her literary executor. But the beautiful Bostonian had enemies as well as admirers. Many colleagues regarded her as imperious in manner and overbearing in her leadership role within the Boston Female Anti-Slavery Society. Chapman's grandson, John Jay Chapman, recalled that his grandmother "looked like a cameo" but also could be intimidating. "She entered a room like a public person," he wrote; "she was a doughty swordswoman in conversation, and wore armor."[10]

The Boston Female Anti-Slavery Society became an effective fundraising group. Its annual fair was described by one abolitionist as "a kind of a ladies' exchange for the holiday week, where each one was sure to meet her friends." In conjunction with the fairs, Chapman edited an annual gift book called the *Liberty Bell,* which contained poems and essays by such notable writers as Harriet Martineau, Elizabeth Barrett Browning, Henry Wadsworth Longfellow, Theodore Parker, and James Russell Lowell. John Greenleaf Whittier, although a confirmed abolitionist, refused to contribute to the *Liberty Bell,* citing Chapman's doctrinaire attitude toward those who disagreed with her philosophy of abolition. Chapman, like Garrison, rejected political action as a means to free the slaves.[11]

In addition to fund-raising, members of the Boston Female Anti-Slavery Society also collected signatures for abolition petitions to Congress. One of their specific goals was the immediate overthrow of slavery in the District of Columbia. Even after the gag rule was passed, members continued to send petitions to Congress through John Quincy Adams in the House of Representatives. One such petition exemplified their persistence. "We respectfully announce our intention to present the same petition yearly before your honorable body," Chapman wrote, "that it may at least be a memorial of us, that in the holy cause of Human Freedom, 'We have done what we could.'" These antislavery petitions, when Chapman sent them around the state of Massachusetts, contained her reminder that women in their roles as wife, sister, and mother "are deeply responsible for the influence we have on the human race." But much of the Boston press was decidedly opposed to Chapman's promotion of women's public role. Boston's *Commercial Gazette* accused her and her antislavery society of attempting " 'to lead captive silly women,' who would be more usefully and profitably employed at home."[12]

If respectable Bostonians regarded women as the weaker sex, this alleged weakness did not protect them from becoming the targets of mob violence. At one 1835 meeting the mayor of Boston begged abolitionist women to disperse. Chapman refused, announcing dramatically, "If this is the last bulwark of freedom, we may as well die here as anywhere." Although the women did take refuge at Chapman's home, they later learned that William Lloyd Garrison had been seized and dragged with a rope around his neck. Garrison was eventually freed by a truckman who delivered him to the mayor for safekeeping.[13]

One of Chapman's compatriots during the 1835 mobbing was her cousin Ann Terry Greene, a young heiress who had lived with the Chapmans since her parents died. In the Chapman household she met the wealthy young lawyer Wendell Phillips, and the two were married in 1837. According to Irving Bartlett, Ann Phillips was largely responsible for cultivating her husband's antislavery inclinations. Wendell Phillips would become the most eloquent of all the abolition orators, in great demand on the lecture circuit, his speeches widely reprinted in sympathetic newspapers. Although Ann Greene was an heiress, Phillips's mother opposed the marriage because Ann was an abolitionist. According to one observer, "The old lady Phillips . . . behaved like a perfect dragon" at the wedding. The Phillips marriage was apparently a happy one. Within a few years Ann Phillips became an invalid, but she always supported and encouraged her husband's abolition activities.[14] Because of her influence over Phillips and her generosity in donating money to abolition projects, women activists often sought her advice and support.

The Philadelphia Female Anti-Slavery Society was organized in 1833. Like Boston, Philadelphia had a committed group of radical abolitionists, though its strong antislavery heritage centered around its Quaker population. It was here that the first meeting of the American Anti-Slavery Society took place, an event which was the immediate stimulus for the formation of the Philadelphia Female Anti-Slavery Society.

When the Philadelphia women assembled for their first meeting, they were so unaccustomed to running a reform society that they automatically turned for help to the well-known male reformers Samuel May and Nathaniel Southard, who gave speeches. The women were too diffident even to preside over the convention. Lucretia Mott later recalled that there was "not a woman capable of taking the chair, and organizing that meeting in due order; and we had to call on James McCrummell, a colored man, to give us aid in the work."[15]

Lucretia Mott soon emerged as the leader of the Philadelphia Female Anti-Slavery Society. Born into a Quaker family on the island of Nantucket, Lucretia Coffin was educated at a religious boarding school in Nine Partners, New York, where she met James Mott, then a teacher at the school. After they were married and she began to raise a large family, Lucretia Mott tried her hand at schoolteaching but quickly became aware of her special gift for the ministry. The Quaker faith encouraged female participation in religious services, and Mott began to preach at the age of twenty-five. Soon she became a prominent speaker at Quaker meetings, where she emphasized the importance of religious experience over dogma. Together James and Lucretia Mott joined the American Free Produce Association, a movement dedicated to the promotion of non-slave-produced goods. Idealistic abolitionists thereby hoped to divorce themselves completely from the sin of slaveholding by eschewing Southern products such as cotton, sugar, and rice. James Mott, who had become a successful commission merchant, refused thereafter to deal in cotton thread or cloth, at considerable financial loss to his business.[16]

Like the Boston Female Anti-Slavery Society, the Philadelphia organization raised money for various abolitionist activities. During its first years, the women created a library of abolitionist newspapers, books, and pamphlets. By November 1834 they had raised enough money to open a school for black children. Soon they began collecting signatures for petitions to Congress calling for abolition in the District of Columbia and in the territories, plus an immediate end to the domestic slave trade. The first Philadelphia fair, modeled no doubt on Maria Chapman's extravaganzas, was staged in 1836 and held annually thereafter until 1861. The Philadelphia women raised a total of $32,000 in this manner.[17]

A number of female abolition societies were founded along the model provided by the Boston and Philadelphia activists. By the mid-1830s Massachusetts women had founded societies in Boston, Lowell, Reading, Groton, Amesbury, Salem, Haverhill, Newburyport, Weymouth, Braintree, Lynn, Dorchester, New Bedford, and Fall River. Philadelphia's female abolitionists inspired a network of societies in Pennsylvania. There were similar organizations in New York City and upstate. Black women were members and active participants of the Boston and Philadelphia societies, as Benjamin Quarles has pointed out. They were not welcome in some of the other female abolition societies, including those at Fall River and New York City, where white women objected to social mixing of the races. Partly as a result of this discrimination, black women founded their own auxiliaries to the American Anti-Slavery Society throughout the northeastern and midwestern states.[18]

Among the most important converts to the antislavery cause in the 1830s was Lydia Maria Francis Child. Born at Medford, Massachusetts, she taught school before turning her efforts toward literary pursuits. In 1824, while still in her early twenties, she published a novel about Indians in pioneer America. Its success made the young author something of a literary sensation in staid, conservative Boston. Child was a prolific writer whose warmth, uncomplicated literary style, and good common sense appealed to many Americans. Her self-help book *The Frugal Housewife* eventually went through more than thirty editions, and her children's magazine *Juvenile Miscellany* was immensely popular. But marriage to abolitionist David Lee Child when she was twenty-six altered her life. Child was a financially unsuccessful attorney, a onetime Massachusetts legislator, and an early member of the New England Anti-Slavery Society. Although Lydia Maria Child may have entertained abolitionist sympathies before marriage, her husband's commitment clearly influenced her. Like the Motts, David Child was involved in the free produce movement, but his attempt to grow sugar beets in Northampton, Massachusetts, failed miserably.[19] Child was always a better philosopher than he was a provider, and his wife's literary output was due in part to financial necessity.

In 1833 Lydia Maria Child published an abolition tract called *Appeal in Favor of That Class of Americans Called Africans,* which evoked praise from radical abolitionists and horror from many readers of her bucolic writing. The fact that Child regarded African slaves as Americans was itself enough to shock many of her devoted followers. In the *Appeal* Child presented a history of slavery. She included engravings of shackles and thumbscrews along with graphic descriptions of their uses in the Atlantic slave trade. In addition to condemning Southern slave owners, she criticized those Northerners who indirectly supported the institution by piously calling it a "lamentable *necessity.*" Slavery, she contended, divided and thus crippled the Union, both financially and morally. Child called for an end to race prejudice. "The removal of this prejudice is not a matter of opinion," she wrote; "it is a matter of *duty.*"[20]

John Greenleaf Whittier, a neighbor and close friend of the Childs, recalled the impact of the *Appeal* on her literary career. "Social and literary circles, which had been proud of her presence, closed their doors against her," he wrote. "She knew all she was hazarding, and made the great sacrifice, prepared for all the consequences which followed." Prepared though she was, Child was still wounded when numerous cancellations of *Juvenile Miscellany* forced her to suspend the eight-year-old publication. Northerners as well as Southerners condemned the *Appeal;* one representative of the Boston Athenaeum hinted that Child was no longer welcome there. And yet she did win some support for the antislavery cause. "This 'Appeal' reached thousands who had given no heed to us before," recalled one prominent abolitionist, "and made many converts to the doctrines of Mr. Garrison."[21]

Lydia Maria Child became a salaried employee of the American Anti-Slavery Society when she accepted the editorship of a new publication, the *National Anti-Slavery Standard.* This official organ of the society was published in New York, where supporters hoped it would attract a wider audience than the Boston-based *Liberator.* Under Child's direction, the

Standard became a well-rounded newspaper with stories designed to appeal to both adults and children, but after two years she resigned, realizing that her perspective was not radical enough to suit Garrison. Uncompromising and determined, Garrison had begun to advocate secession of the North from the morally corrupt South and wanted someone who shared his perspective to take over the newspaper. In 1844 he appointed a troika of Bostonians to edit the *Standard:* Sydney Howard Gay, Edmund Quincy, and Maria Weston Chapman. [22]

If Lydia Maria Child was the abolition movement's great literary recruit of the 1830s, the Grimké sisters of South Carolina were the most dramatic oratorical recruits. Sarah and Angelina Grimké were members of one of South Carolina's landed and politically connected families. Their father, John Faucheraud Grimké, was a plantation owner, lawyer, and judge. The sisters were devoted to one another. Almost thirteen years older, Sarah treated Angelina like a child of her own. The older sister's religious studies led to an interest in the Quaker faith, which must have scandalized her Presbyterian family, and in 1821 she left the South to join a Quaker meeting in Philadelphia. Although Sarah claimed that her abolitionist convictions were formulated during childhood, Gerda Lerner believes these convictions came later; her recollections of slavery, combined with Quaker precepts, probably led her to adopt the abolitionist banner. Angelina Grimké joined her sister in Philadelphia after having been expelled from the Presbyterian church in 1829. [23]

Angelina Grimké became publicly active largely through Garrison's initiative. In 1835 she wrote a letter to the Boston editor praising a recent editorial in the *Liberator.* Ever mindful of a good propaganda opportunity, Garrison published her letter along with biographical details about the Grimké family. Soon it was reprinted in other reform and religious publications. The response that this letter brought stimulated Angelina to write an *Appeal to the Christian Women of the Southern States,* which was published in 1836. [24]

The young Quaker grounded her argument for emancipation in the natural rights philosophy of the Declaration of Independence. In simple, straightforward prose she insisted that women could and should act to free the slaves. "Speak to your relatives, friends, acquaintances," she wrote; "be not afraid . . . to let your sentiments be known. . . . Try to persuade your husband, father, brothers and sons that slavery is a crime *against God and man.*" When, shortly after publication of the *Appeal,* Angelina decided to visit her mother in Charleston, the full impact of her course became apparent. Charleston's mayor informed Mrs. Grimké that if her daughter set foot in the city, she would be jailed until she could be transported back to Philadelphia.[25]

In 1836 the Grimké sisters became the first women professional abolitionists in the United States when the American Anti-Slavery Society hired them as lecturers. Not all members of the society approved of this arrangement. While applauding women for raising money and distributing tracts, they questioned the propriety of women on the lecture circuit. Public speaking was something respectable women did not do in the 1830s. Gerrit Smith, the wealthy and influential New York abolitionist, feared the Grimkés might be compared to the infamous utopian socialist and lecturer Fanny Wright.[26]

However, the sisters were clearly a godsend to the American Anti-Slavery Society. Their family's prominence, their personal experiences with slavery, and the curiosity of many Americans regarding women on the lecture platform combined to ensure large crowds at their engagements. Although the Grimkés' audiences were initially female, they soon began to address mixed or "promiscuous" crowds. Angelina, a persuasive speaker, was sometimes compared to another former slave owner, James G. Birney, though many regarded her as the more eloquent. Wendell Phillips once remarked that she "swept the cords of the human heart with a power that has never been surpassed and rarely equalled."[27]

Despite a pastoral letter from Massachusetts ministers condemning the Grimkés' unladylike behavior, the sisters continued to lecture. In 1837 they started on a whirlwind tour of New England culminating in Boston. On 21 February 1838 Angelina spoke to a capacity crowd at the Massachusetts State House, becoming the first woman ever to address a legislature. She began by reminding her listeners that she was a Southerner and daughter of a slave owner, but one who was "exiled from the land of my birth by the sound of the lash and the piteous cry of the slave."[28]

Grimké did more than simply denounce slavery as an immoral institution. She faced squarely the issue of women's involvement in the abolition movement and at the same time answered her critics in the statehouse, the press, the clergy, and the American Anti-Slavery Society. Clearly rejecting the widely held nineteenth-century view of women as intellectually weak but morally and religiously strong, Grimké adopted a far more radical view of women's role in society. "American women have to do with [slavery]," she said, "not only because it is moral and religious, but because it is *political*, inasmuch as we are citizens of this republic." While Maria

Weston Chapman and her compatriots in the audience applauded the speech, others did not. Angelina was dubbed "Devil-ina" by the New England press.[29]

The Grimkés' notoriety subsided when Angelina married the well-known abolitionist Theodore Weld in 1838. The Friends summarily expelled her for marrying a non-Quaker and dismissed Sarah for attending the ceremony. Both sisters continued to take great interest in the abolition movement, but their appearances were limited by Angelina's family responsibilities and health problems. They both aided Theodore Weld in preparing his compendium of Southern newspaper articles, *Slavery As It Is,* published in 1839.[30]

The Grimké sisters were important role models for abolitionist women. In the aftermath of their 1837–38 lecture tour, women in towns they visited collected signatures on thirty-four antislavery petitions and founded eight new abolition societies. A number of women became American Anti-Slavery Society lecturers, including Abby Kelley, a fellow Quaker who left the faith after being criticized for her abolition activities. Kelley made lengthy trips to isolated areas, stopping to speak whenever she could find an audience. One of the most radical of the Garrisonians, she condemned all who tolerated the institution of slavery, including American churches, which she likened to "cages of unclean birds." Since she was radical and outspoken, Abby Kelley became the target of an unprecedented amount of verbal and even physical abuse. One New York newspaper referred to her as "that monstrosity, a public speaking woman." Other publications were less kind. While she was on a lecture tour of Ohio accompanied by several male and female colleagues, rumors abounded of a "traveling seraglio." Even her marriage in 1845 to abolitionist Stephen Symonds Foster did not silence the critics. It was said that Foster was simply a temporary substitute for her true love, the black abolitionist Frederick Douglass.[31]

Life on the lecture circuit could be grueling even when the audiences were not hostile. Sallie Holley became an agent for the American Anti-Slavery Society when she was recruited by Abby Kelley Foster. In her memoirs Holley recalled the long, uncomfortable days of lecturing in the rural Northeast. "Shall I tell you what anti-slavery hospitality is in Pennsylvania?" she wrote. "It is to be ushered into a small, close, stove-heated room, where seven or eight grown up persons and children have already breathed over the air two or three times." Dinner often consisted of indigestible sausages with thick, doughy pancakes. "And though you have been lecturing an hour and a half that day, besides riding through rain and mud several miles, you are expected to entertain the friends with how delighted you are with anti-slavery in Pennsylvania." At the end of a long day, "you are asked to ascend to a cold, uncomfortable, half furnished apartment." After an unrestful night, "you ride eight or ten miles to the next appointment," where the process was repeated. For her antislavery work, Sallie Holley received only a token salary of ten dollars per week plus expenses.[32]

Black abolitionists suffered many indignities. The experiences of Sojourner Truth are a notable example, for she received a number of insults while on the lecture circuit. A New York slave freed by statewide emancipation in 1827, Sojourner Truth never learned to read or write. For most of her career she did not have a formal identity with organized abolition, yet she became an effective and eloquent crusader. Tall, angular, and very dark skinned, she spoke with a strong Dutch accent. On one lecture tour of Indiana, a male doctor challenged Sojourner Truth to prove she was a woman. Without hesitation, she bared her breasts, to the humiliation of the doctor. In her most famous speech, delivered in 1851, Truth emphasized the disparity between slavery and the comforts of ladydom, asking repeatedly, "A'n't I a woman?" Between 1843 and 1878 she lectured in twenty-one states and the District of Columbia, before retiring at the age of eighty-one.[33]

By the late 1830s women had made an important place for themselves in the abolition movement, through both individual efforts and regional female societies. In order to coordinate these efforts, Maria Weston Chapman suggested that annual conventions be held which would unite abolitionists from across the country. Though some Philadelphia women questioned the idea, arguing that women should gain recognition through the American Anti-Slavery Society, Chapman eventually prevailed.[34]

Annual meetings took place in 1837, 1838, and 1839. The First Anti-Slavery Convention of American Women, held in New York, attracted one hundred delegates from ten states, including Lucretia Mott, Maria Weston Chapman, Lydia Maria Child, Abby Kelley, and the Grimké sisters. Several African American delegates attended as well, among them Sarah Douglass, a Quaker schoolteacher and prominent member of Philadelphia's free black community. She would attend the wedding of Angelina Grimké and Theodore Weld in 1838 and, with them, would protest the discrimination against blacks in the Quaker church. At subsequent national conventions, she would serve as treasurer, while her mother Grace Douglass was selected a vice president.[35]

At the national conventions abolitionist leaders made speeches in support of specific issues such as the free produce movement, a favorite project of Lucretia Mott. They passed resolutions calling for the abolition of slavery in the District of Columbia and the territories. They also demonstrated their growing feminism when they passed a resolution calling on every woman to "act in the sphere which Providence had assigned her, and no longer to rest satisfied with the circumscribed limits in which corrupt custom and a perverted application of the Scriptures had encircled her." Angelina Grimké emphasized the need for women to play a public role when she asked one audience, "Are we bereft of citizenship because we are the mothers, wives, and daughters of a mighty people?"[36] These bold measures are indicative of how far antislavery women had come in the past five years. Once uncertain of how to conduct a reform meeting, they were now increasingly confident and forceful.

Mob violence marred the national conventions just as it had affected smaller gatherings. When more than five hundred delegates met in Philadelphia to attend the Second Annual Anti-Slavery Convention of American Women, a crowd of proslavery vigilantes gathered outside Philadelphia's Pennsylvania Hall to harass the abolitionists. The mob, which grew to seventeen thousand people, set fire to the building, burning it to the ground. Although the home of Lucretia and James Mott was an intended target, it escaped damage. Before the night was over, however, the mob had vandalized a church and an orphanage for black children. Police stood idly by. Undaunted, the delegates met in a schoolhouse to conclude their meeting the following morning. They renewed their commitment to abolition and pledged their support for social mixing of the races. The 1839 meeting, also held in Philadelphia, inspired far less public protest, in part because the lack of a lighted facility precluded evening meetings.[37]

Inspired by the national conventions, women founded antislavery societies in New Hampshire, Maine, Rhode Island, Connecticut, New York, Pennsylvania, and Michigan. Women abolitionists also achieved their most successful petition drives to date during the late 1830s. Petitioning activities reached a peak between 1837 and 1839 when, under auspices of the American Anti-Slavery Society, activists undertook a massive petition campaign. As Dwight Dumond has emphasized, this campaign was launched after Congress passed the gag rule and was in part a response to it. Abolitionists mailed thousands of blank petitions from the American Anti-Slavery Society's New York office; filled petition forms were returned to state antislavery societies, directly to the American Anti-Slavery Society, or to sympathetic congressmen. The petitions covered a wide range of topics, from abolition in the District of Columbia and the territories to prohibition of the interstate slave trade.[38]

The majority of these petitions were circulated by women, a fact noted by Gilbert Barnes more than half a century ago. Moreover, the majority of signers appear to have been female, as Judith Wellman's work on upstate New York has demonstrated. At the Third Anti-Slavery Convention, women had declared that "the only direct influence which we can exert upon our Legislatures, is by protests and petitions. Shall we not, then be greatly delinquent if we neglect *these?*" Where it is possible to discern the gender of the signers, women alone signed 14.5 percent of the petitions and women together with men signed 54.9 percent of a total of 304 petitions. In other words, women by themselves or with men signed nearly 70 percent of petitions received by Congress in the years 1838–39.[39]

Although women attending the Third Anti-Slavery Convention had voted to meet the next year in Boston, there was no meeting; by 1840 a series of philosophical debates within the Garrisonian ranks had caused a schism in the abolition movement. The schism was actually the result of long-standing disagreements, as Aileen Kraditor has pointed out. In 1830 the abolition movement had consisted of a handful of dedicated radicals in the Boston area. By the end of the decade, the movement encompassed the northern United States and was growing philosophically diverse. Although the abolitionist schism was caused in part by disagreement over Garrison's refusal to seek a political solution to antislavery, another important cause for dissension was the role of women in the movement.[40]

An outspoken faction, led by the Reverend Amos Phelps, objected to the growing female influence in what were traditionally male organizations. These men believed that the American Anti-Slavery Society must remain orthodox on all issues except antislavery in order to convince Northerners of the respectability of their cause. Not only were women being appointed as antislavery agents, but some of them were discussing woman's rights. Garrison disagreed. Believing that all barriers to human freedom must be eradicated, he recruited women to the American Anti-Slavery Society and encouraged them to speak out on other reform issues, including feminism. A third position was taken by Theodore Weld and others who believed that woman's rights, though a worthy cause and part of the ultimate goal of human equality, must take a backseat to the immediate goal of abolition. The conflict has been summarized cogently by Lewis Perry: "There was irreconcilable conflict between conservatives, to whom slavery was a singular evil to be eliminated from the basically sound American society, and others who saw slavery as merely the most horrible symptom of America's deep-seated sinfulness."[41]

Although several preliminary confrontations over the "woman question" took place at regional antislavery meetings in the late 1830s, the major battle occurred at the 1840 American Anti-Slavery Society Convention when more than one thousand representatives gathered at New York's Fourth Free Church. Abby Kelley was appointed to the business committee, whereupon a minority of delegates walked out to form the American and Foreign Anti-Slavery Society. Amos Phelps and the wealthy philanthropists Arthur and Lewis Tappan were among the leaders of this new organization, in which women were denied the vote. The American Anti-Slavery Society continued its convention, defying the dissidents by appointing Lucretia Mott, Lydia Maria Child, and Maria Weston Chapman to the executive committee. The convention passed resolutions condemning American churches for "giving undisguised sanction and support to slavery" and criticizing major party candidates in the 1840 presidential election.[42]

The same issues that divided the American Anti-Slavery Society tore apart the Boston Female Anti-Slavery Society. While Maria Weston Chapman continued to support Garrison and raise money for his *Liberator,* those women who favored separate male and female societies formed the Massachusetts Female Emancipation Society. With the triumph of the Garrisonian forces in maintaining control of the American Society, women abolitionists decided not to hold another annual convention. They felt that their voices could best be heard through participation with men in one national convention. The American Anti-Slavery Society lost the cohesiveness that had characterized it during the previous decade and, as Ronald Walters has emphasized, would never again achieve the breadth of activity it undertook in the 1830s, but the legitimacy of female leadership in the movement had been clearly established.[43]

The issue of woman's rights, which had surfaced periodically, became an important reform movement in its own right during the 1840s. There were many reasons for the formation of this movement: the impact of industrialization, which decreased housewives' duties, allowing them more leisure time; discontent over a legal system which prevented married women from owning property; the general reform tenor of the times with its emphasis on perfectionism. By 1840 women had already proved their reformist talents in church-sponsored benevolent societies, in the temperance movement, and in abolition societies.

When delegates to the first woman's rights convention met in Seneca Falls, New York, in 1848, it was the abolition movement that provided the most important precedent. In 1840 the World's Anti-Slavery Convention had convened in London. Women participants, including Lucretia Mott, Ann Greene Phillips, and Elizabeth Cady Stanton, were denied seats on the convention floor and were consigned instead to the balcony. Stanton and Mott remembered their London experience when they decided several years later to hold a woman's rights convention.[44]

The Seneca Falls Declaration of Sentiments included ideas about female independence, education, and legal problems that had been raised by abolition speakers such as Angelina and Sarah Grimké and discussed at the annual Anti-Slavery Conventions of American Women. The *National Anti-Slavery Standard* and the *Liberator* had included articles about feminist issues for years. The abolition movement also helped to create a constituency for feminism, as Ellen DuBois has pointed out. It was no accident that the first national woman's rights convention was planned to convene at the same time as the American Anti-Slavery Society's annual meeting. Abolitionist delegates were thus encouraged to participate in both conventions.[45]

The woman's rights and abolition movements continued to be closely linked until the Civil War. Many abolitionists such as Abby Kelley Foster and the Grimkés quickly and enthusiastically embraced organized feminism. The abolitionist schism of 1840 had convinced many of the need for women to defend their equality within the antislavery movement in order to promote emancipation of the slave.[46] But while older-generation activists would always think of themselves first and foremost as abolitionists, the new generation of women activists were more divided in their priorities, several of them owing their greatest loyalty to feminism. Lucy Stone's career exemplifies this dilemma.

As a young girl growing up in Massachusetts, Lucy Stone was determined to make a life for herself outside the home. Toward that end, she entered Mary Lyons's Mount Holyoke Seminary in 1839, passing out copies of the *Liberator* in her spare time. Stone left Mount Holyoke after only three months when a death in the family forced her to return home, but she later completed her education at Oberlin College. In 1847, speaking from her brother's pulpit in Gardner, Massachusetts, she gave her first woman's rights lecture. Although her message was a radical one, Stone's pleasant appearance, melodic speaking voice, and obvious sincerity made her more acceptable to audiences than some feminist abolitionists such as Abby Kelley Foster, who often was perceived as strident and unfeminine because of her serious countenance and uncompromising nature.[47]

Lucy Stone accepted an offer to become an agent of the American Anti-Slavery Society in 1848. However, some of her superiors soon criticized her for injecting woman's rights into all of her lectures. The young orator agreed to a compromise by which she divided her time, lecturing alternately on abolition and feminism. At the age of thirty-six she married Henry Blackwell, a reformer and brother of one of America's first female doctors.[48]

The women who became most closely identified with the twin causes of abolition and woman's rights were Elizabeth Cady Stanton and Susan Anthony. Stanton was born into one of upstate New York's wealthier families. Her mother was a philanthropist and member of a distinguished colonial family, while her father made his reputation as a legal scholar and judge. Elizabeth Cady was educated at Emma Willard's famous seminary in Troy, an institution which she entered with great reluctance, having set her heart on the all-male Union College. Her interest in reform was encouraged by her cousin Gerrit Smith, whose mansion in Peterboro, New York, served as an Underground Railroad depot. On at least one occasion she was allowed to talk with a slave woman bound for Canada. It was here too that she met abolitionist Henry Stanton, to whom she was married in 1840 at age twenty-four. Her interest in woman's rights can also be traced to her youth. She vividly remembered seeing women come to her father's office in search of legal redress from cruel, often drunkard husbands. Because married women in New York had no property rights and because child custody often favored the father in divorce cases, Daniel Cady could offer them little more than sympathy. During the 1850s Elizabeth Cady Stanton dabbled in various reform movements including abolition and temperance, but she became increasingly preoccupied by woman's rights. In 1854 and again in 1860 she addressed the New York State legislature on this subject.[49]

Though she was born in Massachusetts, Susan Anthony grew up in New York State. Her family, unlike Stanton's, was Quaker, only moderately affluent, and sympathetic to reform. While working as a schoolteacher in

Canajoharie, New York, Anthony joined the Daughters of Temperance. She gave her first public speech in 1849, in which she called upon women as moral and religious teachers of the family to "cast their United influence" toward the eradication of liquor.[50]

Susan Anthony was not present at the historic Seneca Falls convention, but members of her family attended a later woman's rights meeting in Rochester and undoubtedly gave a sympathetic report. Her interest in organized feminism also was inspired by her experiences at an Albany meeting organized by the Sons of Temperance, where she was denied the podium because of her gender. Elizabeth Cady Stanton, whom she met in 1850, encouraged her interest in feminism. The two became devoted friends and coworkers in the abolition and woman's rights movements. Their relationship was not entirely an equal one, however, for Anthony was often overshadowed by her more forceful and articulate friend. Throughout their lives Anthony addressed her colleague as "Mrs. Stanton," while Stanton referred to her unmarried friend, who was just five years younger, as "Susan."[51]

In November 1856 Elizabeth Cady Stanton wrote a letter to her cousin complaining about the government's continuous efforts to appease the slave states. Stanton believed these measures were ineffective. "I am becoming more and more convinced," she wrote, "that we shall be in the midst of violence, blood, and civil war before we look for it. Our fair republic must be the victim of the monster, slavery, unless we speedily rise in our might and boldly shout freedom."[52] Stanton's prediction was correct. Almost four years to the day would bring the election of Abraham Lincoln, and the secession of eleven slave states would soon follow.

Women played an important role in the prewar abolition movement, though their numbers were far smaller than those involved in church-related benevolent organizations. Forming auxiliary societies to the male abolition groups, they raised money, wrote letters, and circulated petitions. Gradually women began to step away from this purely supportive role to engage in lecturing and philosophizing. As the old taboo against mixed-gender antislavery activity faded, especially after 1840, women took important leadership positions in the American Anti-Slavery Society.

Although many female abolitionists regarded woman's rights as their first priority after 1848, this order was reversed with the outbreak of war. The woman's rights conventions that had taken place annually in the 1850s ceased, and female abolitionists vowed to throw their full efforts behind the final eradication of slavery. Nevertheless, many of the more radical activists found themselves unable to ignore their feminist inclinations, and they managed to keep women's issues before the public throughout the war. Elizabeth Cady Stanton hoped that women's wartime patriotism and work on behalf of the slave would lead to political gains for women in the postwar period.

In the next five years the alliance between abolition and feminism would undergo profound changes. Women abolitionists would work tirelessly on behalf of the slave, and their efforts would involve an unprecedented degree of organization. Ultimately, the alliance proved to be decidedly uneasy. Having subordinated, though never abandoned, their feminist concerns, many women abolitionists would emerge from the Civil War not with a sense of triumph over slavery's demise but with feelings of bitterness over the Civil War's impact on women. The 1860s would provide a mixed legacy both for African Americans and for women.

From Secession to War

Is it possible to make a union of liberty & slavery? Has not the
experiment been fully tried, & its failure made apparent to all
philosophical observers?
—Elizabeth Cady Stanton, "Speech on Slavery," 1861

The secession crisis brought new challenges for abolitionist women: the
terrorist activity of John Brown, the election of a free-soil president and
the disunion that followed; the start of what they would come to regard as a
holy war; and throughout the tumultuous months following Harpers Ferry,
an undercurrent of debate over the role of women in times of public crisis.

Because Republicans were the first major political party to endorse a
free-soil platform, the creation of this party in 1854 was an encouraging
sign for some abolitionists. While doctrinaire Garrisonians such as Abby
and Stephen Foster continued to shun any political involvement, others
showed marked interest in the new party. Lydia Maria Child supported
John C. Frémont's 1856 presidential campaign enthusiastically. "I would
almost lay down my life," she wrote, "to have him elected."[1]

Elizabeth Cady Stanton had mixed feelings about the new Republican
party. Her husband advocated political action to end slavery, but she
usually had followed Garrison's nonpolitical approach. In a letter to Susan
Anthony, she complained about the attitude of some abolitionists regarding the Kansas controversy. "You Garrisonians are such a crotchety set that
generally, when all other men see cause for rejoicing, you howl the more
grievously," she wrote. "How it is now? I desire to know, for as I am one of
you, I wish to do what is most becoming to one of the order. Shall I fire off
my boys' cannon and a bundle of crackers," she asked, "or shall I wear
sackcloth and ashes?" Anthony's response is unknown, but Stanton appears to have thrown in her lot with the Republicans, for she wrote in 1855
that "I am rejoiced to say that Henry is heart and soul in the Republican
movement" and noted that she had "attended all the Republican meetings."[2]

Many abolitionists became involved in the movement to promote the
free settlement of Kansas. Lydia Maria Child sent provisions to the terri-

tory and wrote a novella, *The Kansas Emigrants,* which was serialized by
Horace Greeley in the New York *Tribune.*[3] Some abolitionists became so
impassioned in their promotion of a free Kansas that they were sympathetic toward John Brown. Others were skeptical. When Brown sought
the advice of prominent abolitionists regarding his scheme to initiate a
slave insurrection in the South, Frederick Douglass advised him on potential flaws in the plan. Abby Hopper Gibbons, a New York abolitionist,
questioned its practicality. And what would he do with the mothers and
their children, she asked? "Not hurt a hair of their heads" was his reply.
Brown finally gained financial support from a group of New England
philanthropists, among them Samuel Gridley Howe, Theodore Parker,
Thomas Wentworth Higginson, and Gerrit Smith.[4]

On the evening of 16 October and the early morning of the following
day, Brown, commanding an "army" of twenty-two, captured the federal
arsenal at Harpers Ferry, Virginia. The operation was ludicrously ill-
conceived, and Brown was captured, tried, and hanged. But his remarkable degree of composure and courage during the ordeal of his trial and
execution helped to make him the most important abolitionist martyr
since Elijah Lovejoy. The execution touched off a wave of public mourning
in the North; Emerson and Thoreau each likened Brown to the crucified
Christ. Lydia Maria Child, who had curtailed her antislavery activities
when she left the editorship of the *Standard,* was inspired by Brown's raid.
In fact, she tried to visit the imprisoned man shortly before his trial. Her
correspondence with Virginia's governor on this subject was released to the
press, influencing Margaretta Mason, wife of a Virginia senator, to chal-
lenge the Northern writer. The *Correspondence between Lydia Maria Child
and Governor Wise and Mrs. Mason, of Virginia,* was published by the
American Anti-Slavery Society and sold 300,000 copies, the largest sale of
Child's career. Believing these troubled times required her best efforts, she
called this publication the "most notable of all my anti-slavery doings."[5]

Jean Fagan Yellin believes this exchange, emphasizing women's role in
times of national crisis, represents "Child's major contribution to the
ongoing debate over definitions of true womanhood." Margaretta Mason
condemned Child as a villain for "attempting to sooth with sisterly and
motherly care the hoary-headed murderer of Harper's Ferry." She implied
that Child's sympathy and that of other abolitionist women implicated
them in Brown's treachery. Mason and her slave-owning sisters were true
women, she contended, because of the care they showed for slave women
during times of illness and childbirth. The abolitionist author responded

by condemning slavery on biblical and humanitarian grounds, citing Sarah Grimké's personal experiences. She defended Brown as a man of principle. Regarding the issue of true womanhood, Child upheld the benevolent activities of Northern women when she wrote, "Here at the North, after we have helped the mothers, we do not sell the babies."[6] Child would remain an active participant in the public debate over slavery during the coming months.

Most of the abolitionists did not participate in the election of 1860, though some, including David and Lydia Maria Child, ignored Garrison's advice and endorsed the Republican candidate. But whether or not they supported Lincoln during the campaign, many abolitionists were openly enthusiastic about his victory. Whittier celebrated Lincoln's election as "the triumph of our principles—so long delayed." Even Wendell Phillips, who only months before had called Lincoln "The Slave-Hound of Illinois," now told a cheering crowd at Boston's Tremont Temple, "If the telegraph speaks truth, for the first time in our history the *slave* has chosen a President of the United States." Harriet Beecher Stowe was slightly more circumspect. "We are aware that the Republican party are far from being up to the full measure of what *ought* to be thought and felt on the slavery question," she wrote. "But they are for *stopping the evil*—and in this case to arrest is to cure."[7]

Shortly after Lincoln's election, South Carolina left the Union, encouraging several other slave states to secede. During the winter of 1860–61, at the same time that many in the North were trying to comprehend what was happening, assess the South's commitment to secession, and think of ways to end the crisis, the abolitionists stepped up their antislavery activities. They advocated peaceable separation of the North and South, using as their universal rallying cry the Garrisonian slogan, "No Union with Slaveholders!" During the lame-duck presidency of James Buchanan, their greatest fear was that a compromise would once more be made to appease the slave states. This course of action had to be avoided at all cost. Maria Weston Chapman's views matched those of many abolitionists. "We are well & in high spirits," she wrote in January 1861. "Civil war, if we are to have it (which I do not think) is not so bad as Slavery. Public opinion is so rapidly consolidating under the recent & the present revelations," she concluded, "that I augur nothing but good."[8]

The abolitionists' insistence on separation from the South involved faulty logic, as James McPherson has pointed out, since an independent South would be unlikely to grant emancipation. However, the abolitionists argued that the South would never survive as an independent nation. Because the United States Constitution and therefore the army protected slavery, a Southern nation, deprived of the protective force of the army, could not prevent slave insurrections and might find it difficult to prevent fugitives from escaping to the North. The slave-based economy would collapse. Furthermore, an independent South would become a pariah among nations, condemned by the world for its despicable form of servitude. The abolitionists found justification for their stance in the words of the founding fathers, who had once argued that a government which did not serve the will of the people, and which denied the natural rights philosophy of the Declaration of Independence, must be abolished and a new government substituted.[9]

Lydia Maria Child clearly believed that the national crisis called for women's public activism. She demonstrated her own commitment by working tirelessly writing tracts in support of abolition and disunion. Her pamphlet *The Duty and Disobedience to the Fugitive Slave Act: An Appeal to the Legislature of Massachusetts* was published in the fall of 1860. "As sure as there is a Righteous Ruler in the heavens," she pleaded, "if you continue to be accomplices in violence and fraud, God will *not* 'save the Commonwealth of Massachusetts.'" Also in 1860 she edited *The Patriarchal Institution,* a compendium of runaway slave notices from Southern newspapers, slave state laws pertaining to the peculiar institution, and quotes from Southern apologists, all designed to convince Northerners that slavery was indefensible. "Slavery and Freedom are antagonistic elements," she concluded. "One must inevitably destroy the other. Which do you choose?" Child's treatise *The Right Way the Safe Way* describes emancipation in the British West Indies during the 1830s. In contrast to slavery's defenders, Child claimed that West Indian emancipation was accomplished without any major disruption to the islands' economy and that free blacks had become industrious workers and productive members of society. *The Right Way the Safe Way,* first published in 1860, was reprinted during the Civil War.[10]

In addition to writing political tracts, Child also edited a narrative designed to pull at the heartstrings of American women, entitled *Incidents in the Life of a Slave Girl, Written by Herself.* Its author was the remarkable runaway slave Harriet Jacobs, who related horrifying tales about her life in bondage. Once owned by a North Carolina doctor who subjected her to constant sexual harassment, Jacobs resisted his advances and devised an escape plan. With the assistance of black and white friends, she ran away from her master's home, but she paid a considerable price for her freedom; in order to elude capture, she claimed to have spent almost seven years hiding in the crawl space of her grandmother's home. Ultimately she escaped to the North and found employment as a domestic servant in the home of New York publisher N. P. Willis. Jacobs succeeded in presenting a book which is dramatic and deeply moving. The narrative includes vivid details about the white master who attempted to recapture her; the help she received from white abolitionist women, especially the first and second wives of N. P. Willis; and Jacobs's extraordinary family: her grandmother, who was a freed slave; her parents, who lived and died in bondage; her brother, a fiery Northern abolitionist; and the two children who were products of the illicit liaison with a white attorney she had while still in bondage.[11]

Although she emphasized racial injustice, Jacobs also underscored the cult of true womanhood. Because she was writing for a white, Northern, and largely female audience, she portrayed black women as having the same instincts of purity, domesticity, and maternity as their Northern sisters, instincts that were violated by slavery. In the preface to her book, she denied having any wish to "excite sympathy for my own sufferings"; instead, she said, "I do earnestly desire to arouse the women of the North to a realizing sense of the condition of two millions of women at the South, still in bondage." Admitting remorse over violating nineteenth-century sexual standards, Jacobs nevertheless defended herself on the grounds that women subjected to the horrors of slavery should not be judged by the standards of middle-class morality.[12]

In her recent analysis of Jacobs's book, Elizabeth Fox-Genovese has cast doubt about the factual accuracy of some of Harriet Jacobs's contentions, particularly the length of her period of hiding—the proverbial seven years—and the likelihood that she successfully avoided all of her master's sexual advances. Fox-Genovese concluded that Jacobs probably "embellished an account that was true in its essentials." The book's strength lies not so much in the truthfulness of Jacobs's depiction of slavery as in its inspiration as a narrative of resistance to oppression.[13]

In the early 1850s Rochester abolitionist Amy Post urged Jacobs to publish an account of her life in slavery. Jacobs approached Harriet Beecher Stowe for assistance but rejected Stowe's offer to include her story as part of the forthcoming *A Key to Uncle Tom's Cabin*. Lydia Maria Child, whom Jacobs met through the black abolitionist William C. Nell in 1860, was impressed by the former slave, a highly articulate woman who had learned to read and write as a child. The high quality of writing by a woman born in slavery caused many to question the authorship of the book; but the careful research of Jean Fagan Yellin, editor of the most recent edition of *Incidents,* has established that Jacobs was indeed the author. Though Child's editorial assistance on the manuscript appears to have been minimal, her endorsement of the book undoubtedly helped Jacobs in finding a publishing house. Unfortunately Thayer and Eldridge Publishers went bankrupt before any copies had been bound. Jacobs ultimately managed to buy the plates herself, but distribution of the privately printed book was difficult.[14]

Child did what she could to promote the volume. Writing to her "much esteemed friend" John Greenleaf Whittier, she noted that Jacobs's story was "more interesting than any biography of a Slave, that I ever read." Pleased to learn that Whittier liked the book, she wrote of her "good deal of pains" in trying to circulate it. Child believed that her efforts were well founded because *Incidents* was exactly the sort of emotional narrative that could appeal to Americans not swayed by legal and moral "arguments" against slavery.[15]

Although Child complained about what she perceived to be a lack of enthusiasm by the *Liberator* and *National Anti-Slavery Standard* in promoting the book, *Incidents* was favorably reviewed in the antislavery press. Writing in the *Liberator,* William C. Nell described *Incidents* as "more attractive than many of its predecessors purporting to be histories of slave life in America." The book would appeal especially to women, who "may learn yet more of the barbarism of American slavery and the character of its victims." Although Jacobs's book was available for sale at the offices of antislavery societies, sales figures are not known.[16] During the war Harriet Jacobs would devote herself to the plight of the freedmen, ministering to refugees living in and around Washington, D.C. Her work was financed in part by Philadelphia Quakers. She wrote letters to Lydia Maria Child, reprinted in the antislavery press, describing both the suffering of the freedmen and their exemplary character.[17]

Mary Putnam, sister of the poet James Russell Lowell, published a melodramatic abolition novel in 1861. *Record of an Obscure Man* is the story of a Northern gentleman who was injured while traveling in the South and was taken in by a white Southern family and their free black servant. Clearly written for a Northern audience, *Record of an Obscure Man* emphasizes the black man's rich African cultural heritage and his potential for intellectual achievement. Garrison applauded Putnam's work, noting that "it has all the charm of fiction with all the assurance of truth." "The African," he concluded, "is contemplated as a man apart from his accidents."[18]

While writers such as Lydia Maria Child, Harriet Jacobs, and Mary Putnam were using their pens to extol the virtues of African Americans and advocate immediate emancipation, abolitionist speakers were using their voices to do the same. Throughout the secession winter of 1860–61, orators praised the slave, vilified the slaveholder, condemned the South, and urged the disunion of the states. The result was mob violence reminiscent of the 1830s. For the most part these mobs consisted of propertied men, who faced the prospect of losing money if the South seceded, and urban laborers, whose deep-seated racial hatred was based in part on fear of black competition for jobs.[19] The character of the mobs had changed somewhat. In the 1830s abolitionists were dragged through the streets with ropes or subjected to tar and feathering. Now rioters broke up antislavery lectures by attending them in large numbers, shouting, stomping, and clapping so loudly that the speakers could not be heard. In many instances, the rioters assumed complete control of the meetings, even passing their own proslavery resolutions.[20]

In December, for example, abolitionists rallied at Boston's Tremont Temple, only to have a mob seize control of their platform and pass resolutions conciliatory to the South. In January, Wendell Phillips addressed a mixed audience of abolitionists and troublemakers at Music Hall, announcing that secession represented "the jubilee of the slave"; in another speech the following month, he stated simply, "Disunion is honor." Worried about his personal safety, Phillips carried a gun during those turbulent months, and friends often acted as unofficial bodyguards.[21]

Women abolitionists were vitally involved in this propaganda crusade and risked their personal safety in participating. Like Wendell Phillips they embraced an uncompromising disunionist stance, thereby alienating many listeners. But then gender set them apart from Phillips and his male colleagues in the public eye. By being active and female, they further alienated those who, in this time of national crisis, were profoundly uncomfortable with women's public activism.

Susan Anthony organized a lecture tour of upstate New York in January 1861. The lecturing party included the Reverend Samuel May, the Reverend Beriah Green, Stephen Foster, Aaron Powell, and Elizabeth Cady Stanton, in addition to Anthony. Stanton could lecture only intermittently because her brood of seven children, one of them still a baby, kept her at home in Seneca Falls, but Anthony urged her to participate.[22] Even when child-care responsibilities kept her at home, Stanton managed to remain active in the abolition cause. In 1860, for example, she published a tract called *The Slave's Appeal.*

After condemning slavery on biblical and humanitarian grounds, the abolitionist pamphleteer called upon New York citizens to defy the fugitive slave law. "When the panting fugitive shall touch your soil, his chains must fall forever," she wrote. Included in *The Slave's Appeal* were petitions demanding an end to "slave hunting." Stanton urged New Yorkers to collect signatures and send the petitions to their state legislators. Colleagues were impressed by Stanton's work. Lydia Mott, sister-in-law of the Philadelphia minister, wrote of the "excitement" created by *The Slave's Appeal.* She promised to send each member of the House and Senate a copy when Congress convened.[23]

During the secession lecture tour, Elizabeth Cady Stanton demonstrated her radical disunionism, her monolithic view of the South, and her effectiveness as a platform speaker. Again and again she condemned the South for allowing slavery to sully the reputation of the American republic. Slavery "has corrupted our churches, our politics, our press," she said in one speech, and "laid violent hands on northern freemen at their own firesides." In addition, slavery had "gag[g]ed our statesmen, stricken our northern senators dumb in their seats. Yes beneath the flag of freedom," she continued, "liberty has crumbled with fear. That grand declaration of rights made by William Lloyd Garrison while yet a printer boy was in a far higher plane than that of 76."[24]

Although Stanton's message was a radical one, she was capable of tempering it. Throughout her career, Stanton showed an uncanny ability to couch her theories in the acceptable parlance of the day, at least when she found it expedient to do so. Nowhere was this more evident than in a speech which she composed in 1861. Addressing her comments to female listeners, she tried to lessen fear of Southern secession by comparing the breakup of the Union with the breakup of a family. Neither was desirable, but both were sometimes necessary. She likened South Carolina to a "hot headed willful boy," determined to leave the family, jeopardizing the happiness of the other children if forced to stay home. Wise parents, Stanton claimed, should let the headstrong boy go in peace, with "plenty of clothes & good advice," for the sake of family harmony. For those who found the probability of disunion too appalling to contemplate, Stanton asked which concept of the United States was preferable: a large nation characterized by "strife & violence or a small christian republic with clean hands."[25]

Stanton encouraged female activism during this time of national peril. "It is immensely important that at this hour every woman should understand the true position of this nation," she declared, "& give . . . her intellect & moral power in the right direction." She appealed to "true women" as mothers and as patriots, reminding her audience that while party politics might not be part of women's realm, morality certainly was. Furthermore, she encouraged listeners not to underestimate their abilities, for "one must not go through college or law school or spend years at the bar or the bench to learn what is right."[26] In the coming months, Stanton would repeat this theme. Ultimately her commitment to the crusade would lead her to devise a specific strategy in order to draw women toward public activism.

Although Susan Anthony preferred to organize abolition meetings rather than address them, she did give many speeches during the New York tour. Believing, perhaps, that the exigencies of the hour demanded plain talk, she abandoned the rhetoric of true womanhood and instead emphasized Garrisonian ideology. Using the "No Union with Slaveholders" theme, she declared that slavery "makes our professedly Christian, Democratic, Republican America, *a lie,* —a hissing and a by-word in the mouth of all Europe, and an offense in the sight of High Heaven!" Anthony frequently called on her audiences to refuse support for the "slave-holding Constitution" by reminding them that the United States was founded on compromises over slavery. Finally, Anthony no doubt alienated many by advocating the political and social equality of African Americans, one of the most controversial aspects of Garrisonian doctrine. Stressing blacks' "*inalienable right* to *Liberty & Equality,*" she called on Americans to permit their entrance into law, medical, and divinity schools, church pews, offices, and jurors' boxes.[27]

The first meeting of the New York campaign was held in early January 1861, at Buffalo's St. James Hall. Susan Anthony and Elizabeth Cady Stanton were joined by the Reverend Beriah Green for the two-day meeting. The convention, including its frequent disruptions, was given full coverage in the Buffalo press. The *Commercial Advertiser* condemned Stanton as an activist woman by alleging that she learned about slavery from one even lower in social esteem, a "nigger gal." As for Anthony, she "and her coadjutors have an undoubted right to express their opinions," but "the policy of holding these miscalled 'conventions' is very questionable." Antiabolitionist elements finally wrested control of the convention by turning off the gas, thereby plunging the crowd into darkness. Finally, the usurpers passed a resolution stating that in future, Anthony, Green, Stanton, and their colleagues must "utter their treasonable sentiments" in "some other locality than the city of Buffalo."[28] Stanton was incensed by the crowd's behavior. Noting that junior members of the Millard Fillmore and Horatio Seymour families were among the disrupters, she wrote caustically that "Northern Buffaloes have come forth in their might" and have "trampled the right of free speech in the dust."[29]

Abolitionists met with similar heckling and disruption in Rochester, when a convention of five hundred gathered there 11–13 January. When Stanton rose to speak, she was greeted with hisses. The Reverend Samuel J. May then attempted to address the convention, but he too was drowned out, despite the efforts of Rochester's mayor, sheriff, aldermen, and police to instill order. The convention adjourned until the following day, when resolutions calling for the "dismemberment of the Slaveholding Confederacy" were introduced.[30]

Henry Stanton, now a Washington correspondent for the New York *Tribune*, was concerned for his wife's safety. Writing from the capital after hearing of the Rochester convention, he urged her to stop holding abolition meetings. "There is so much rowdyism," he wrote; "the mobocrats would [as] soon kill you as not." Furthermore, Stanton insisted that the rioters were secessionist rather than Unionist in their sentiments, and thus their commotion ultimately aided the antislavery cause. Like many abolitionists, Stanton naively thought that emancipation was imminent. "Me thinks above the general din I hear old John Brown knocking on the lid of his coffin & shouting 'let me out,' 'let me out!' The doom of slavery is at hand," he wrote. "It is to be wiped out in blood. Amen!"[31]

The Utica abolition convention, scheduled for 14 January 1861, had to be canceled when the directors of Mechanics' Hall decided to deny Anthony, Green, and others admittance. In order to save face, a few of the faithful met in a private home, passing the obligatory abolitionist resolutions. "We all feel that we must go on," Anthony wrote to Stanton, who had missed the meeting; "the liberal people are stirred to the core." Accompanied by Aaron Powell and Stephen Foster, she traveled to Rome, New York, to address a small meeting of thirty to forty men and three women. As Anthony stood at the door collecting a small admission fee from each entrant, a man quickly shoved her aside and led a band of troublemakers into the hall. Unable to continue, Anthony returned to her hotel, where the proprietor assured her that the mob action would bring more converts to abolition than a hundred peaceful meetings.[32]

Mob attacks on the abolitionists grew steadily worse. In Syracuse, Samuel May was attempting to speak in Convention Hall when a group of antiabolitionists seized control of the proceedings and passed resolutions guaranteeing Southerners full constitutional rights "both in States and Territories." Regarding free speech, "what does it mean?" one speaker declared. "Does it mean an unbridled tongue licensed by law to teach our people treason and rebellion?" The convention disrupters soon took to the streets, where two hundred marched, shouted, and carried banners demanding "Freedom of Speech, but not Treason" and "Abolitionism no Longer in Syracuse." The proceedings took an even uglier turn when the mob condemned abolitionist and female activism by burning effigies of Samuel May and Susan Anthony, after having represented them in the performance of sexual intercourse. Of the Syracuse newspapers, the *Courier and Union* clearly sided with the mob, while the *Daily Journal* sided with the abolitionists, decrying "outrages upon public decency."[33]

If the abolitionists feared for their personal safety on the New York lecture tour, they certainly did not show it. Because many of them were seasoned public orators who had lectured on the controversial subject of abolition for years, they had long since become accustomed to the jeers and pranks. Self-righteous about their cause and their right to promote it, many abolitionists seemed to thrive on the controversy they aroused, even in this time of national peril. During a riot in Auburn, New York, Susan Anthony addressed a gathering of hostile men. Burned in effigy the previous week after being represented in lewd sexual poses, she felt no compunction to take refuge in the rhetoric of ladyhood. "Why, boys, you're nothing but a *baby mob*," she said. "You ought to go to Syracuse, and learn how to do it, and also learn how to get before the Grand Jury." Indeed, Anthony seemed almost to relish the tumult. "Mrs. Stanton, Susan & Co. are giving Anti-Slavery lectures in New York," Lucy Stone wrote to her sister-in-law Antoinette Brown Blackwell. "They have been mobbed in Buffalo, Utica, and Rochester. Won't Susan enjoy it?"[34]

New York abolitionists met at Albany for their Fourth Annual Anti-Slavery Convention, 4–5 February 1861. Among the delegates were Lucretia Mott and her sister Martha Wright, Frederick Douglass, Elizabeth Cady Stanton, Gerrit Smith, and Susan Anthony. Despite the best efforts of Albany mayor George H. Thacher to preserve order, speakers were heckled and interrupted by cheers for slavery and compromise. Elizabeth

Cady Stanton, whose rhetoric still included images of the family but whose invective was growing more venomous as a result of audience hostility, likened slave owners to "polygamists, who have many wives," and "cannibals who sell babies by the pound." But this tirade was tempered by Stanton's eloquent appeal against the restraint of free speech. "If it were possible thus to cut the jugular vein of abolition," she declared, "it would be at a fearful cost, for once admit the principle that one man may hold another[']s [right of] speech, & its sacredness is gone." Stanton delivered this address in Orleans County, New York, as well. It was later published in pamphlet form.[35]

Abolitionists also campaigned actively in the Midwest. In Cleveland, Abby Kelley Foster lectured in Chapin's Hall, apparently without opposition. Scoffing at the notion that "cotton is king," Foster emphasized the superiority of free labor over slavery.[36] But in Michigan antislavery orators were faced by angry mobs. Josephine Griffing and Parker Pillsbury led sessions in Ann Arbor that included resolutions demanding the formation of a Northern confederacy and the immediate abolition of slavery. The mob scene that followed was "one of the fiercest I ever encountered," according to Pillsbury. In Farmington their meeting was disrupted when troublemakers lit a match covered with cayenne pepper. When order was finally restored, Pillsbury concluded the meeting by accusing the slave states of a massive plot to assassinate President-elect Lincoln and General Winfield Scott, take the capital, and establish despotic rule in Washington.[37]

Josephine Griffing was a little more restrained than Pillsbury in discussing the South. Writing to the *Liberator* in May, she admitted that "slavery could not have lived without the aid of the North." Griffing was one of the most prominent female abolitionists in the Western Reserve. During the 1850s she was a paid agent of the American Anti-Slavery Society, lecturing in Ohio and Indiana. She also wrote articles for the *Anti-Slavery Bugle*, published in Salem, Ohio, and participated in woman's rights conventions. Her home near Cleveland was a western depot of the Underground Railroad.[38]

In December 1860 Josephine Griffing toured northern Indiana, where she found citizens of Lagrange, Noble, and Steuben counties suitably opposed to compromise with the South. The following June she found less cause for optimism. Having convinced Sojourner Truth to accompany her on a lecture tour of the state, Griffing was appalled when her colleague was arrested shortly after the two crossed the Ohio/Indiana state line. It was said that Sojourner Truth violated the state's black laws. Southern sympathizers were numerically significant in Indiana's legislature, which may help to explain why the black woman was arrested several more times in the course of her lecture tour. The first two times Griffing managed to win freedom for her friend, but the final arrests were handled by prominent attorneys. Reflecting on the hostility that the women encountered on their tour, Griffing remarked, "In my experience with mobs, I have never seen such determination. . . . At all our meetings for three weeks, we have been told that armed men were in our midst, and had declared that they would blow out our brains." During the war, Sojourner Truth would collect food and clothing for black volunteer troops near her Battle Creek, Michigan, home and later serve as a counselor for former slaves living in a Virginia refugee camp. [39]

As Phillip Paludan has emphasized, the winter and spring of 1860–61 became, for many Americans, a crisis of law and order. Some optimists, including President Lincoln, believed that Southerners were being duped by radical fire-eaters; Unionists at heart, the people of the South would soon reject secession. However, thousands of Americans feared the dissolution of the Union and anticipated that it would lead to chaos, anarchy, and the probable end of democratic government. Self-government, particularly on the local level, was a basic and cherished American value. Few were willing to jeopardize America's governmental system for the sake of the slave. Abolitionists were vilified during the winter months of 1860–61 for allegedly having pushed the South into secession. At a time when thousands feared civil war, abolition orators were openly encouraging disunion. At a time when Negrophobia was high, abolition orators were talking about political and social equality for blacks. [40]

Although the use of violence against abolitionists would seem to be antithetical to a belief in law and order, vigilantes in the Jacksonian Era had mobbed Indians, Mormons, immigrants, Masons, blacks, and, of course, abolitionists, all in the name of preserving the established order. During the early months of 1861, mob anger was focused on antislavery whites and free blacks living in the North. At the Syracuse convention in January, one resolution introduced by the antiabolitionist element emphasized democracy. "Firmly believing in 'the capabilities of man for self-government,' we hope the sunshine will soon, in undimmed splendor, break through the clouds that now hang darkly over us." Having committed themselves to participatory democracy, the mob proceeded to burn the abolitionists in effigy. [41]

Although the abolitionists themselves were not guilty of using physical violence, they did make vituperative, often exaggerated, and occasionally false accusations against the South. Their bellicosity linked them to the Southern radicals in the public mind, a fact which damaged their credibility. Their belligerence certainly contributed to the hysteria of the times, making compromise with the secessionists all the more unlikely. The abolitionists were, first and foremost, agitators. They were always self-righteous and always more effective at staging protests than at formulating practical solutions. Altruistic though their motives might have been, their determination to keep the abolition question in the public mind placed them and many free northern blacks in physical danger. In short, even those Americans who defended the abolitionists' right to free speech deplored both their tactics and their sense of timing. And many undoubtedly deplored the visibility and vehemence of Stanton, Anthony, Griffing, and the other female lecturers who insisted on flaunting their public activism and thereby challenging the basic tenets of true womanhood in this most perilous time in the nation's history.

With the fall of Fort Sumter in April 1861, most abolitionists rallied to the Union cause. They quickly abandoned their earlier endorsement of secession and their predictions of the imminent failure of an independent South. Suddenly they saw a new way to liberate the slaves: a holy war. This concept had great appeal for abolitionists who had long regarded their thirty-year struggle as a religious crusade. The war would serve as a form of nationwide atonement, followed by the final victory, freedom for the slaves.

Because abolition was not an official war aim, some reformers were hesitant about supporting the Union effort. Moreover, since many abolitionists had been active in the peace movement for decades, the advent of war caused them to reassess their traditional pacifism. Some took comfort in the words of John Quincy Adams, who had once declared the government's prerogative to abolish slavery in wartime. Wendell Phillips agonized for days after the fall of Fort Sumter. His speech endorsing the Union war effort was reprinted in newspapers across the nation and helped to transform his public image from radical agitator to patriotic orator. Lydia Maria Child supported the war but expressed her pacifist beliefs by hanging a white flag from her gate. When several observers once mistook her flag for a Copperhead symbol, she was furious at the implication that she would ever favor compromise. William Lloyd Garrison endorsed the war but continued to publish pacifist articles in the *Liberator,* including one message from the Peace Society of London declaring that war "bequeaths to posterity a sinister legacy of hatreds."[42]

Quaker abolitionists sometimes had pangs of conscience about supporting the war. Susan Anthony was raised as a Quaker. Her father was disowned for permitting a dancing school on one floor of their house, and although she never formally broke with the Quaker faith, she did not adhere to its somber dress code or its strict emphasis on pacifism. "It is strange to go in for the Union," Anthony admitted to Wendell Phillips after the fall of Fort Sumter, "but the War *is* glorious."[43]

Acceptance of the war was not so easy for Lucretia Mott, whose pacifism was deeply rooted in her Quaker beliefs. Mott could never endorse the war wholeheartedly, but she aided the abolition cause in many ways. Camp William Penn, a military training base for black troops, was organized in early 1863 near Mott's Philadelphia home. Although she could not bring herself to visit this military installation very often, she did befriend many individual officers and enlisted men. When on one occasion several of the regiments assembled to begin their march toward the battlefront, Mott ran into her house, gathered up all of her baked goods, and handed each soldier a slice of gingerbread until the supply was gone. Theodore and Angelina Weld, despite the latter's Quaker identity, were deeply disappointed when their son Charles declared himself to be a conscientious objector. Angelina Weld became convinced that war was necessary to free the slaves.[44]

When Abraham Lincoln was inaugurated president, abolitionists who had rejoiced in his election quickly became distrustful, for the president reiterated his pledge not to interfere with slavery in the states where it existed. "Lincoln's Inaugural makes *me* very doubtful of him," Lydia Maria Child wrote in a letter to Whittier. "I made great allowance for the extreme difficulty of his position, but it did seem to me that he bowed down to the Slave Power to an unnecessary degree."[45]

Abolitionists had even more cause for pessimism when, in July 1861, the Union army suffered a resounding defeat at the battle of Bull Run. Antislavery advocates ruefully acknowledged that their holy war would not be a short one. Not only had they underestimated Southern military power, but they also overestimated the willingness of slaves to take arms against their masters, a lesson they should have learned after John Brown's abortive insurrection. Nevertheless, abolitionists soon mobilized to exert pressure on the Lincoln administration to declare emancipation an official war aim.[46]

Abolitionist tolerance for President Lincoln, waning since the inauguration, finally changed into open hostility in the fall of 1861. On 30 August John C. Frémont, commanding Union troops in Missouri, declared martial law and freed all the slaves of rebel sympathizers in the state. Abolitionists and Republican liberals were jubilant. Abraham Lincoln was not. The president's policies were always tempered by his concern for the border slave states, whose secession could seriously endanger the Union cause. Frémont had acted without consulting the president, and his emancipation edict overstepped the First Confiscation Act, which allowed generals to seize those slaves directly involved in the Confederate military effort. Lincoln's consternation over the affair was compounded by a visit from the general's wife, Jessie Benton Frémont, who was convinced her husband's enemies had misrepresented him in Washington. The meeting was filled with tension. The president modified Frémont's proclamation, ordering the general to revise his slavery edict in keeping with the law. Lincoln relieved Frémont of his command later that year upon learning that the general had awarded military contracts to several of his California friends without formal bidding.[47]

The abolitionists were infuriated by Lincoln's actions. Martha Wright wrote to her daughter that she hoped every antislavery commander in the Union army would resign his commission rather than choose the role of "slave driver." Lydia Maria Child insisted that Frémont "be sustained by every friend of freedom. . . . We ought never to forget that he was the *first* man to utter the word, which millions long to hear." Garrison's *Liberator* contended that Frémont's decree of martial law took precedence over the Confiscation Act. Garrisonians continued to insist that the only way to end the war speedily was through emancipation of all the slaves.[48]

Another abolitionist hero was General David Hunter, who commanded the Department of the South. An admirer of Harriet Tubman, the runaway slave who had helped dozens of others to escape, he allowed her free transport on all government vessels. Tubman became a scout and spy for the Union army.[49] Hunter delighted abolitionists when he ordered the emancipation of all slaves in the states of Florida, Georgia, and South Carolina. President Lincoln negated the order, and many began to fear that divine punishment would be visited upon the Union for its failure to liberate the slaves. "This country will have to pass through shameful stages of degenerance," Lydia Maria Child wrote to Jessie Frémont, "if we blindly and recklessly throw away the glorious opportunity for atonement which the Divine Ruler has placed within our reach." Amy Post noted that military defeats had followed Lincoln's revocation of Hunter's proclamation. "Perhaps defeat is the means to bring the nation to its senses," she speculated; "this nation must suffer for all these multiplied wrongs [but] for how long or how severely is not seen as yet."[50]

The abolitionists had reason to feel despondent. After more than thirty years of hard work and agitation, they had achieved their goal of separation from at least most of the slave states. A free-soil president occupied the White House, and yet emancipation was still not within their grasp. Fully aware of the importance of the conflict, activist women would search for a way in which to influence its direction.

Abolition's Joan of Arc

I regret that Providence has furnished only one woman for such a crisis
as this. I wish we had 50 Anna E. Dickinsons scattered all over the
country telling the people the truth.
—Benjamin F. Prescott, Chairman of the
New Hampshire State Republican Committee,
to Anna Dickinson, 24 June 1863

The appearance of a new platform lecturer, Anna Elizabeth Dickinson of
Philadelphia, gave beleaguered abolitionists something to cheer about.
She was young, earnest, fresh-faced, and articulate. From her modest
origins in Quaker Pennsylvania, she rose to become an orator of national
reputation, often compared to a wartime heroine of another time and
place, Joan of Arc. She would become the most popular woman lecturer of
the abolition cause and a role model for those who believed the national
crisis called for increased female activism. Although Dickinson's contribution to the Republican party in 1863–64 has long been recognized,[1] her
importance as a feminist abolitionist has never been thoroughly investigated.

Born in 1842, Anna Dickinson was the fifth child and second daughter
of Quaker parents John and Mary Dickinson. John Dickinson, a business-
man of modest means, had dedicated himself to the abolition movement.
His untimely heart attack and death came while he was still in his forties,
after he had given a rousing antislavery speech. His youngest child Anna
was just two years old. Although she had no memories of her father, she
relished the stories others told her about his "brilliant" oratorical abilities.[2]

Mary Dickinson struggled to support her children by taking in boarders
to meet expenses. She taught her daughter to revere the Bible and appreciate the works of Shakespeare. Young Anna hid under the bed to read the
verses of Lord Byron, of whom her mother presumably did not approve.
Growing up in an abolitionist home, she undoubtedly read all the newspaper stories about slavery and the Union that appeared so regularly. One
of the newspapers she read was the Liberator, and at age thirteen she
submitted an antislavery essay which appeared in the 22 February 1856
issue.[3]

Dickinson left school at age fifteen to find a job. As a middle-class girl forced by the death of her father to seek employment, she would gain an identity with the working classes which would set her apart from other abolitionists. She would also begin to develop ideas about the role of women that would make her a woman's rights advocate and a role model for young women of her generation. Securing a position as assistant teacher in New Brighton, Pennsylvania, Dickinson soon learned of another job in a nearby school. She applied, only to find that her salary would be just sixteen dollars per month, although the man who held the job previously had received twenty-eight dollars. "Are you a fool or do you take me for one," she allegedly said to the supervisor, adding, "I would rather go in rags than degrade my womanhood by accepting anything at your hands."[4]

Dickinson then found work as an adjuster at the United States Mint in Philadelphia. According to Catherine Clinton, Civil War mobilization of troops led to more than 100,000 job vacancies in industry and government to be filled by Northern women. Like teaching positions, these jobs paid women about half the salary men had received. Although the Mint paid Dickinson twenty-eight dollars per month—relatively high wages for women's work—the job involved long hours of tedious work. The young adjuster's thoughts turned increasingly toward woman's rights and the abolition movement, a cause whose immediacy was made clear to her by the outbreak of war in April 1861.[5]

Anxious to participate in both antislavery and woman's rights activities, Anna Dickinson began to speak at reform conventions in the Philadelphia area. She was assisted in her oratorical efforts by several mentors. One of them was Lucretia Mott, like Dickinson a Quaker raised in a religious tradition which emphasized female preaching. Mott introduced the eighteen-year-old woman when Dickinson gave her first full-length address, 27 February 1861. Entitled "The Rights and Wrongs of Women," the speech helped to set an oratorical pattern for her subsequent addresses. She spoke at great length, more than two hours, delivering the speech extemporaneously and with great dramatic flourish. Advocating woman suffrage, she posed a question to her audience. If women could stand in line to pay their taxes, why was it "unladylike" for women to go to the polls and vote? On the subject of prostitution, a delicate one in Victorian America, she suggested that the practice resulted from female poverty rather than moral decay. Audience and press reacted favorably to the speech, although the Philadelphia *Press* commented that "it was the words of mediocrity spoken through the lips of genius." Dickinson was disappointed in her own

performance, believing her speech to be too lengthy and lacking in structure and organization. The young orator still had much to learn.[6]

Three male abolitionists also became Dickinson's supporters: William
Lloyd Garrison, Miller McKim, and Oliver Johnson. Garrison, a longtime
advocate of woman's rights and a firm believer in women's ability to appeal
to audiences on the subject of antislavery, had helped to launch Angelina
Grimké's career in the 1830s. He saw in Anna Dickinson a woman of rare
oratorical gifts who held his belief in immediate abolition. Sharing the
podium with Dickinson at a meeting of the Pennsylvania Anti-Slavery
Society in October 1861, Garrison heard her emotional appeal for making
emancipation an official war aim of the North. Without such a war aim,
she argued, "we have no war-cry—no noble motive. . . . While the flag of
freedom waves merely for the white man, God will be against us."[7] Dickinson also warmed the hearts of abolitionists because of her sharp criticism of
General George B. McClellan. Radicals despised the Union commanding
general because of his well-known sympathy for slave owners, his belief
that the sole purpose of the war was reunification of the states, and his
military caution. In a speech late in 1861, Dickinson charged the Northern general with treason in the Union loss at the battle of Ball's Bluff,
Virginia. The allegation, which was totally unfounded, received raves
from the abolitionists but evoked hisses from members of the audience who
probably perceived Dickinson as unpatriotic. The speech also cost Dickinson her job at the United States Mint. She later contended that the
dismissal was a blessing in disguise, for it forced her to make oratory her
total livelihood.[8]

Having decided on a favorite target, Dickinson continued to give
speeches in which she lambasted General McClellan. She drew a crowd of
one thousand at Concert Hall, 11 March 1862, where she pilloried Mc-
Clellan while praising abolitionist general John C. Frémont. "She thought
it time to recognize the only true leader the people had in this cause," the
Liberator recorded, "one who was not afraid to inscribe on his banner
freedom and liberty."[9] Perhaps Dickinson identified with the abolitionist
general. She believed he was fired for defending emancipation, just as she
had been.

Five days later Dickinson wrote a letter to William Lloyd Garrison
relating the details of her dismissal from the Philadelphia Mint and asking
his help in securing lecture engagements in the Boston area. Garrison
arranged a number of lectures, the first of them at Fall River, Massachusetts, where the audience received her enthusiastically and a local

newspaper announced "The New Star." The following evening in New-port, Rhode Island, Dickinson "kept the full house spellbound" according to one source. "Even the *rough* element, so often blatant, was completely hushed." A Democratic reporter for the Providence *Press* praised Dickinson's intellect and eloquence and then added, "It is a stroke of policy . . . the sending forth of this modern Joan of Arc to preach the crusade against slavery and in favor of promoting and fostering slave insurrections, and it will have its effect on some."[10]

Returning to Boston after her lecture tour, Dickinson became a welcome guest in the Garrison home, writing to her sister Susan that "Mr. Garrison has treated me like a father since I came." She seemed to appreciate Garrison's paternalism, perhaps because she never knew her own father. Dickinson may have been attracted to William Lloyd Garrison, Jr., whom she described as a "splendid . . . specimen of simple, natural, dignified, attractive manhood," while denying any romantic involvement. Clearly the young orator relished the friendships she was making with prominent New Englanders, enjoyed her new opportunities for travel, and seemed a willing protégé of Garrison, who coached her on lecturing techniques, vocal projection, and abolition philosophy.[11]

Garrison's coaching was more timely than either of them expected because Dickinson was called upon to address Theodore Parker's Twenty-eighth Congregational Society one week earlier than scheduled. Wendell Phillips was expected to deliver the address in Music Hall, 20 April 1862, but was forced to cancel due to exhaustion resulting from a western lecture tour. Dickinson agreed to substitute, although she was so nervous and distraught that she could neither eat nor sleep before the lecture.[12]

Her fear was unfounded. The audience of four to five thousand included Phillips himself, and, she later recalled, "all the literary fragments about Boston floated up there to listen." The speech was a "magnificent success." Calling on Dickinson the following day, Wendell Phillips told her that "actually my dear Anna brought tears into my eyes, they had almost forgotten the sensation." As for Garrison, he received many accolades for having discovered the new lecturer. But not all observers praised Dickinson's performance. The Boston *Post* objected to her abolitionist ideas, "almost all of which have been exploded."[13]

The following month Dickinson traveled with Garrison to New York City, where she addressed the twenty-ninth meeting of the American Anti-Slavery Society. It was her most important speech to date. In her address, she examined the causes of the war. Denying that Northern abolitionists had forced the South into secession, she insisted that aristocratic slave owners in the South bore entire responsibility for the present conflict. They had demanded compromise after compromise from the United States government. When the government refused to compromise further, the slavocracy forced the Southern state legislatures to issue secession ordinances. The slave power had even poisoned the minds of many Northerners, as witnessed by the recent mobbing of Wendell Phillips in Cincinnati. [14]

Like all abolitionists, Anna Dickinson naively believed that emancipation would bring the war to a speedy close, though she offered no specific program toward that end. She feared the spread of militarism that the war was promoting, warning her audience, "It rests with you to say whether [the republic] shall grow gradually more and more despotic—for the training of military men never runs toward Democracy."[15]

Believing with other Garrisonians that slavery was morally wrong, Dickinson quizzed her audience as to whether black people were fit for freedom. Answering her own question, she asked what right any white American had to claim that slaves were unfit for emancipation when blacks had never been afforded the opportunity to demonstrate their fitness. By 1863 she began to argue persuasively in favor of black enlistment in the Northern army, and after the war she published a novel in which she pleaded for tolerance of interracial marriage. [16]

Dickinson's themes were not unlike those of dozens of other abolitionist lecturers, yet few speakers drew audiences the size of her crowds. Her youth, gender, timely appearance on the lecture circuit, and considerable oratorical skills combined to make her an abolitionist of unprecedented popularity.

At nineteen, Dickinson was younger than most female orators and more attractive than some. She was short and slight and had expressive gray eyes and brown hair, which she parted in the center with curls falling back toward her shoulders. She dressed in simple Quaker style. Contemporaries usually did not describe her as pretty, though *Frank Leslie's Illustrated Newspaper* and the *Home Journal* characterized her as beautiful save for her prominent "Napoleonic" jaw. Still, her appearance was youthful, fresh, and unsophisticated. That Dickinson's appeal was in part visual may be seen in the fact that newspaper accounts of her lectures often included lengthy accounts of her facial features and clothing. [17]

In all of her speeches, Anna Dickinson presented issues in very simplistic terms: the Southern slave power caused the war; emancipation would end the war quickly; continued war threatened American democracy. Time and time again she repeated these themes. Never an original thinker, she was dependent on abolition's more gifted philosophers both for her ideas and even her facts. Dickinson's correspondence includes a number of letters to William Lloyd Garrison and others requesting information on a wide variety of topics.[18]

If the young Quaker leaned heavily on the Garrisonians for ideas, her platform manner and delivery were uniquely hers. By contrast to her girlish and rather innocent appearance, she was not afraid to condemn, in the most sarcastic terms, leaders of the government and military who she felt were forestalling Union victory. General McClellan became the brunt of her most vigorous condemnation, but even the president himself did not escape her ire. When Lincoln revoked General David Hunter's emancipation edict, she concluded that the president was "not so far from [being] a slave catcher after all." Dickinson's sarcasm was always tempered, however, by her patriotism. After lambasting one or more Union generals, she might inspire pathos with descriptions of military courage or evoke pride with her rendition of the capture of Fort Donelson, including the "final gallant charge and glorious triumph" of General Ulysses S. Grant's troops.[19]

In spite of the fact that she was just nineteen years old, Dickinson was poised and self-assured on the lecture platform. None of her stage fright was apparent to her audiences. She spoke extemporaneously, referring only occasionally to a few written notes, a fact which was invariably noticed by the press. Her voice was low, but her inflection varied depending on the subject. She had no trouble making herself heard even in the large lecture halls. A journalist for the New York *Times* once reported that "no reporter's pencil is dexterous enough to follow the magical rapidity of her vocalization." Horace Greeley's *Tribune* was equally complimentary. "She has the skill to please her auditors with wit, humor, pathos, argument, anecdote, history and philosophy," one reporter wrote in 1863, "and the power to control them by that influence which exists in the voice, thought, manner and presence of those who are truly eloquent."[20]

Given Anna Dickinson's youthful appearance, her undisputed speaking ability, and her emotional appeal, comparison with the Maid of Orleans was inevitable. A Northern public which was often contemptuous of female abolitionists appearing on the lecture platform before the war now welcomed the young Philadelphian with the sarcastic tongue. She was a novelty, and her pleasing appearance coupled with her direct, melodramatic manner appealed to the senses of many in wartime. As for the veteran abolitionists, whose performances she now so frequently upstaged, they welcomed her warmly. Wendell Phillips remarked that "she was the young elephant sent forward to try the bridges to see if they were safe for older ones to cross." Audiences that all too often rejected Phillips's approach to abolition cheered Anna Dickinson when she espoused abolition in a more dramatic, less intellectual way. Garrison, who was clearly pleased by the crowds his young protégé was drawing, could not help admitting privately that he was somewhat surprised by her phenomenal success. "Is it not curious what a popular enthusiasm she has created whenever she has spoken?," he wrote to a friend. "It is without a parallel."[21]

Dickinson was exhilarated by her oratorical achievements. Having been raised in poverty by a family still fighting to pay basic expenses, she dreamed of financial security. Having tasted success, she quickly rejected nineteenth-century notions of woman's "rightful sphere" and instead dreamed of becoming even more accomplished as an orator and even more popular with her audiences. Nevertheless, Dickinson knew that she had a long way to go before she reached these goals. Writing to her sister in May 1862, she complained that by the time her expenses were paid, there was not enough money left to buy a summer silk dress. "However," she added, "I am satisfied I have made an opening which will be worth hundreds to me next winter & probably thousands afterwards."[22] She returned home to Philadelphia in the summer to spend several months with her family.

Marriage, domesticity, children, and the gentle arts such as needlework and music clearly were not Anna Dickinson's interests, nor was she very enthusiastic about benevolent activities, long an accepted public outlet for women. Although she visited Union army hospitals in Philadelphia many times during the summer of 1862, she seemed more interested in talking with soldiers and collecting anecdotes than changing bandages and dispensing medicines. Dickinson gathered enough material to offer a new lecture on "Hospital Life," but the multitude of lecturing engagements that she had optimistically predicted in the spring did not materialize.[23]

If nursing and charity work did not interest her, issues involving women's inequality did. When she received an invitation to speak to the Twenty-eighth Congregational Society in Boston, the same organization which had sponsored her May lecture, she chose the topic "A Plea for Woman." Much of her lecture on 11 November 1862 encompassed the plight of women in the work force, an issue about which she could speak from personal experience. Dickinson argued persuasively in favor of better compensation for women workers. Turning to the subject of war, she contended that if women had held responsible positions in America from its foundation, the war would never have occurred. Like Elizabeth Cady Stanton, she appealed to audiences of traditional Americans by comparing government to the home. She alluded to the North's problems with finding a commanding general when she said, "It would not have taken a woman or housekeeper two years to discover that a person was incompetent, and to discharge him." Dickinson, it was reported, "is a graceful and earnest speaker" who held her audience's attention for two hours.[24]

Although Dickinson enjoyed meeting prominent abolitionists during her Boston trip, including Theodore Weld, Charles Sumner, and John Greenleaf Whittier, the eagerly awaited lecture invitations were all too few and far between. Her sister wrote of the family's desperate financial situation, even suggesting that Anna might wish to return to schoolteaching. But Dickinson's determination to continue lecturing was apparent when she managed to secure another series of engagements through the help of the Reverend Samuel May, Jr. Traveling through New England, she spoke on "Slavery and the War" and "Woman's Voting" in December 1862. In Concord, New Hampshire, the assembled crowd was so large that many stood for two hours while she lectured on "The Nation's Peril." The young speaker took advantage of the opportunity to denounce one of her favorite targets, General McClellan, along with other Democratic officers in the Northern army. Although this tour of Massachusetts, New Hampshire, and Rhode Island was moderately successful, Dickinson was finding neither the financial nor the political glory that many had predicted for her the previous year.[25]

Anna Dickinson and virtually all the abolitionists were jubilant when Lincoln's Emancipation Proclamation went into effect on 1 January 1863. It was not the type of sweeping emancipation edict for which the abolitionists had hoped, nor one which they felt would end the war quickly. At the same time, it was clearly a step in the right direction, especially coming from a president who had given them precious little reason for hope before that time. Anna Dickinson joined with Frederick Douglass and other abolitionists at Tremont Temple in celebrating the victory. "The contest can have but one ending," she said, "no compromise, no conciliation, but either the Palmetto or the Stars and Stripes from one end of the country to the other."[26]

President Lincoln and his Republican party gained new stature in the eyes of the abolitionists. Speaking at Fall River, Massachusetts, 7 January

1863, Dickinson commented on Lincoln's presidential record. "The President has listened to Sumner one day, to Crittenden the next, then to the Border State men," she declared. "He has wavered and faltered, and we have seen defeat and disaster. At last he has said this can go no further. There is but one thing left. The president decrees justice and the Almighty answered him with victory."[27] Because of Lincoln's apparent change of heart, Dickinson had no hesitation about campaigning for his party in the forthcoming state elections.

Republicans believed that success in the 1863 elections was crucial to the party's ability to continue its war policies. Opposition to Lincoln's implementation of the draft, his suspension of habeas corpus, and his issuance of the Emancipation Proclamation, combined with Union military defeats in the war, all contributed to Republicans' political vulnerability. New Hampshire and Connecticut were pivotal states. Both held early spring elections, and in each instance peace Democrats launched ambitious campaigns to defeat the Republican candidates. If these two New England states fell to the antiwar Democrats, other states might follow.[28]

Republican state chairmen, first in New Hampshire and later in Connecticut and other states, took a careful look at Anna Dickinson and concluded that a young female orator might add a charismatic element to their campaigns. Dickinson, dreaming of stardom as a speaker, eagerly accepted their offers to lecture in the spring of 1863. She continued to speak out in favor of abolition, but her emphasis shifted to partisan politics.

Benjamin Prescott of New Hampshire arranged for Dickinson to speak twenty times in the state. Convinced that she had special appeal for women as well as men, he believed women could influence votes even if they did not cast ballots. In February 1863 he noted that "the women of this state who have sons in the war are considerably nervous and want the war closed. . . . Please encourage them in all possible ways." As for the men, one New Hampshire Republican emphasized Dickinson's novel appeal when he wrote that "such men as we want to hear a lecture will not turn out to *hear a man.*" Although the Republican votes cast by furloughed soldiers and the presence of a third-party candidate were probably significant, Republican leaders gave the young orator a good deal of credit for their victory in the state election.[29]

Dickinson went on to campaign in Connecticut, Pennsylvania, and New York. Often her audiences outnumbered those of more distinguished speakers from the ranks of politics, journalism, and the military. In New

Hampshire, she outdrew abolitionists Theodore Weld and Stephen Symonds Foster; in Connecticut, she was more popular than Governor Joseph Wright of Indiana and congressmen William D. Kelley of Pennsylvania, E. H. Rollins of New Hampshire, and J. F. Farnsworth of Illinois. In her native Pennsylvania, Dickinson's competition included John W. Forney, editor of the Philadelphia *Press*, Horace Greeley of the New York *Tribune*, and generals John A. Logan and Benjamin Butler.[30]

Everywhere she received newspaper coverage, its tone usually set by the paper's political orientation. In Connecticut, for example, the *Daily Times* lambasted her as a "*spirit medium*" who was "48 hours from the presence of Wm. Lloyd Garrison." In addition to "Black Republicanism" and her defense of the blacks, occasionally referred to as "Woolleys" by the *Daily Times*, Dickinson, like the notorious feminist Abby Kelley, favored the "abominable heresies" of woman's right to vote and hold office. The *Connecticut Courant*, a Republican organ, defended Dickinson, referring to her "matchless eloquence" and her able discussion of the "political and military history of the rebellion." Charles Dudley Warner, flamboyant editor of the Hartford *Press*, gushed about this "American woman, cultivated, trained, endowed, devoted to the noblest cause since the Christian era began." Her purpose in Connecticut was divinely inspired, Warner concluded, for she "is sent as from on high to save the state."[31]

In addition to her novelty as a woman speaker, Dickinson was also unique among antislavery orators because of her working-class background. Whereas the more learned abolitionists had trouble communicating with laborers, Dickinson appealed to them in language they could understand. She was almost the only abolitionist who had genuine ties to the working class and could address audiences as one who knew what it meant to work eleven hours a day, six days per week. Recognizing this, the Republican party sent her into the small towns and the "mechanics' halls" in the cities of New Hampshire, Connecticut, and Pennsylvania.

In addressing working-class audiences, she rarely presented much ideological breadth but was often dramatic and inspirational. Dickinson was at her best when she used humanitarian arguments, as when she rhetorically asked one largely immigrant audience in Connecticut, "Shall it be said of you who have come from foreign shores—you who have fled from despotism and tyranny at home—that you have come to this country to crush out the 4,000,000 human beings whose fate is infinitely worse than yours ever was?"[32] The young orator was sincere, she was persuasive, and her audiences were almost always responsive.

In Pennsylvania, where she spent two weeks campaigning in fifteen different towns, she faced several audiences of miners. Many of them were Irish, and most were violently opposed to the Union war effort in general and the draft in particular. Dickinson used her trademark combination of sarcasm and emotion, first by condemning the Southern slave power for causing the war and alleging Democratic party ties to the Confederacy. Later she balanced her tirades with moving tales of hospital life based on her personal experiences and touching stories of martial courage based on her recent tour of Gettysburg, the scene of battle only three months before.[33]

Thirteen thousand copies of one of her speeches were distributed throughout Pennsylvania, and one Republican assured Dickinson that she had influenced many voters. "Your lecture," William Hay wrote 16 October 1863, "had a good effect upon the union men whom you addressed." Alluding to the fact that the Quaker orator's effectiveness lay not in the logic of her arguments but rather in her dramatic appeal, Hay added: "Persons often entertain opinions and feel satisfied of their correctness without being able to give 'a reason for the faith that is in them.' It is well to enable such to be able to defend their faith." Even in the smallest towns, Dickinson often drew working-class crowds well in excess of one thousand.[34]

Often she used economic arguments. Aware of working-class fears regarding the draft and potential job competition from blacks, she frequently reassured audiences by insisting that if slaves were emancipated, they would continue to live in the South. On the other hand, if the Confederacy won the war, the land it gained would be closed forever to free institutions. Never troubled by oversimplification or inconsistency, Dickinson appealed to the patriotic sentiments of the immigrant Irish in Connecticut yet told the Protestant workingmen of Maine to grant black suffrage as a balance to the votes of the "ignorant Irish."[35]

During the Connecticut campaign, Dickinson proved her ability to think quickly and use economic arguments to her advantage. While addressing a largely immigrant audience of Democratic voters in Waterbury, she said, "In the old country you worked for ten cents a day; and Mr. Buchanan, late Democratic President, said that was enough for you." An Irish listener called out from the back of the hall, "That's all we get now," to which the spirited orator replied, *"You must be working for a Democrat!"* Much laughter resulted since Brown Brothers' factory, owned by Democrats, was the only one of Waterbury's large companies to withhold wage increases from employees. Dickinson also liked to point out the beneficial aspects of the Republicans' protective tariff program. She was one of the few, if not the only orator, in the Connecticut campaign to discuss tariff protection versus free trade.[36]

Anna Dickinson undoubtedly helped the Republicans in the states where she campaigned, especially in Connecticut where the gubernatorial election was extremely close and where momentum seemed to swing to the Republicans at the end of the campaign. Pennsylvania's Republican governor also won reelection, and while the Democrats held on to the New York governorship, Republicans won control of the state legislature.[37] Although the young Quaker's public stature clearly was rising, her public image does not tell the entire story.

Always subject to stage fright, although she kept it well hidden, Dickinson often paced back and forth across the stage to relieve her tension. Although she seemed genuinely to thrive on the verbal combat of public speaking, in private she suffered from loss of appetite and sleeplessness.[38] Once forced to work for low wages to support her family, she worried constantly about money.

In several instances her physical safety was threatened. During the Pennsylvania state election campaign, she ventured into the western coal-mining region of the state, where antidraft violence was a common occurrence. When one audience refused to quiet down enough for her to speak, Dickinson, as was her usual pattern, waited patiently for the furor to subside. All of a sudden, one miner who disapproved of women lecturers pulled out a pistol and fired at her, clipping off one of her brown curls. Amazed by the courage and composure of the young speaker, the miner became an instant admirer.[39]

Although Republican organizers were thrilled with Dickinson's public addresses—at one point the Connecticut Republican chairman had cabled to his New Hampshire counterpart: "MISS DICKINSON SPOKE TO A CROWDED HOUSE LAST NIGHT. SHE HAS NO EQUAL IN CONNECTICUT. PEOPLE WILD WITH ENTHUSIASM."—the Republicans often failed to back their enthusiasm with hard currency, even when they had promised to do so. A pattern was set in her first campaign, when, in New Hampshire, Dickinson was rewarded with membership in the all-male Union League of Concord but with disappointing financial rewards. The Republican chairman regretted that lack of funds prevented his paying her more. She was paid well in Connecticut, receiving $100 per speech and $400 for her final address. But in her native state of Pennsylvania, organizers promised her $12,000 for twelve addresses, and Dickinson never received anything close to that amount. In New York she received $150 and a matching brooch and earrings.[40]

The abolitionists were, of course, euphoric over Anna Dickinson's latest successes. The *National Anti-Slavery Standard* was struck by the changes that had occurred since the 1830s when the Grimké sisters were denounced by ministers across the state of Massachusetts for speaking in public. Now, thirty years later, Anna Dickinson had won the enthusiastic endorsement of politicians and religious leaders, including Hartford's most eminent theologian, Horace Bushnell. Wendell Phillips waxed eloquent when he announced, "The Goliath of Connecticut Copperheads has been killed not by a stripling but by a Girl." Elizabeth Cady Stanton focused on Dickinson's importance as a role model in a glowing letter to her friend Martha Wright. "I am thoroughly satisfied with this noble girl, and have not one criticism to make. How many life-long hopes and prayers I realized as I listened to her eloquence: for whatever any woman does well, I feel that I have done it. Just as any poor negro listening to Douglass loses himself in pride, of race, so do I in womanhood."[41] Ironically, when Dickinson spoke on behalf of the Republican slate at St. James Hall, Buffalo, receiving favorable press coverage and being compared with Edmund Burke, it was the very same hall in which Elizabeth Cady Stanton and Susan B. Anthony had been heckled and derided almost three years before. Audiences unwilling to accept women speaking in public during the secession crisis now seemed willing to judge Anna Dickinson a patriot—at least those with Republican party loyalties.

In addition to making campaign orations, Dickinson accepted invitations to give her interpretation of the war for large metropolitan audiences. She shared the platform with William Lloyd Garrison in Boston, and at New York's Cooper Institute she delivered several speeches in the spring of 1863, introduced at one function by Mayor George Opdyke and at another by the Reverend Henry Ward Beecher. Newspaper accounts of the lectures indicate that every seat was taken, every doorway filled, and even the outer lobby of Cooper Institute was crowded. Speaking on the "Three Methods of Peace," in May 1863, Dickinson asserted that the North had several alternatives: concession, which she said was "simply impossible"; separation, which would leave slavery intact, imply that aristocracy was preferable to democracy, and could never be the basis for lasting peace; and vigorous prosecution of the war, the only viable solution. Dickinson's audiences had come to expect biting rhetoric, and the young orator did not disappoint her New York crowds. She blamed the South for the war, including the "manifold concessions of the North to slavery, and . . . the continuing aggressions of the slave power." She condemned the usual array of Union generals, including, of course, the luckless McClellan.[42]

Copperheads also had become a favorite target of Dickinson's, since they opposed a vigorous prosecution of the war. "They ought to be compelled to take one side or the other openly and not be permitted to depreciate the Government currency, to oppose the Conscription Act, to ridicule and embarrass the Government, to attempt to divide the North," she insisted. Indeed, she believed that Copperheads challenged God's wishes by deliberately opposing Abraham Lincoln and the war. Continuing these themes in Brooklyn at the end of May, she declared that "there are but two parties in the country to-day—patriots and traitors." Although she had once complained that before the war abolitionists were denied their rights of free speech and press when attempting to protest the fugitive slave law, she stated categorically that Copperheads had no right of assembly; in fact, their meetings "*should be broken up, even though it be done at the point of the bayonet.*" This tirade brought forth applause from the audience.[43]

The New York *Times* and *Tribune* each praised Dickinson's oratorical ability, while the *Independent* emphasized her feminine appeal. "Miss Dickinson is not a woman speaking like a man. . . . She thinks and feels like a woman. And she proves beyond all controversy that there are elements of truth, and phases of public affairs, important to be known, that can be given from no other stand-point than the heart of a true woman." The *Standard* reacted similarly to another Dickinson address, noting her "most womanly way of rendering a speech."[44]

Because of Dickinson's campaign successes and widespread public acclaim, the Democratic press occasionally ridiculed her. While many had initially scoffed at her potential to influence public opinion, the recent Republican victories combined with the size of her audiences made her a threat to the Democrats. "Somebody has said that a woman's name should appear in print but twice—when she is married and when she dies," scoffed the New York *World*. "Miss Anna E. Dickinson, of Philadelphia, is evidently of the contrary opinion." While admitting that the young Quaker "did no injustice to her theme," the *World* condemned her as "a woman unsexed."[45]

In an article entitled "Anna E. Dickinson and the Gynaekokracy," an upstate New York newspaper, the Geneva *Gazette*, decried "the absurd endeavors of women to usurp the places and execute the functions of the male sex." This movement of "Amazons" had its first proponent at the beginning of the century in the notorious freethinker Fanny Wright. Anna Dickinson and her colleagues were "advocates of every form of fanaticism. . . . They are in turn socialists, spiritualists, bloomerites, free lovers, Abolitionists: in short, agitators in general whenever and wherever they can find people silly enough to hear them." The Geneva paper commented quite correctly that Dickinson's addresses lacked originality, that she borrowed heavily from the speeches of Wendell Phillips, Horace Greeley, and Charles Sumner with a good deal of "flippancy and boldness" added for dramatic effect. Although the *Gazette* took comfort in its belief that "respectable ladies" did not condone such unfeminine behavior,[46] the size of Dickinson's audiences would seem to indicate that some ladies did attend her lectures.

By the fall of 1863 Anna Dickinson had become a speaker of national prominence, but one whose career had focused exclusively on the eastern states. Her first exposure to the West came at the invitation of the Chicago Sanitary Commission, an organization devoted to fund-raising for the benefit of Union soldiers. Mary Livermore, a Chicago reformer and abolitionist, had written to Dickinson in August with details of the "great Northwestern Fair," which was to be "not only a money-making agency, but a great moral demonstration rebuking disloyalty, and upholding Freedom." Because Dickinson would be forgoing potentially lucrative lectures in the East, the sanitary commission agreed to pay her $600 for her two November lectures.[47]

Chicago awaited Anna Dickinson's arrival with great anticipation. "The press had raised the expectation of the people very high by the narration of her oratorical triumphs in the East," Mary Livermore later recalled. Her fans apparently were not disappointed. In her first of two lectures Dickinson spoke "On the Duties of the Present Hour" to a capacity crowd at Metropolitan Hall. The focus of the address was on patriotism. The present conflict was "a war between good and evil, between liberty and slavery," she declared. "The first duty of every man, woman and child at this hour was unconditional loyalty." "Immense cheers" ensued, the local paper reported. After a lengthy discourse on the treasonous qualities of the Democratic party, Dickinson recounted several instances of personal courage by black soldiers, illustrating the readiness of black men for freedom. The meeting closed with three cheers for the Union, followed by three cheers for the loyalty of women.[48]

The Chicago *Tribune*, a Republican newspaper, lauded Anna Dickinson for her Chicago lectures. The *Tribune* was careful, however, not to be caught in the potentially embarrassing position of encouraging female participation in the public sphere. Editorializing about Dickinson's Chicago tour, the *Tribune* began by insisting that "society at large has an honest horror of the assumption by women of the functions which belong strictly to men . . . it is founded on that high regard for the purity and gentleness of the female sex." The *Tribune* was especially concerned because "of late years there has seemed to be a greater necessity for the cultivation of the sentiment alluded to, because of a dissemination amongst us of exaggerated notions concerning woman's sphere." Having made the obligatory stand for the hearth and home, the *Tribune* proceeded to insist that Anna Dickinson was a woman of "extraordinary talents," whose contribution to the Union cause was worthy of a "Roman matron." Her oratorical ability was compared to that of the great Edward Everett of Boston. Though she lacked Everett's polish, she could "deliver as much matter as Edward Everett . . . in double the time and her voice neither faltered nor shook." Indeed, "she has a mind that can grapple with the most subtle arguments—a voice of rare sweetness, strength and endurance—and a combination of power that never fails to magnetize the most careless audience."[49]

Mary Livermore also was impressed by Dickinson's oratorical talents. While noting her addresses were not memorable for originality or for logic, Livermore recalled the "magnetic power" of Dickinson's voice. "With a fearful array of indisputable facts, she exposed the subterfuges of those who planned the rebellion at the South, and those who defended it at the North. With the majesty of a second Joan of Arc, she invoked the loyalty, patriotism, and religion of the North to aid in quelling it."[50]

The Democratic press, angered no doubt by Anna Dickinson's effectiveness in campaigning for Republican candidates, accused her of profiteering at the expense of the sanitary commission. The loyal Mrs. Livermore wrote to the Chicago *Tribune*, explaining that Dickinson had interrupted her eastern lectures in order to travel at her own expense to Chicago. Her fee of $600 was not an exorbitant amount of money under the circumstances, especially considering the fact that Dickinson's lectures brought proceeds of $1,300 to the sanitary commission. In addition, Anna was a fatherless girl who "earns her own living and supports her mother"; during the six months of the year when she was not lecturing, Dickinson frequently volunteered her time, working in Philadelphia hospitals as a nurse. Her patriotism was clearly beyond reproach.[51]

Newspapers across the United States lined up for and against Anna Dickinson. In Hartford, Connecticut, the scene of the Republican electoral triumph some eight months before, the Chicago trip was a front-page story in the Republican *Connecticut Courant.* The Democratic Hartford *Times* sarcastically condemned Dickinson as "the wandering female Black Republican stump speakeress" who "charges $100 a night for her harangues; and for her speeches at fairs, for the benefit of sick and wounded soldiers, she charges—$300." In New York, Greeley's *Tribune* editorialized that "we think the slurs and flings whereof Miss Dickinson has been the subject . . . are most unworthy." Commenting on Dickinson's Chicago lecturing fees, the New York *World* sneered, "She is about the only woman in the country capable of the act." In spite of the sanitary fair's noble purpose, Dickinson persisted in issuing "diatribes against the party to which half of our soldiers belong." Even in Portland, Maine, newspapers debated Dickinson's trip. The Portland *Argus* accused her of taking money "for rendering a service to sick and wounded soldiers," while the *Press* accused the *Argus* of "copperhead slander of a patriotic, whole-souled, sacrificing young lady."[52]

Although the furor over the incident soon died down, the press reaction was indicative of Dickinson's rising stature as a speaker. Her reputation had grown tremendously as a result of the recent state elections. Whether or not her political impact in New Hampshire, Connecticut, and Pennsylvania elections had been pivotal, the Democratic press took her work seriously. Not only was Dickinson a threat to them politically, she was also a threat to them because she was female. Democratic newspapers invariably condemned her as an abolitionist and a woman. Republican newspaper editors generally supported her, but while some gave her their unequivocal support, a few such as the Chicago *Tribune* qualified their praise by showing uneasiness with the increasing tendency toward female participation in the public sphere. The national crisis seemed to justify the activities of this Joan of Arc, but the *Tribune* did not wish to see Dickinson begin a trend.

As the year 1863 drew to a close, Anna Dickinson could take great pride in her accomplishments. She had helped the Republican party to eliminate the threat posed by the peace Democrats in New Hampshire, Connecticut, Pennsylvania, and New York. She was nationally acclaimed as the Joan of Arc of the Union cause.[53] In an era when it was very difficult

for a single woman to eke out a living through schoolteaching, factory work, and other such low-paying jobs, this gifted young woman was earning fees of $100 per address and more. She earned as much per lecture as the highest paid male speaker in America, Henry Ward Beecher.[54]

Success altered Dickinson's life-style considerably. Gone were her simple Quaker costumes and her modest living quarters. In Boston she was reported to have worn point lace and diamonds to one speech, while in New York "she was attired in a splendid light purple moire" dress, and in Portland, Maine, she appeared in "rich drab silk, cut high in the neck, and trimmed with black lace." In Philadelphia she rented an elegant house for her family at 1710 Locust Street, paying first $500 and later $1,000 per year in rent. If her extravagant life-style seemed excessive in wartime, her charitable donations were also extravagant. Dickinson gave hundreds of dollars to charity, including a contribution to a children's home in west Philadelphia.[55]

Once the protégé of William Lloyd Garrison, Lucretia Mott, and others, Dickinson was increasingly confident and independent-minded. Furthermore, she was quickly attracting a following among women, who perhaps saw her as a heroine. So many women flocked to hear her speeches during the Connecticut state election campaign that they were asked to stay home on election eve, allowing enough lecture-hall seats for voting men. Journalists frequently noted the presence of large numbers of women in her audiences, including one Cooper Institute speech where they were numerically dominant.[56]

While some women may have come simply to admire her lace and diamonds, others liked what she had to say, admired her speaking ability, and perhaps supported her willingness to defy convention and speak out on subjects about which she felt strongly. Although prewar female activists such as the Grimké sisters, Abby Kelley Foster, and Elizabeth Cady Stanton were gifted orators, they often had been dismissed as shrill and unladylike. Dickinson, with her sumptuous clothes and dramatic lecture style, was seen by many as patriotic, theatrical, and feminine; in short, a true woman. One women's magazine likened her intellectual gifts and oratorical powers to those of William H. Seward and Edward Everett, while another called her "this most charming of female Demosthenes."[57] Astute Republican organizers such as Benjamin Franklin Prescott were well aware of Anna Dickinson's appeal for male voters and for women as well. While women did not vote, their powers of persuasion were believed to be significant, and their support for a vigorous prosecution of the war could be a great asset to the Republican party.

Success had its darker side as well. While she was confident, self-assured, and quick-witted before even the most hostile of audiences, privately Dickinson suffered from bouts of depression. She appeared genuinely to thrive on the verbal combat of lecturing in wartime; when alone she was often plagued with self-doubt and fear of failure, occasionally suffering from loss of appetite and insomnia. These symptoms were a reminder that while she had become a seasoned lecturer, she had barely reached the age of twenty-one. In spite of financial success, she was frequently victimized by political organizers, such as those in Pennsylvania who promised her thousands of dollars and then failed to deliver. The very qualities that contributed to Dickinson's success—youth, vitality, vulnerability—made her easy prey for unscrupulous promoters.

Abolition's Joan of Arc clearly captured the imagination of many in the war-weary North. She was young and female, which made her a relative novelty on the lecture circuit. In contrast to her fresh-faced appearance, she often issued sarcastic tirades against men who she felt were responsible for the Union's military defeats early in the war. Perhaps the Portland, Maine, *Transcript* best summarized Dickinson's lecture style when one reporter wrote of her "voice of remarkable power and sweetness," while also noting her "propensity to use the tongue *as a lash.*"[58]

On 1 January 1864 Stephen Symonds Foster wrote a letter to his adolescent daughter Alla urging her to follow the example of Anna Dickinson. "To charm is to captivate," he wrote, and "to captivate is to command. . . . This it is chiefly to which Anna Dickinson owes her success. She has neither learning, nor philanthropy, but a happy faculty of clothing the most common & obvious truths with uncommon beauty & thus giving them the effect of originality."[59]

Foster's description was accurate. A hardworking, energetic Philadelphia teenager, Dickinson was catapulted into the national limelight by a public which was hungry for inspiration and desperate to be told the meaning of the terrible carnage around them. Anna Dickinson fit the bill. She seemed to thrive on conflict and controversy and loved the attention lavished upon her by the public, the press, and the politicians.

Dickinson was not an original thinker, and yet her reliance on Garrison and others was understandable. When the war broke out, she was eighteen. She did not have the benefit of thirty years' experience in the

abolition movement. Although Dickinson may have been the only abolitionist ever to make a substantial income from her lecturing, she was a
child of poverty. Her early experiences with teaching and factory work,
coupled with the financial demands of her family, made her determined to
succeed on the lecture platform.

Abolition's Joan of Arc was a creation of the Civil War. If there had not
been a war, her name would never have become a household word.
Although her commitment to antislavery and woman's rights was genuine
and she would continue to promote both racial and gender equality in later
years, Dickinson was a dramatic orator first and foremost. Her postwar
career included several attempts to win acclaim as an actress, a natural
progression for her flamboyant personality.

At the turn of the century, Ida Tarbell wrote of Anna Dickinson's
contribution to the Republican victories in New Hampshire and Connecticut, concluding that "her usefulness to the Union cause in the war cannot
be questioned."[60] On New Year's Day, 1864, the day that Stephen Foster
wrote so revealingly about Anna Dickinson, abolition's Joan of Arc was
still preparing for her greatest triumph.

Elizabeth Cady Stanton and her daughter Harriot in 1858. (Courtesy of the Library of Congress)

Susan B. Anthony during the Civil War. (Courtesy of the Department of Rare Books and Special Collections, University of Rochester Library)

Anna Dickinson
(1860s) and an
expression of her
youthful
enthusiasm.
(Courtesy of the
Library of
Congress)

The World belongs to
those Who take it.
Truly Yours
Anna Dickinson

One of Anna
Dickinson's
oratorical rivals,
Emma Webb
(*right*), with her
sister Ada.
(Courtesy of the
Dramatic Museum
Portrait Collection,
Rare Book and
Manuscript Library,
Columbia
University)

Hannah Tracy Cutler photographed by Mosher in old age. (Courtesy of the Chicago Historical Society)

Sarah Parker Remond. (Courtesy of the Essex Institute, Salem, Mass.)

Harriet Beecher Stowe in 1862. (Courtesy of the Stowe-Day Foundation, Hartford, Conn.)

Fanny Kemble as a middle-aged woman. (By permission of the Houghton Library, Harvard University)

Lydia Maria Child
during the 1860s.
(Courtesy of the
Trustees of the
Boston Public
Library)

Julia Ward Howe.
(Courtesy of the
Schlesinger Library,
Radcliffe College)

Ellen Wright and her brothers. (Courtesy
of the Sophia Smith Collection, Smith
College)

Wendell Phillips during the Civil War. (Courtesy of the Chicago Historical Society)

Charles Sumner. (Courtesy of the Chicago Historical Society)

William Lloyd Garrison and his daughter Fanny Garrison Villiard, c. 1866. (Courtesy of the Sophia Smith Collection, Smith College)

ANNIVERSARY

OF THE

Women's Loyal National League.

———·•·———

The Anniversary of the Women's National League will be held in New York on Thursday, May 12, at 10 o'clock A.M., at the Church of the Puritans, Union Square.

Representatives from Auxiliary Leagues, and women who believe in a Democratic form of government, are invited to attend.

The work of the hour is not alone to put down Rebels in arms, but to EDUCATE THIRTY MILLIONS OF PEOPLE INTO THE IDEA OF A TRUE REPUBLIC Hence every influence and power that both man and woman can bring to bear will be needed in the reconstruction of the nation on the basis of justice and equality.

As the educators of future statesmen, heroes, and martyrs, it is the duty of women to inform themselves on all questions of national life, that they may infuse into the politics of the nation a purer morality and religion.

This revolution has thrown on woman new responsibilities, and awakened in her new powers and aspirations, no longer to be expended, as now, in mere surface work, but to be developed into a broader, deeper, and higher range of thought and action than has yet been realized.

The nation's destiny now trembles in the balance, and waits the electric word that shall rouse the women of the Republic to make themselves a POWER FOR FREEDOM in the coming Presidential Campaign. That all our sacrifices of wealth and ease and home, and the blood of our first-born, may not have been in vain, let us, earnest and heroic through suffering, now make haste to pronounce the doom of Slavery, and ring the death-knell of caste and class throughout the land.

E. CADY STANTON, President.

SUSAN B. ANTHONY, ⎱ Secretaries.
CHARLOTTE B. WILBOUR, ⎰

Broadside of the Woman's National Loyal League (also called the Women's Loyal National League) announcing the anniversary meeting in 1864. (By permission of the Houghton Library, Harvard University)

Women's Voices Appeal to England

Universal freedom for all dawns like the sun in the distant horizon: and
still no voice from England.
—Harriet Beecher Stowe,
"A Reply to 'The Affectionate
and Christian Address,'" 27 November 1863

One important aspect of the abolitionists' propaganda crusade involved
Great Britain, which to the surprise and horror of many declared official
neutrality in the War Between the States. Worse yet, many Britons were
openly sympathetic toward the fledgling Confederacy. Although opposition to slavery was strong in Britain, few believed slavery to be a significant
element in the war. Some conservatives favored Confederate nationhood
because the South seemed to represent gentility and culture, while the
North was perceived as big, boisterous, aggressive, ethnically diverse, and
dangerously democratic. Liberals such as William E. Gladstone supported
the Confederacy because of a commitment to the principle of national self-
determination. Even Samuel Wilberforce, the bishop of Oxford whose
father had been Britain's greatest abolitionist leader, favored the South's
independence. While some Englishmen sympathized with antislavery sentiment in the North, they did not believe the Lincoln administration
should fight a war to free the slaves. [1]

Outraged by Britain's lack of sympathy for the North's cause, several
activists believed that the national crisis called for women's involvement
in the diplomacy of the war. One such woman was Hannah Tracy Cutler.
A native of Massachusetts, she had married an abolitionist lawyer who
died after being attacked by a proslavery mob. Left with several children,
she followed Lucy Stone's footsteps by attending Oberlin College in the
1840s. She served as matron for the Deaf and Dumb Asylum at Columbus,
Ohio, for several years, but marriage to Colonel Samuel Cutler led her to
settle in Dwight, Illinois. During the Kansas statehood controversy, she
helped to organize a Woman's Kansas Aid Convention in Chicago. [2]

In July 1862 Hannah Tracy Cutler wrote a letter to the prime minister of
England. She was "pained beyond expression," Cutler wrote, "to see such
manifestation of bitter feeling as your press has spoken . . . while the

barbarisms of those who war against us, are passed by without remon-
strance." Her immediate provocation for writing was Lord Palmerston's
expression of sympathy for Southern women living in occupied New
Orleans. In May, Union general Benjamin Butler had decreed that any
New Orleans woman who insulted Union troops would be "regarded and
held liable to be treated as a woman of the town, plying her avocation."
This order evoked protest throughout the South and in Britain. Cutler's
letter was reminiscent of Lydia Maria Child's correspondence with Margaretta Mason three years before. Southern women were not true women,
according to Cutler, and she intended to drive home her point with
Palmerston. She reminded him that gracious Confederate hostesses were
also slave owners who "delight in chastising" their slaves "and inflicting
tortures at which even a callous man would shrink."[3]

Cutler contended that America was a nation founded on liberty and a
country whose early commitment to antislavery might be seen in the
passage of laws prohibiting the African slave trade. Sadly, this initial
momentum was negated by the South's economic rise, stimulated by the
invention of the cotton gin. Britain shared in America's guilt because of
the nation's incessant demand for raw cotton. With the growth in Northern antislavery sentiment and the election of a free-soil president, the
South determined to destroy the Union and provoked the present conflict.
Aware of British arguments against using war as a method of achieving
abolition, Cutler reminded Lord Palmerston that "we may perchance,
borrow our passion for internecine war from the venerable example of our
mother, whose wars of the red and white roses have garlanded our common
history." The antislavery activist concluded her letter by asking that Britain "stand aside and let the judgment of heaven against evil doers take its
unobstructed course."[4]

Most women who appealed to England did so by addressing the people
rather than the government directly. Among the more persuasive voices
was that of Sarah Parker Remond. Born in Salem, Massachusetts, in 1826,
Remond was the daughter of free black parents who prospered as a result of
shipping and trade. Growing up she was surrounded by antislavery activity.
Her father was a member of the Massachusetts Anti-Slavery Society; her
brother Charles Lenox Remond became well known as an abolitionist
agent; and Salem's Female Anti-Slavery Society was very active. Sarah
Remond made her debut on the antislavery lecture platform as part of a
group of abolitionists canvassing New York State in 1856.[5]

Three years later she sailed for Liverpool, one of a host of distinguished black Americans who traveled to England in the two decades before the war to plead the cause of the slave. One of the first prominent African Americans to make this trip was her brother Charles who had attended the famous 1840 World's Anti-Slavery Convention. Sarah Remond's oratorical gifts combined with the novelty of a black woman lecturer assured her large and enthusiastic crowds when she spoke in numerous cities in England, Ireland, and Scotland. Although she had planned to stay in England for only one year, friends persuaded Remond that her voice was needed to drum up English support for American antislavery.[6] With the outbreak of war, that voice was needed more than ever.

Like Harriet Jacobs, whose *Incidents in the Life of a Slave Girl* was published in an English edition in 1862,[7] Remond often appealed to the sensibilities of white women by discussing the emotional and sexual abuse of female slaves. In a major address before the International Congress of Charities, Correction, and Philanthropy in 1862, she referred to "nominal wives," for "there is no such thing as legal marriage" for slaves. She declared that slavery denied to black Americans the natural rights inherent in the Declaration of Independence and reminded her listeners that black people had never been allowed to test their real capabilities. At Chesterfield, shortly after the outbreak of war, she emphasized that slavery was the cause of the conflict; abolition was the only basis for peace and prosperity. Finally, the most pressing and recurrent theme in her wartime lectures was the need for Britons to give their sympathy and "moral influence" in support of American antislavery. As she declared in 1862, "The negroes and their descendants, whether enslaved or free, desire and need the moral support of Great Britain, in this most important but hopeful hour of their history."[8]

Far and away the most important female voice appealing to England was that of Harriet Beecher Stowe, whose Civil War activities have long been neglected by historians and literary critics, despite the hundreds of books about her life and works. Although scholars often paraphrase the famous line attributed to Lincoln about the little woman who caused the big war, the little woman's role in the big war has remained somewhat obscure.

Harriet Beecher Stowe's early life has been well documented. Born in Litchfield, Connecticut, in 1811, she was the seventh child of the prominent Connecticut minister Lyman Beecher. As a young girl, she was an avid reader, eagerly discovering the adventures of *Don Quixote* and *The Arabian Nights*. She loved Cotton Mather's monumental *Magnalia Christi Americana*, which, she said, made her believe the "very ground she walked on was consecrated by some special dealings of God's providence." Religion was always an important part of her life. As an adolescent, she was "awakened" into religious faith after hearing her father's sermon "Jesus as a soul friend offered to every human being."[9]

Harriet Beecher's formal education began at age five, when she was sent to dame school with her younger brother Henry Ward. Several years later she attended Litchfield Academy, and in 1824 she joined her oldest sister Catharine in Hartford, where she first studied and later taught at the Hartford Female Seminary. When in 1832 Lyman Beecher was offered the presidency of Lane Theological Seminary in Cincinnati, the Beecher clan moved west. Again she joined her sister, becoming an instructor at Catharine Beecher's newest educational institution, the Western Female Institute. The Cincinnati women's school closed in 1837 for lack of funds.[10]

It was in Cincinnati that Harriet Beecher had the time, the inspiration, and the encouragement to begin serious writing. The Beecher clan believed she had talent and told her so; moreover, she joined the Semi-Colon Club, a literary group which included most of the aspiring writers in the Queen City. With the publication of a short story about her colorful Uncle Lot Benton in 1834, Beecher joined the growing ranks of women writers. Mary Kelley has aptly named them "literary domestics." Like other such writers, Harriet Beecher was initially insecure about her writing, but Semi-Colon Club members were encouraged to submit pieces anonymously, which undoubtedly reassured her. Like that of E. D. E. N. Southworth, Sara Parton, and others, her fiction focused on domestic themes. And like other women writers, she published, in part, out of financial necessity.[11]

In 1836 Harriet Beecher married Calvin Ellis Stowe, a widower and professor at Lane Seminary. Years later she described her groom as "a man rich in Greek and Hebrew, Latin and Arabic, and alas! rich in nothing else." Absentminded and hypochondriacal, Calvin Stowe began admonishing his wife in the 1850s that she bore primary responsibility for supporting the family and managing its financial resources. With a household that eventually included seven children, Stowe felt increasing pressure to write for profit as well as self-fulfillment.[12]

Harriet Beecher Stowe's conversion to abolition was a gradual one. As a child, she had heard stories about her Aunt Mary Hubbard, whose marriage to a British emigrant in Jamaica had ended when she discovered he had mulatto children. Nevertheless, the Beecher clan had little sympathy for Garrisonian abolitionism, at least during the movement's early years. Lyman Beecher supported the American Colonization Society, believing its policies provided a moderate yet workable answer to the race problem. Catharine Beecher opposed Angelina Grimké's abolition activities during the 1830s on the grounds that public speaking on such a topic was un-ladylike. Harriet Beecher Stowe spoke critically of the abolitionists while on an 1837 visit to her brother William in Putnam, Ohio. Having observed the town's many abolitionists and having seen a copy of the proceedings of the 1837 Anti-Slavery Convention of American Women, Stowe expressed her views in a letter to her husband. "There needs to be an *intermediate* society," she wrote. "If not, as light increases, all the excesses of the abolition party will not prevent humane and conscientious men from joining it."[13]

Although Stowe's firsthand knowledge of slavery was limited, she did learn something about its cruelties during her years in Cincinnati. In July 1836 a mob vandalized an abolitionist press, sparking a riot which Stowe feared would provoke "war to the knife." The slavery question was further personalized after she employed a runaway slave to help with the housework. When the young servant's Kentucky master attempted to press her back into slavery, the Stowe family helped her to escape.[14]

Increasingly concerned about the slavery question, Stowe began to write articles on this topic. Her story "Immediate Emancipation" was published in the *New York Evangelist* in 1845. A few years later the family moved to Brunswick, Maine, where Calvin Stowe had accepted an appointment at Bowdoin College. The antislavery climate was far more radical in the Northeast than it had been in Cincinnati, especially after passage of the Fugitive Slave Act in 1850, which outraged even those who took a moderate antislavery stance. Stowe was among them. When Gamaliel Bailey, editor of the *National Era* in Washington, offered her $100 to produce a special antislavery piece, she wrote *Uncle Tom's Cabin*. It appeared in the *National Era* in weekly installments beginning in May 1851. Book publication came the following March.[15]

Harriet Beecher Stowe once wrote that "the heroic element was strong in me, having come down by ordinary generation from a long line of Puritan ancestry." Her patriotism, her strong commitment to Christian precepts, and her unwavering belief in the immorality of slavery provided the inspiration for *Uncle Tom's Cabin*. Indeed, she often contended that God had guided her hand when she wrote the novel. Stowe firmly believed that slavery demoralized both the South and the North. It corrupted the South by promoting idleness and indulgence; it corrupted the North by encouraging moral detachment. Stowe was not the first novelist to describe slavery's immorality, but she was the most successful. As Eric Sund-quist has written, "Her novel perfectly combined the tradition of the sentimental novel and the rhetoric of the antislavery polemic."[16]

Uncle Tom's Cabin was an instant success in the northern United States, becoming the first American novel to sell more than one million copies. Because the book was so popular internationally, it eventually was trans-lated into forty languages, and British sales exceeded American. Harriet Beecher Stowe made three transatlantic trips during the 1850s and was greeted with respect and acclaim in England and on the Continent.[17]

Thousands of Englishwomen were moved by *Uncle Tom's Cabin.* Deter-mined to let their American sisters know of their feelings, a group of prominent British women gathered in London to discuss the slavery ques-tion. This group, which was advised by the Tory philanthropist Lord Shaftesbury, included the duchess of Sutherland, a personal friend of Queen Victoria. Viscountess Palmerston, the duchesses of Bedford and Argyll, and the wives of Charles Dickens and Lord Tennyson also partici-pated. They composed a letter in 1853 which they called "An Affectionate and Christian Address of Many Thousands of Women of Great Britain and Ireland to Their Sisters, the Women of the United States of America." The document was also called the Stafford House Address because it was written at the London home of the duke and duchess of Sutherland. Af-ter acknowledging the delicate nature of the slavery issue, these British women insisted that slavery must be ended, for it denied the sanctity of slave marriages, separated children from their parents, and prevented slaves from receiving a proper Christian education. In all, 562,848 women representing all classes of British society signed the address. It was sent to Stowe in twenty-six leather-bound volumes, which she later loaned to Maria Weston Chapman for her Boston Anti-Slavery Fair and eventually displayed in an oak case at her home. Stowe received other petitions from the women of Leeds, Edinburgh, and Glasgow.[18]

Although the Stafford House Address was praised by many Americans, others condemned it. The New York *Observer* reprinted the document after changing every reference from "Negro slavery" to "white slavery." Mrs. John Tyler, a Virginian and a former First Lady, suggested that the duchess of Sutherland "leave it to the women of the South to alleviate the sufferings of their dependents while you take care of your own." Harriet Beecher Stowe was dismayed by attacks on the English aristocracy that the Stafford House Address engendered. Realizing the extent of poverty in Britain, she blamed intemperance and not the English class system. "It is my belief from observations and travel in England and Scotland," she wrote in 1856, "that almost all the poverty and misery of the lower-classes now arises from the traffic in intoxicating drinks."[19]

Stowe took advantage of her new fame to promote the antislavery cause. When the Kansas-Nebraska bill was before the United States Congress, she issued an appeal to the women of America. "Shall the whole power of these United States go into the hands of slavery?" she asked. Stowe urged women to familiarize themselves with the subject of slavery, gather signatures on congressional petitions, and arrange lectures. Above all, she urged women to pray for abolition.[20]

Despite her increasingly active public role in the antislavery cause, Stowe never formally associated herself with the radical abolitionists. This daughter, wife, and sister of clergymen could never separate her antislavery sentiments from her religious beliefs, and abolitionist leaders criticized Christianity far too often for her taste. In 1851 she wrote a letter to Frederick Douglass taking him to task for his condemnation of the church as "pro-slavery." She was equally disturbed by William Lloyd Garrison's repeated condemnations of both the church and the Union in issue after issue of the *Liberator*. Eventually Stowe invited Garrison to visit her home, where their two-day meeting did much to erase the negative feelings she had for him.[21]

In addition to her religious objections to Garrisonian abolitionism, Stowe was not temperamentally suited to work in an organized movement. She was a creative writer who composed when inspired. She never aspired to be a public speaker, and she was always too busy to do routine organizational work, even though she might sympathize with the cause. Writing to Anne Weston about the annual Boston Anti-Slavery Fair, Stowe promised to do her best to attend but warned that Weston should not count on her. "My family is a large one always," she wrote, "& lately there have arisen in it claims which I could find none but myself able to satisfy." Six of Stowe's children lived to maturity, and it was often all she could do to manage her children and the absentminded Calvin. Despite Stowe's refusal to play an active role in the organized antislavery movement, abolitionists admired her greatly. Elizabeth Cady Stanton declared *Uncle Tom's Cabin* to be "the most affecting book I ever read," while Lydia Maria Child wrote, "My favorite author, *par excellence*, is Mrs. Stowe."[22]

In 1852 Harriet Beecher Stowe began writing a column for the New York weekly paper, the *Independent*. Her brother Henry Ward Beecher became the editor-in-chief of this influential newspaper in 1861. With the outbreak of war, Stowe increasingly used the medium of political commentary rather than fiction to promote the antislavery cause. The *Independent* was an excellent instrument for her commentary; its circulation, which was just thirty-five thousand at the outbreak of the war, climbed to seventy-five thousand under the editorship of Beecher and his young assistant, Theodore Tilton.[23]

Stowe wrote guardedly of the presidential election of 1860. While admitting that the Republican party was not committed to immediate emancipation, she pointed out that at least it favored "*stopping the evil.*" She urged her readers to place their faith in God, "not in politicians or fleets or armies or elections or Presidents any further than they are indications of His mighty will who hath sworn to break every yoke, and let the oppressed go free." But in addition to prayer, Stowe advocated a more active stance, urging that "friends of anti-slavery principle should not relax [their] labor."[24]

In the ensuing months Stowe's writing centered around one basic theme: the Civil War was a holy crusade to emancipate the slaves. Warning Americans in April 1861 of the need to practice "self-denial" and "unselfish devotion" in the war effort, she placed the American war in a millennialist perspective. "It is one part of the *last* struggle for liberty—the American share," she said, "of the great overturning which shall precede the coming of HIM." In a similar vein, she wrote a poem called "The Holy War" in which she emphasized the high moral purpose of the Northern war effort.

> To the last battle, set, throughout the earth!
> Not for vile lust of plunder or of power
> The hosts of justice and eternal right
> Unfurl their banner in the solemn hour.[25]

Stowe was shocked upon learning that many Englishmen were sympathizing not with the North's "Holy War" but rather with the young Confederacy. She could scarcely believe that the English people, who had welcomed her so graciously in their country and had sent her an antislavery petitioned signed by more than half a million women, could befriend the South. "We are sending our very heart's blood out of our homes . . . to do battle against this slaveholding Babylon," she wrote in the *Independent.* "Where are the voices of our former friends in England?" But Stowe urged her readers to view the British position rationally. The *Times* with its

Southern proclivities did not represent the views of all Englishmen. The British government's declaration of neutrality was certainly regrettable, but it did, after all, amount only to an affirmation that the Confederate States were a belligerent power. England must be informed as to the true issues of the American conflict.[26]

With the education of the English people in mind, Stowe addressed a letter to Lord Shaftesbury. The earl had taken an active role in the "Affectionate and Christian Address" sent to the author of *Uncle Tom's Cabin* in 1853. Her letter to Shaftesbury, written from her home at Andover, Massachusetts, 21 July 1861, received attention on both sides of the Atlantic despite the public's preoccupation with news of the first battle of Bull Run.

The earl of Shaftesbury was one of those Englishmen who demonstrated an alarming degree of sympathy for the South. Stowe could only conclude that the earl and many others "misunderstood" the North's position. Insisting the North's cause grew directly out of the historical Anglo-American antislavery movement, Stowe wrote, "This war is a great Anti-Slavery war, not in form, but in fact; not in proclamation, but in the intense conviction and purpose of each of the contending parties, and still more in the inevitable overruling indications of divine Providence." The election of President Lincoln had sent a clear message to the South: "NO MORE SLAVE TERRITORY"; thus the "doom of their peculiar institution was sealed." Once the "slave party" found it could no longer manipulate the American government, she continued, it vowed to destroy the Union. Confederate vice president Alexander Stephens had stated unequivocally that slavery was the cornerstone of the Confederacy. Finally, Stowe spoke of the sacrifices many Northern boys were making for their holy cause. "There is not a thought or shadow of regret at the sacrifice we are making," she declared, "for now, if ever, we have a country that is worth dying for, and a cause in which we count nothing too dear."[27]

According to the *Independent*, Stowe's letter had "an almost unexampled circulation" in England. This was no doubt an exaggeration, though many commentators reacted immediately and often negatively to Stowe's missive. Pamphleteer Henry Richards, for example, decried war as an instrument of change and claimed that emancipation, if adopted at all, would represent a "cunning war-measure against the South" rather than an ideological commitment to abolition.[28] Among the scathing editorials published, the *Saturday Review's* was both critical and patronizing.

In a September 1861 editorial entitled "Mrs. Stowe's Wounded Feelings," the *Saturday Review* noted that Stowe's letter to Lord Shaftesbury was "a very ladylike document," for she adopted "all the tempestuous violence of feeling, the carelessness about facts, the one-sidedness" of a lady whose pride has been hurt. What she needed was to have her "say," along with "a good cry, an appeal to the feelings, and a flounce out of the room." After giving Stowe "credit" for helping to cause Southern secession, the *Saturday Review* took issue with Stowe's claim that the Union was fighting a "Holy War" to abolish slavery. "The North has not hoisted for its oriflamme the Sacred Symbol of Justice to the negro; its *cri de guerre* is not unconditional emancipation." The newspaper undoubtedly wounded Stowe's feelings still further by huffing, "The Governmental course of the British nation . . . is not yet directed by small novelists and their small talk."[29]

Along with Stowe, the *Saturday Review* also criticized Thomas Hughes, the well-known author of *Tom Brown's School Days*, for having defended the Union. Hughes replied the following week by writing a letter to the *Spectator*. Calling Stowe a "very distinguished American lady," Hughes condemned the *Saturday Review* for its "flippant and contemptuous serenity" toward the American writer and her cause. England, he wrote, must encourage the North in its antislavery sentiments. Most English newspaper writers, like Hughes, showed their respect for Stowe even if they disagreed with her position. The London *Sun*, which had little faith in the North's commitment to antislavery, commented at length on Stowe's letter, concluding that her "hope gives us hope."[30]

The Southern bent of the *Times* probably bothered Stowe more than the views of any other newspaper. The mighty *Times* with its long and prestigious journalistic record showed no sympathy for Stowe's directive to Lord Shaftesbury. In a letter to the editor, one member of Parliament who claimed to have "unfeigned respect" for the American author asked if her rebuke of England was deserved. After suggesting that the conflict between "free soil" and "slave soil" during the 1850s had been primarily a power struggle for control of Congress and also a "protectionist struggle" of free white labor against black competition, the writer questioned whether the North was truly interested in helping black people. Time after time fugitive slaves who escaped to Union lines had been returned to their owners. What better example could be shown that the North regarded blacks as chattel? Exhibiting a marked distaste for the very notion of an "antislavery war," the writer instead urged the peaceable emancipation of American slaves and insisted that England did not sympathize with the

South. Later in the war the *Times* went so far as to defend the institution of slavery.[31]

Criticism of Stowe was not confined to London publications. One newspaper in the industrial city of Leeds was not impressed by Stowe's contention that emancipation was a de facto war aim of the North. Englishmen would believe Lincoln's commitment to abolition when antislavery was "warmly avowed . . . not when it is kept skulking behind vague generalities." In the meantime, Britons would continue to regard the American war as a mere civil strife.[32]

The *Economist's* review of Stowe's letter, specifically citing British interests, criticized the North's adherence to the protective Morrill tariff and feared the impact on British manufacturing of a prolonged blockade of Southern cotton. While doubting the North could "reconquer" the seceded states, the *Economist* claimed that Britain's respect for the Union would grow markedly if antislavery became a war aim.[33]

The *Freeman*, a Baptist newspaper, admitted slavery was the basis of the American war but complained that "Mrs. Stowe does not see with European eyes" the North's history of territorial aggrandizement and the "bullying, bragging style" of American diplomacy. The *Freeman* reprinted Stowe's letter to Lord Shaftesbury in full. The *Nonconformist* was equally critical of Stowe for endorsing the extreme methods of the American abolitionists and what the paper termed the "anti-slavery party in the North." While praising Stowe as a writer, the paper nonetheless concluded that "we cannot but regret this mistimed exemplification of American tartness, as a mistake calculated to damage her object." Finally, the irrepressible *Punch* dismissed Stowe's "long and grandiose" letter in a three-sentence paragraph. If, as the American writer claimed, the North was united as one man, why was it that he "ran away like one woman" at the battle of Bull Run?[34]

Even American abolitionist journals were critical of Stowe's letter to Shaftesbury. The *Independent* admitted Stowe's work contained "serious mistakes," while the *Standard* attacked the author of *Uncle Tom's Cabin* on more specific grounds. To say that the North's "purpose" was emancipation of the slaves was a distortion of fact, according to the *Standard*. Nor was Stowe correct in implying that abolitionists and Republicans stood shoulder to shoulder against slavery. In fact, the Republican party had done nothing more than limit the spread of slavery in the territories. "We fear that Lord Shaftesbury's judgment of us is correct," lamented the *Standard*. "Anti-slavery feeling on the part of English people must be continued to be expressed by faithful admonition and rebuke to our nation" and "by help, for the present, to the American Anti-Slavery Society, instead of the American Government."[35]

The prominent and respected Mrs. Stowe clearly had earned for herself a degree of unwanted criticism. English newspapers, many of them anxious about America's growing power in the world, uninspired by the new president from Illinois, yet impressed by the fledgling Confederacy and its military heroics, were not inclined to accept Stowe's contention that emancipation was a de facto war aim. As for the abolitionists, many of them were still concerned with preserving their ideological purity, with keeping their distance from Abraham Lincoln and his Republican party. At least one abolitionist applauded Stowe's efforts. Lydia Maria Child wrote to her friend Sarah Shaw: "Didn't you like Mrs. Stowe's letter to Lord Shaft[e]sbury? I did *amazingly*. I thank God for Mrs. Stowe."[36]

Stowe's anger toward the British was considerable. In 1862 she wrote to her friend the duchess of Argyll, a Union sympathizer. "You see I am bitter," Stowe admitted. "It is our agony; we tread the winepress alone & they whose cheap rhetoric has been for years pushing us into it now desert 'en masse.'" Publicly, however, she controlled her temper, while still criticizing Southern sympathizers in England and promoting immediate emancipation through her column in the *Independent*. She praised the Liberal member of Parliament John Bright whose constant support of the Union was a source of comfort for many in the North. "John Bright represents a power and opinion in England greater than that of *The Times*," she wrote. Indeed, the *Times* had become "too contemptible to be replied to." Turning to the war itself, Stowe urged black enlistment in the Union army and emancipation as a "gift," not as a "cowardly expedient."[37]

As the war continued, with mounting destruction and a shockingly high death toll, Stowe's columns for the *Independent*, often based on biblical parables, turned ever more deeply religious. She implored her readers to sympathize with the slaves, to accept blacks as children of God. Not always emphasizing charity and love, her writing took on a far graver tone when she foretold God's punishment of the guilty nation. "This God of our Fathers is guiding the tempest and directing the storm," she wrote in August 1862. "We are being educated into faith in God by a terrible discipline." But Stowe urged her readers not to despair. She implored Americans to unite in prayer meetings all across the United States and to pray that Abraham Lincoln might obey the wishes of God and free the slaves.[38]

Like all abolitionists, Stowe questioned Lincoln's judgment during his first months in office. Lauding General Frémont for his emancipation edict, she had written in the *Independent*, "The hour has come, and the man!"³⁹ Lincoln's revocation of the Frémont edict angered her, but the president's decision to issue the Emancipation Proclamation was a step in the right direction despite its limitations. Stowe decided to use this presidential decree as the basis for an open letter to the people of Great Britain. She had never replied to the "Affectionate and Christian Address" sent to her by antislavery advocates in England back in 1853, and she would do so now. But first she wanted assurances from "'Father Abraham' himself" that the proclamation was "a reality & a substance, not to fissle out at the little end of the horn." She determined to call on the president in November 1862 to assess his commitment to abolition. After informing her friend James T. Fields, editor of the *Atlantic Monthly*, that she intended to write a "Reply to The Affectionate and Christian Address," for publication in his journal, Stowe set out for Washington.⁴⁰

En route to the capital, Harriet, along with her daughter Hatty and son Charley, stopped in Brooklyn for a week's visit with Henry Ward Beecher and his family. These two prominent members of the Beecher family found time to call on Mary Todd Lincoln, then visiting New York. In a letter to her husband, Stowe described the president's wife as "a good hearted weak woman fat, & frank. She denounced McClellan with a will (Seward also)." Frankness was clearly a trait that Mrs. Stowe shared with Mrs. Lincoln. Before leaving Brooklyn, Stowe managed to complete about two-thirds of her "Reply." "I would willingly send you the first part for the press before I leave for Washington," she wrote to Fields, "but think it best on the whole to wait till I see how things lie there and then send all together."⁴¹

Stowe and young Charley were ushered into Abraham Lincoln's study and introduced to the president by Massachusetts senator Henry Wilson. "Is this the little woman who made this great war?" Lincoln said, according to Stowe family legend. When their conversation turned toward the war, Stowe must have told Lincoln of her "Reply to the Affectionate and Christian Address," and he undoubtedly assured her that he would sign the Emancipation Proclamation in one month's time. On the whole, Stowe seems to have been convinced of Lincoln's sincerity. Before the November meeting, the only meeting between these two great humanitarians, she occasionally had ridiculed the president as "Father Abraham." To the duchess of Argyll she had complained, "Lincoln has been too slow." After their meeting, she wrote to friends that the proclamation was an "expectation" and a "glorious expectancy." In later months, when many abolitionists still referred to Lincoln as an uncouth baboon and an ass, Stowe wryly remarked, "Even the ass can kick safely and joyfully at a lion in a net."[42]

Stowe remained in Washington for two days completing her fourteen-page "Reply," which was published in the January 1863 issue of *Atlantic Monthly*. It was a brilliant piece of political propaganda, in which she combined history and current events, logic and subtle sarcasm to point out the absurdity of English sympathy for the Confederacy. The "Reply" was also published as a pamphlet in England.[43]

The theme of her discourse was that the American war was a conflict between slavery and freedom. The Southern government, she argued, had acknowledged that slavery was its cornerstone. The United States government, on the other hand, was dedicated to "restoring the Union as it was," meaning as it was in the eyes of the antislavery framers of the Constitution. Overstepping the evidence, Stowe claimed that America's founding fathers intended for slavery to be abolished gradually; she pointed to the specific examples of progress toward that end, including the emancipation of all slaves in the District of Columbia and in the territories, the Anglo-American treaty to end the slave trade, and President Lincoln's acceptance of the idea of compensation for Southern slaveholders. Stowe listed several examples of martial courage on the part of black troops and the joyous reactions of Georgia Sea Islands slaves to their liberation by the Union army. She then turned her attention toward Great Britain.[44]

"It is an unaccountable fact," she wrote, "that the party which has brought the cause of Freedom thus far on its way . . . has found little or no support in England. Sadder than this, the party which makes Slavery the chief corner-stone of its edifice finds in England its strongest defenders." While admitting that public sympathy often leans toward small nations struggling for their rights, Stowe asked, "If these [rights] prove to be the right of selling children by the pound and trading in husbands and wives as merchantable articles, should not Englishmen think twice before giving their sympathy?"[45]

Early in the war, Stowe continued, many Britons asked only for evidence that the North was committed to emancipation. Now, some one and one-half years later, the American government had moved closer to the time when "universal freedom for all dawns like the sun in the distant horizon: and still no voice from England." No voice, she added, except for the voice of Confederate ships being constructed in British dockyards. She signed the "Reply," "in behalf of many thousands of American women,

Harriet Beecher Stowe." It was dated 27 November 1862, Thanksgiving Day in America.[46]

John Bright, perhaps the North's most loyal supporter in Parliament, thanked the American author for sending him a copy of the *Atlantic Monthly*, claiming he read "every word" of her manifesto "with an intense interest" and assuring her that "its effect upon opinion here has been marked & beneficial." Bright insisted that despite England's official position of neutrality, "large & earnest meetings have been held in all our towns in favor of abolition and the North." The end of slavery was sure to bring an end to war. Anglican archbishop Richard Whately of Dublin wrote more cautiously, explaining to Stowe the varied opinions in Britain about the war and lamenting that North and South "should be making so much greater an expenditure of life and property than can be compensated for by any advantage they can dream of obtaining."[47]

Stowe's "Reply" was reprinted in many British publications in January 1863, often accompanied by the news that the Emancipation Proclamation was signed on 1 January. Many papers criticized Stowe's manifesto just as they had criticized her letter to Lord Shaftesbury. The lofty *Times* declined to comment, while the London *Morning Post* and *John Bull* questioned the sincerity of Mrs. Stowe's government. The *Saturday Review*, which stood out among British publications for its persistent criticism of Stowe's gender, complained that "only a woman could have hit upon this peculiarly telling and monstrously annoying rejoinder." Even if emancipation was a Northern war aim, abolition of slavery was not worth the toll in human life of this, "the bloodiest, the most purposeless, the most hopeless [war] in history." The *Athenaeum*, though it admired Stowe, shared with the *Saturday Review* a rejection of war as a means to end slavery. The London *Sun*, in echoing these sentiments, complained not only of the "horrors" of the Civil War but also about "inconveniences that ensue from the disruption of engagements with foreign countries."[48]

Punch, which spared no effort in satirizing both North and South during the Civil War, responded to Stowe's "Reply" by printing an "exchange of letters" between Lord John Russell, Britain's foreign secretary, and Lord Palmerston, the prime minister. Labeling Stowe's work a "woman's one-sided and incomplete way of putting a matter," Russell, according to *Punch*, nevertheless admitted that "it is not a bad hit, and all this comes of our allowing females to exceed their functions." The First Lord of the Treasury reportedly responded by telling his colleague to "keep cool" and by concluding, "I will never be angry with anything a woman does until she is unnatural enough to attempt to think." This and other caricatures of Stowe amused the American author, who wrote to a friend: "Have you seen the letters in Punch on my letter. They are more to the Point than Bishop Whately, & very funny."[49]

The Manchester *Guardian* was in no way amused by Stowe's manifesto. Anti-Northern sentiment ran strong in Lancashire, where unemployed cotton workers favored Southern independence as a means of revitalizing the depressed cotton-manufacturing industry. Many people in Manchester and neighboring cities regarded Lincoln's emancipation edict as hypocritical, as an expedient measure to undermine the Confederacy.[50] The Manchester *Guardian* criticized Stowe as a "raving priestess of havoc and destruction" because she promoted the "miseries of fratricidal war." In her "Reply" to the Stafford House Address, Mrs. Stowe "never wrote a truer word than that the party whose defence she undertakes have found little or no support in England during the past eventful year." The Birmingham *Daily Gazette* agreed, commenting sarcastically on the "sin England is said to commit in sympathizing with the South." This anti-Stowe newspaper excerpted the *Saturday Review* critique, while the Liverpool *Mail* borrowed the Russell/Palmerston exchange from *Punch*.[51]

Other newspapers were sympathetic. The London *Record* reprinted excerpts of the "Reply." The *Daily News,* discussing Stowe's work at length, concluded that "we are now in a position to see why the sympathy of this and every civilised people is asked, and even claimed as a right, for the North against the South." Those signers of the "Affectionate and Christian Address" in 1853, now supporting the Confederacy, showed more emotionalism than judgment, according to the *Daily News*. The *Spectator* echoed these sentiments. Aristocratic women signers of the 1853 manifesto who had "prayed in public places" for their erring American sisters to see the light of freedom for the enchained slave were now curiously silent. "Fashion," the *Spectator* noted tartly, was "now on the side of the Southern aristocracy."[52]

The *Freeman* and the *Nonconformist* had both criticized Stowe's letter to Lord Shaftesbury. Each newspaper reprinted lengthy excerpts of the "Reply." The *Freeman* assured Stowe that England was unshakable in its antislavery sentiments and advised the American government to cease espousing the virtues of reunion and to make universal emancipation its immediate priority. The London *Dial* was more openly laudatory toward Stowe. "Mrs. Stowe's 'reply' is not merely a sentimental address," one journalist wrote in the *Dial*. "She pleads with a woman's feeling, but she argues with a logician's mastery of her theme." The *Times*, after all, had criticized even Stowe's masterpiece, *Uncle Tom's Cabin*. Despite its power and prestige, the *Times* did not represent the feelings of the English people, for the "heart of England still beats true to the cause of freedom." These sentiments were echoed by the London *Morning Star* as well.[53]

It is clear that a number of British newspapers supported Stowe. Several, including the *Spectator*, emphasized the hypocrisy of many Britons whose prewar antislavery sentiments were now called into question by their support for the South. Two British newspapers, the *Freeman* and the *Nonconformist*, had softened, however slightly, in their attitudes toward the North, as evident from a comparison of their criticisms of Stowe's letter to Lord Shaftesbury and their later affirmation of antislavery in publishing her "Reply." If British press reaction to Stowe's manifesto did not indicate enthusiastic support for the Union, perhaps it did at least demonstrate a waning of support for the proslavery Confederacy.

A number of pamphleteers also addressed Stowe's "Reply." An anony-mous writer, characterizing himself simply as an English citizen, published a *Voice from the Motherland* in March 1863. Emphasizing England's com-mitment to antislavery, "Civis Anglicus" criticized Stowe for overlooking that part of the Stafford House Address which stressed the need for gradualism in slavery's abolition. Continued war could only bring more death, destruction, and governmental corruption. Urging separation of the North and South, the writer concluded, "The Federal States may start on a long and glorious career of freedom."[54]

By contrast, a committee of British women led by Frances Power Cobbe wrote a *Rejoinder to Mrs. Stowe's Reply* in the winter of 1863. This pam-phlet, published by Victoria Press of London, was reprinted in America in the April 1863 issue of *Atlantic Monthly*. Though the *Rejoinder* was un-signed, its authors claimed to represent the sentiments of British women on the subject of slavery. "The failure of English sympathy whereof you complain is but partial at the most," they wrote to Stowe. "The nation at large is still true. . . . Our hearts are with you in unchanged sympathy for your holy cause." Conspicuously absent from the *Rejoinder* was any men-tion of the aristocratic signers of the 1853 document.[55]

Because of the eventual success of the Union forces and passage of the Thirteenth Amendment freeing the slaves, historians have tended to exaggerate the extent of English support for the Union during the war. Passage of the Emancipation Proclamation is sometimes seen as a turning point, a time when English skeptics fell into line behind the Northern cause. Revisionists have challenged this view, pointing out that many leaders such as Gladstone supported the South until well after this time.[56]

Stowe's impact on British public opinion helps to clarify this matter. The American author was criticized—harshly criticized—by some newspapers, giving credence to the revisionist emphasis on British coolness toward the Union. On the other hand, it is hard to avoid believing that America's image in Europe improved, even if only slightly, with passage of the Emancipation Proclamation. Although the proclamation freed only those slaves in areas still in rebellion against the Union, slaves over which Lincoln had no control, the official declaration of emancipation as a war aim captured British interest, for abolition, far more than Union, was a goal with which the British public could identify. More important, after the proclamation was signed, the British government found it virtually impossible to aid the South without appearing to support the forces of slavery against the forces promoting its abolition.[57]

When, in 1862, the Confederate diplomat William Lowndes Yancey returned from London after months spent in an unsuccessful attempt to win British support for the South, he told Jefferson Davis sarcastically that too many Britons had read *Uncle Tom's Cabin.*[58] Harriet Beecher Stowe was a well-known figure in England, a writer who had touched the hearts of millions with her antislavery novels. The opportune publication of Stowe's "Reply" and its reprinting in a number of newspapers, coupled with the impact of her phenomenally successful fictional writings, undoubtedly helped to establish the moral superiority of the Union cause in the eyes of some English readers.

In America, Stowe's "Reply" was not widely reprinted, though antislavery journals excerpted some British reviews of the manifesto.[59] Nathaniel Hawthorne wrote to Stowe: "I read with great pleasure your article in the last 'Atlantic.' If anything could make John Bull blush, I should think it might be that, but he is a hardened and villainous hypocrite. I always felt that he cared nothing for or against slavery, except as it gave him a vantage-ground on which to parade his own virtue and sneer at our iniquity." Hawthorne's cynicism aside, Stowe found much cause for celebration in January 1863. She had written a powerful statement about slavery based on her deepest moral, religious, and political convictions. Senator Charles Sumner, one of abolition's strongest voices in Congress, congratulated Stowe on her "most timely" publication and reinforced her belief that the president would indeed "stand by his Proclamation."[60]

On 1 January 1863 she was seated in the gallery of Boston Music Hall attending a celebratory concert when word from Washington came across the telegraph that the Emancipation Proclamation had been signed. The crowd clearly credited the author of *Uncle Tom's Cabin* with helping to lead popular support in favor of emancipation, for people suddenly began to shout her name from all parts of the auditorium. Modestly she acknowledged the cheers, bowing and waving to the enthusiastic applause.[61]

After that memorable day, Stowe returned to a quieter life, publishing articles about housekeeping and novels set in the New England she knew so well. Without comment, she ceased to contribute columns for the *Independent* or to speak or write about the issues of slavery and war. Influenced by her sister Catharine's interpretation of the female sphere, Stowe did not think of herself as a political activist. Abolitionism was a moral crusade, and she was willing to make an exception to help emancipate the slaves. Having met with Lincoln in 1862 and having become convinced of his commitment to end slavery, Stowe had tried to help the president by speaking to the people of England. Once her objective was accomplished, it was time to step out of the public spotlight, return to her family and her novel writing, and let the president run the war.

Frances Kemble was one of those Englishwomen who had been deeply moved by Harriet Beecher Stowe's novel *Uncle Tom's Cabin.* But unlike most of her countrywomen, Kemble had firsthand knowledge of slavery. Her feelings about *Uncle Tom's Cabin* were so strong that she wrote a letter to the *Times* attesting to the accuracy of Stowe's descriptions. Because of the unhappy events of Kemble's life, she was unable to allow her letter to be printed in 1852. Instead she waited until 1863, some four months after Stowe's "Reply" had appeared in England, before she told her fellow Britons about her own experiences with slavery, including her views about *Uncle Tom's Cabin.*

Frances Anne Kemble was born in 1809, two years before Harriet Beecher Stowe. The Kembles were England's best-known theatrical family. Both of her parents were actors, and her aunt, Sarah Siddons, was the most celebrated Shakespearean actress in England from 1782 until she left the stage thirty years later. As a teenager, Fanny Kemble decided to join the family profession, motivated by the desire to assist her family financially rather than by any great love of acting. Nevertheless, she quickly became an exceptionally popular actress in England. Dark-haired Fanny Kemble was not beautiful, but she was shapely, agile, intelligent, and self-confident—and she knew how to capture an audience. In 1832 she trav-

eled to America, opening her tour at New York's Park Theater playing
Bianca in Henry Hart Milman's tragic play *Fazio*. Phillip Hone, the diarist,
wrote the next day, "We have never seen her equal on the American
stage." Baltimore, Philadelphia, and Washington audiences were equally
enthusiastic. In Boston, Harvard students were so enraptured with Fanny
Kemble that they pawned jewelry, even overcoats, to buy tickets for her
performances. Two of those scholars were Charles Sumner and Wendell
Phillips, both of whom walked seven miles in order to watch Fanny
Kemble act.[62]

In spite of her phenomenal success, Fanny Kemble was desperately
unhappy as a traveling thespian. Several months after the sudden death of
her traveling companion and confidante, she married the wealthy Philadelphian Pierce Mease Butler and left the stage. The marriage was a disaster almost from the start. She was intelligent, vivacious, quick-tempered,
and romantic, while he was narrow-minded and provincial. But the persistent American had been infatuated with the English actress ever since
she began performing in Pennsylvania and had pursued her relentlessly.
Fanny found in him the financial and emotional security she needed to quit
acting.[63]

Fanny Kemble Butler claimed that at the time of her marriage, she did
not know the source of her husband's wealth. Given the rapidity with
which Pierce Butler met, courted, and married her, coupled with the fact
that married women had few legal rights and could not own property in
their own names, this is possible. But she soon found out. Pierce Butler
and his brother John were absentee landlords. They lived in Philadelphia,
but their livelihood was based on Georgia rice and cotton. The Butlers
owned two plantations in the Georgia Sea Islands and nearly seven hundred slaves. In June 1835 Fanny Butler wrote to her friend Anna Brownell
Jameson about her discovery of Pierce Butler's slaveholdings. "The family
into which I have married are large slaveholders; our present and future
fortune depend greatly upon extensive plantations in Georgia. . . . As for
me, though the toilsome earnings of my daily bread were to be my lot again
to-morrow, I should rejoice with unspeakable thankfulness that we had not
to answer to what I consider so grievous a sin against humanity." John
Butler died of dysentery while serving in the American army during the
Mexican War, and Pierce inherited some of his brother's slaves.[64]

Fanny Butler's objections to slavery were deep-seated. As an Englishwoman, she had grown up in an era when Great Britain came to terms with

slavery. In 1833, the year after her emigration to America, Parliament abolished slavery in the British empire. Her distaste for the peculiar institution was heightened by her acquaintance with the Unitarian divine William Ellery Channing. Pierce Butler, who was a Unitarian, initially approved of his wife's friendship with Channing. In 1835 Channing published a volume entitled *Slavery* in which he urged Christians to help slave owners perceive the sin of slaveholding and repent their sin. The former actress, deeply influenced by the book, hoped to convince her husband that slavery was evil.[65]

In 1835 Fanny Kemble Butler published the diary of her first two years in America. Originally she planned to include an antislavery essay, but Pierce Butler was scandalized and she relented, fearing that an angry mob might "tear our house down, and make a bonfire of our furniture." There was much material in the 1835 *Journal* which bothered Americans even without the essay, including a series of unflattering descriptions of American women who dress "very much like French women gone mad" and American men who tended to be "very obnoxious chewers of tobacco."[66] No doubt Pierce Butler would have preferred that his wife suppress the entire volume; with his traditional ideas about gender roles, he did not approve of married ladies acting on the stage or writing books.

Filled with idealism, having adopted antislavery as her cause célèbre, Fanny Butler was determined to visit her husband's Georgia plantations. She found an opportunity when the Butlers' longtime overseer resigned, necessitating a new appointment. Pierce Butler was forced to make the trip south and decided to take his wife and young daughters. They arrived in late December 1838, dividing their visit between the family's plantations on Butler Island and St. Simons, where Pierce and John Butler were among the largest landowners and where slaves comprised 80 percent of the population. Fanny Butler started writing her journal sometime in January 1839. She wrote periodically throughout the Butlers' fifteen-week stay in Georgia. Her individual entries were addressed in letter form to her friend Elizabeth Sedgwick, who lived in Lenox, Massachusetts, and whose sister-in-law, Catherine Maria Sedgwick, was a well-known author. She never actually sent these letters to Elizabeth Sedgwick, but the journal was dedicated to Elizabeth when it was finally published.[67]

From the outset, Fanny Butler made no attempt to hide her dislike of slavery. Shortly before leaving for Georgia she wrote, "Assuredly I *am* going prejudiced against slavery, for I am an Englishwoman, in whom the absence of such a prejudice would be disgraceful." At the same time she hoped to find "mitigations in the practice to the general injustice and cruelty of the system." She found few mitigations.[68]

Like Harriet Beecher Stowe, Fanny Butler wrote when she was inspired. Often pressed for time, she jotted down her thoughts and did little editing. Her journal consists primarily of vivid descriptions of slave life as seen by a woman who expected to find poor conditions but still was shocked by the harsh reality of slavery. There is evidence that she intended the journal for publication from the outset. In one early entry she likened her efforts to those of Monk Lewis, a novelist and diarist whose *Journal of a West Indian Proprietor* was published in London in 1834.[69]

Butler described the plantation slave quarters in great detail. Each cabin, she wrote, consisted of a main room, twelve feet by fifteen feet, and several tiny closetlike partitioned areas for sleeping. While most cabins contained bedsteads, the mattresses were made of moss and the blankets were "pestilential-looking." Two families of up to ten members each lived in every cabin. Though garden space was provided, few slaves tended gardens.[70]

Butler was appalled by the hygienic standards of the plantations. The Butler slaves went to the fields at dawn and carried their noonday food with them. This they cooked and ate as best they could, often dipping from iron pots with broken spoons. The children used their fingers. "A more complete sample of savage feeding I never beheld," Butler wrote, and yet she commented that her husband's slaves were "generally considered well off." Even more upsetting were conditions in the estate infirmary, where Butler found a filthy room filled with dirty women and children. With her usual energy, she undertook to wash every baby in sight and "worked my fingers nearly off" stitching baby clothes for the newborns.[71]

The women were Fanny Butler's special concern. In the infirmary she observed one slave woman whom she could not help. The poor slave suffered from epileptic fits, lying on the floor barking "like some enraged animal on the ground." Another woman evoked her deepest sympathy. She had given birth to fifteen children, nine of whom had died, and now she suffered from chronic rheumatism. Unable to offer the woman freedom from work, she gave her medicine to rub on her swollen limbs. In another instance she interceded on behalf of a couple about to be separated by Pierce Butler's decision to give the husband to his departing overseer as a gift. "Poor Joe's agony while remonstrating with his master was hardly greater than mine while arguing with him," Fanny Butler wrote. "How I cried, and how I abjured, and how all my sense of justice, and of mercy, and of pity for the poor wretch . . . broke in torrents of words from my lips and tears from my eyes!" Her arguments must have been convincing, for the couple was not separated.[72]

Fanny Butler commented about the plantation aristocracy of the Georgia Sea Islands as well. Describing a duel between two local planters which resulted in the death of one, she noted that it was "a good sample of the sort of spirit which grows up among slaveholders." But her comments were not always critical, for she described in detail an incident of plantation folklore in which Pierce Butler's grandfather had bestowed a handsome silver cup upon a faithful slave. And the Englishwoman, who had the romantic's respect for nature, was moved by the beauty of the Georgia islands. She loved the outdoors and went riding and fishing whenever she could. Her sense of humor can clearly be seen in her comments about catfish. She described the "slimy beasts" in some detail: "They hiss, and spit, and swear at one, and are altogether devilish in their aspect and demeanor." During her fishing sojourns, she enjoyed the company of a slave guide named Jack, whose death some months later caused her much sorrow.[73]

The Butler family left Georgia in April 1839. For the next twelve months Fanny Butler edited and copied her journal, hoping to return to the plantations the following winter so that she could record more observations. Pierce Butler's family, led by his brother John, refused to grant this request. John Butler believed she had meddled in slave affairs. Still, there is evidence that the outspoken woman hoped to publish her work. On 26 October 1840 she wrote to her friend Harriet St. Leger, "I have sometimes been haunted with the idea that it was an imperative duty, knowing what I know, and having seen what I have seen, to do all that lies in my power to show the dangers and evils of this frightful institution."[74]

By 1840 the Butlers' marriage was floundering, with Fanny's literary interest and disagreements over slavery as precipitating factors. When Lydia Maria Child wrote to her requesting permission to print excerpts from the Georgia journal in the *National Anti-Slavery Standard*, she weighed the request carefully. While she had never met Mrs. Child, the two had mutual friends.[75] In fact, a number of antislavery sympathizers were aware that the former actress had kept a journal of her experiences with slavery, and some had even read the manuscript. The Grimké sisters had proved the appeal of Southern women speaking out against slavery. The diary of so glamorous and intelligent a public figure as Mrs. Butler, containing personal observations of plantation slavery, could be invaluable as a propaganda tool.

Pierce Butler was appalled by Lydia Maria Child's request and his wife's response stating she was not at liberty to print her journal but would submit the letters she wrote while traveling to Georgia, which contained observations about slavery that might prove illuminating. She backed down and refused to submit anything to the *Standard* after her friend Elizabeth Sedgwick intervened on Pierce Butler's behalf. "However great your contempt may be for my want of purpose," she wrote to Lydia Maria Child, "it cannot possibly exceed my own."[76]

The Butlers' separation and subsequent divorce was one of the most sensational legal battles of the 1840s. Supplementing their personality differences and their arguments over slavery was Fanny Butler's discovery of her husband's repeated infidelities. Charles Greville, the English diarist, wrote in 1842 that "she has discovered that She has married a weak, dawdling, ignorant, violent tempered man," yet Greville also criticized Fanny Butler for having "no tact, no judgment, no discretion." The antislavery diarist had hoped to obtain custody of her beloved daughters, but the divorce settlement of September 1849 granted her child custody for just two months of the year.[77] Although feminists such as Elizabeth Cady Stanton were keenly interested in divorce reform, child custody was still often granted to men.

With her usual indomitable energy, she returned to the stage under the name Mrs. Frances Anne Kemble. In contrast to her American debut more than fifteen years earlier, Kemble was now middle-aged; she had, moreover, gained considerable weight. Though she was no longer able to play Shakespeare's young heroines, she had no desire to do so. Rather than acting in plays, she turned increasingly to dramatic reading, a creative medium which she enjoyed and at which she excelled. "The fashionable world is all agog again upon a new impulse," Phillip Hone wrote in New York. "Mrs. Butler, the veritable 'Fanny Kemble,' has taken the city by storm." Each of Kemble's theatrical readings attracted hundreds of men and women from the fashionable world and netted her as much as $2,000 to $3,000 per week.[78] Having secured a divorce, Pierce Butler could make no claims to his former wife's considerable earnings.

Although Fanny Kemble was now free of financial worries and marital concerns, she was still unwilling to publish the Georgia journal. While she was legally entitled to spend two months each year with her children, Kemble did not wish to jeopardize these visits by enraging the volatile Pierce Butler. In 1853 she was asked to sign the "Affectionate and Christian Address" to be sent to Harriet Beecher Stowe by concerned Englishwomen, but she declined to do so. The "Womanifesto against Slavery," as Thackeray dubbed it, was sure to accomplish no purpose. Kemble feared that it might arouse "bitter feeling" among Northerners because of the "assumed moral superiority which it would be thought to imply."[79]

Although her feelings about slavery were as strong as ever, Kemble still believed that the decision to emancipate the slaves must come from slave owners themselves. During the Civil War she wrote to Charles Greville, "I have no claim to be ranked as an abolitionist in the American acceptation of the word." Although she never succeeded in convincing Pierce Butler of the evils of the slavery system, financial reverses in the panic of 1857 forced him to sell more than half of his slaves. In 1859 Butler oversaw the auction of 436 men, women, and children, the sale of whom brought the Philadelphian more than $300,000. "My children ceased to be among the richest girls in America," she recalled; indeed, the girls left their Philadelphia estate to move into a boardinghouse with their father. The sale caused Pierce Butler "extreme pain and mortification" because of the national publicity involved in a slave auction of such proportions. The facts of the Butler slave sale were quickly incorporated into abolitionist lectures, including those of Sarah Remond who told one English audience in 1861 that Pierce Butler, "known in this country as the husband of Mrs. Fanny Kemble Butler," had sold hundreds of slaves at auction but did not lose his standing "either in the Church or in society."[80]

After Abraham Lincoln won the presidential election of 1860, Kemble scoffed at Southern threats of secession. "Their bluster is really lamentably ludicrous," she wrote 24 November 1860, "for they are without money, without credit, without power, without character—in short, *sans* everything." With the outbreak of hostilities, however, she became increasingly alarmed by the South's military victories as well as the surprising amount of sympathy Great Britain showed for the fledgling Confederacy. "I hope to God that neither England nor any other power from the other side of [the] water will meddle in the matter—but, above all, *not* England," she wrote in September 1861. Her elder daughter agreed with her. Sarah Butler, who had married the prominent Philadelphia physician Owen Wister, was a fervent Unionist. Commenting on England's sympathy for the Confederacy, Sarah Wister wrote in the spring of 1861, "I cannot speak or even think of the English without almost going into spasms." The younger daughter, Fan Butler, adopted her father's Southern sympathies.[81]

When Fanny Kemble visited her native England in June 1862, Anglo-American relations were at a low point. She was shocked at the anti-

Northern tone of the British press and wrote that "the people among whom I lived were . . . Southern sympathizers." In private discussions with Charles Greville and Lord Clarendon, a liberal in the House of Lords who had once served as foreign minister, she argued the North's cause. Determined to influence a larger audience, Kemble decided the time was ripe for publication of her Georgia journal. She reached her decision to publish sometime between Lincoln's issuance of the preliminary Emancipation Proclamation, 22 September 1862, and the end of the year. Her decision was based largely on the course of events in the war but also on the fact that her younger daughter was legally of age. Pierce Butler no longer could dictate the frequency or the length of her visits to Kemble.[82]

Kemble's *Journal of a Residence on a Georgian Plantation in 1838–1839* was published in London in late May 1863. Like Harriet Beecher Stowe, Kemble invoked the words of Confederate vice president Alexander Stephens by including his famous "Slavery the chief corner stone" statement on the title page of the book. Her brief preface, dated 16 January 1863, indicated that the Georgia plantations were now occupied by Union troops. The journal was printed with few revisions, much as she had written it in 1839, along with her letter to the *Times* attesting to the accuracy of *Uncle Tom's Cabin*.[83]

Clearly, Kemble wrote her book in such a way as to emphasize slavery's most reprehensible characteristics—the separation of families, squalid living conditions, and above all the absolute control of master over servant. Because she was such a skillful writer, it is easy to lose sight of the polemical aspect of her text and accept the *Journal* as the unbiased account of a foreign observer. And yet Kemble herself never claimed to have written without bias. Like Harriet Jacobs, she intended her work to be a contribution to antislavery propaganda, and her diary stands out among such works. Harriet Beecher Stowe had written a powerful novel about slavery, but *Uncle Tom's Cabin* was fiction. Other writers had produced volumes based on personal experiences with slavery, but none had lived on one of the largest plantations in the South with a slave population which exceeded seven hundred men, women, and children. Nor did any previous chroniclers match Kemble's descriptions in vividness and detail.[84]

Extravagant conclusions have been made as to the *Journal*'s impact on Britain. One author has credited the book with no less than "diverting English sympathy from the cause of the Confederacy and helping to hasten the Surrender at Appomattox." Another writer believed that John Bright, having read the Georgia *Journal*, addressed the House of Commons in a speech that "turned the tide against the South." Such claims are greatly exaggerated. While the antislavery parliamentarian may have read Kemble's book, he did not mention it in any of his famous pro-Union speeches. A descendant of Fanny Kemble, writing in 1970s, claimed that excerpts of the Georgia diary were recited before the House of Commons. In addition, the cotton manufacturers of Manchester allegedly ceased to buy Southern cotton after reading Kemble's *Journal.*[85] Both claims are unsubstantiated. Neither Kemble's name nor her *Journal* appear in Hansard's *Parliamentary History.*

However, it is undoubtedly incorrect to assume, as one historian has, that Kemble's diary created "no stir."[86] The glamour and the notoriety associated with the Kemble name could attract a readership for anything the English actress published. It is also significant that the Ladies London Emancipation Society soon published an abridged version of the *Journal* in pamphlet form under the title *The Essence of Slavery* by F. A. Kemble.[87] Charlotte Forten, a black abolitionist from Philadelphia, was working as a teacher of newly liberated slaves on South Carolina's Sea Islands when she read Fanny Kemble's *Journal.* The book had special relevance for Forten, since Kemble's narrative encompassed the very black community that Forten had traveled south to serve. Describing Kemble's diary as "painfully interesting," Forten recorded in her own diary that "such a thorough exposé of slavery must do good, in this land, and in England as well."[88] Undoubtedly Kemble's *Journal* was a useful piece of propaganda for supporters of the North, and its publication just four months after the Emancipation Proclamation went into effect further emphasized the disparity between the virtuous North and the slave-owning Confederacy.

Several English journals of opinion reviewed the Kemble diary. The *Saturday Review,* which had criticized Harriet Beecher Stowe so scathingly as both a Northern apologist and a woman author, now upbraided Kemble for writing explicitly about such delicate subjects as maternity leave for field hands and illegitimate births and pointed out that slaves on the Butler plantations were probably no less fortunate than the agricultural poor in many English towns. The British *Quarterly Review* praised the Georgia *Journal* as an "antidote and corrective" to those British writers who attempted to romanticize the institution of slavery. The *Athenaeum* shared this view, dismissing those "mealy-mouthed apologists, whose function it is to 'make things pleasant' with regard to slavery." Kemble "uses plain terms . . . and we thank her for so doing." The *Spectator* was equally laudatory, praising the English actress for a "condemnation of slavery more severe than any in which professed philanthropists would venture to indulge."[89]

The American edition of *Journal of a Residence on a Georgian Plantation* was published by Harper and Brothers in July 1863. While sales records for the book are no longer extant, it sold well enough to warrant a second edition in 1864. Excerpts of Kemble's *Journal* were also printed in pamphlet form in the United States under the title *The Views of Judge Woodward and Bishop Hopkins on Negro Slavery at the South, Illustrated from the Journal of a Residence on a Georgian Plantation.* As a companion piece to Fanny Kemble's diary, the well-known narrative of Pierce Butler's slave auction, first published by the American Anti-Slavery Society before the war, was reprinted in 1863 by the Union League of Philadelphia.[90]

Abolitionist women rejoiced at the appearance of Kemble's *Journal*, for it provided them with further evidence of the evils of slavery. Elizabeth Cady Stanton used Kemble's diary in her lectures. Speaking on "The Future of the Republic," Stanton remarked, "No better blow has been dealt on our common foe during the war than she has given." Lydia Maria Child, recalling Kemble's refusal to print the *Journal* in 1840, now applauded her sense of timing. "It will do a hundred-fold more good now," she wrote to Oliver Johnson, editor of the *Standard*. "It came out in the very nick of time. I think it will prove one of the most powerful of the agencies now at work for the overthrow of slavery." Child faulted the Englishwoman, however, for her belief that only the slaveholders themselves could take the initiative for emancipation.[91]

Antislavery weeklies praised Kemble's *Journal* as an accurate and dramatic exposé of slavery. The *Independent* reprinted numerous extracts, lauding the English actress for her "plain, clear, outspoken diary." Horace Greeley, a regular columnist for the *Independent*, believed that "the intense *meanness* of slaveholding has never been more forcibly exhibited than in Mrs. Kemble's *Journal.*" The *National Anti-Slavery Standard* also reprinted lengthy excerpts from the book, along with favorable reviews from both sides of the Atlantic.[92]

American journals embraced the diary enthusiastically. *Littell's Living Age* reprinted the *Spectator's* favorable review. *North American Review* believed the work to be valuable because Kemble was more than a mere transient observer of Southern slavery. *Harper's New Monthly Magazine* regarded Kemble's diary as "the most powerful anti-slavery book yet written," while *Atlantic Monthly*, which had printed Harriet Beecher Stowe's "Reply" in January 1863, devoted four pages to a review of Fanny Kemble's account. *Atlantic* was struck by the uniqueness of the *Journal*. Frederick Law Olmsted had written persuasively about slavery, yet he was only an observer. Mrs. Stowe's book was a novel, powerful though it was. Theodore Weld moved many readers with his compendium of newspaper accounts, *Slavery As It Is*, in 1839. Yet only Fanny Kemble could write about slavery from the perspective of one who had actually lived with the institution. *Atlantic* viewed the *Journal* as further evidence that the current struggle between government and slavery could not end before the destruction of one or the other.[93]

Kemble's Georgia *Journal* was an important contribution to antislavery literature. Her diary was printed in the same month that the North turned the tide of the war by winning battles in both the eastern and western theaters. The first American printing sold out within a year, and the *Journal* was warmly received by leading journals of opinion. Furthermore, Kemble's book was used by the American Freedmen's Inquiry Commission, established by Secretary of War Edwin Stanton, to investigate the status of the former slaves. Fanny Kemble was cited by committee members Robert Dale Owen, Samuel Gridley Howe, and James McKaye as an expert on the impact of slavery on women. The report of this commission led to passage of the Freedmen's Bureau Act of 1865.[94]

The issue of Anglo-American relations was an important one during the American Civil War. Although Britain came close to war with the Union only once during the 1860s, after two Confederate diplomats were removed from a British ship in 1861 and taken to the North, the threat of war remained.[95] British recognition of the Confederacy could have had disastrous consequences as well. Many Englishmen sympathized with the Confederacy at the outset of the war, a fact which both confused and angered those abolitionists who believed emancipation to be a war aim of the North. Hannah Tracy Cutler, Sarah Parker Remond, Harriet Beecher Stowe, and Fanny Kemble thought that England must be forced to realize that slavery was the cornerstone of the Confederacy and, conversely, that emancipation was the ultimate goal of the United States government. Each added a powerful voice to those of the diplomats and statesmen who argued successfully against British intervention in the American Civil War.

In the process they provided abolitionists with new arguments and antislavery women with additional role models. When Elizabeth Cady Stanton decided it was time that women took a more active role in the war, she highlighted the importance of the Georgia *Journal* and urged women to "exalt the eternal principles on which a republic rests, with word & pen, as that great hearted woman Fanny Kemble has done."[96] In the same month in which Kemble's *Journal of a Residence on a Georgian Plantation* was published in England, Stanton would launch a nationwide feminist abolitionist organization which would involve thousands of American women in the moral and political issues about which Cutler, Remond, Stowe, and Kemble wrote and spoke so effectively.

The Woman's National Loyal League

Women can neither take the ballot nor the bullet to settle this
question; therefore, to us, the right to petition is the one sacred right
which we ought not to neglect.
—Susan B. Anthony, American Anti-Slavery Society
Third Decade Meeting, 4 December 1863

In the summer of 1862, Ellen Wright wrote a letter to her close friend Lucy
McKim. Both women were the daughters of well-known abolitionists, and
both would later marry sons of William Lloyd Garrison. On 15 August
1862 Ellen Wright expressed her disappointment at being unable to play
an active role in what she regarded as the war to liberate the slaves. "Think
how our boys are all going!" she wrote. "Is it not stifling, irksome work, to
remain quietly at home."[1] Her letter demonstrated the exuberance and
impatience of youth, but she also touched upon something more far-
reaching. Many women felt a sense of frustration during the war. Fully
aware of the importance of the conflict for both antislavery and the future
of democratic government, many believed the national crisis called for
female participation beyond the traditional tasks of nursing, sewing, and
bandage rolling.

It should be noted that abolitionist women by no means shunned charity
work. Abigail Hopper Gibbons, the New York reformer who had questioned John Brown about the practicality of his proposed abolition scheme
in 1859, became a nurse at the age of sixty. She was assigned to Union
army hospitals first in Virginia and later in Maryland. To her friends at
home, Gibbons wrote poignant letters about her hard work and sympathy
for the wounded soldiers.[2]

Many abolitionist women worked for the contrabands, those slaves who
escaped through the Union lines. While many were returned by the army
to their masters, thousands streamed into Washington and other Northern
cities. Frightened, confused, and often destitute, these men, women, and
children provided a natural outlet for abolitionist charity. The Ladies
Anti-Slavery Society of Rochester devoted its time and money to sponsor-
ing a school for freedmen in Washington. Members also donated money to
Harriet Tubman, the black abolitionist who was working with former

slaves at Hilton Head, South Carolina. Martha Wright of Auburn, New York, gave so many of her family's clothes to the freedmen that her husband and children began to feel the shortage of wearing apparel. Lydia Maria Child, who used her pen time and again to help the abolition cause, published a self-help book about growing old gracefully, the proceeds of which went entirely to freedmen's relief.[3]

Women abolitionists participated in other types of abolition-related war work as well. The Grimké sisters became strong advocates of black enlistment in the Union army. Lucretia Mott attempted to integrate public transportation in Philadelphia by staging a public protest, while Sojourner Truth played a similar role in Washington. After Charles Sumner had an ordinance passed prohibiting segregation on streetcars in the District of Columbia, the black abolitionist attempted to ride one streetcar. She was shoved against a door by its brutal conductor but succeeded in having the man arrested and fired from his job.[4]

Fund-raising, freedmen's relief work, and nursing were valuable outlets for female philanthropy during the Civil War. Women also turned to writing, oratory, and petitioning to support the antislavery cause. One such woman was Julia Ward Howe. Born and raised in New York City, Julia Ward grew up in a wealthy, religious, and loving home. Her marriage at age twenty-three to Dr. Samuel Gridley Howe produced several children but proved to be stormy, and Sam Howe proposed a formal separation. His wife would not hear of such an arrangement, for, she wrote, "I am no Fanny Kemble—I can suffer and die with my children, but I cannot leave them till God calls me from them." Even with her domestic responsibilities and marital turmoil, Julia Ward Howe, like Harriet Beecher Stowe, found time to write. In 1854 Ticknor and Fields published her first volume of poetry, entitled *Passion Flowers.*[5]

As a child, Julia Ward regarded the abolitionists as "wicked" and "crazy," but in the 1840s, influenced by the transcendentalist Theodore Parker, she began to sympathize with the antislavery position. Like many New Englanders, the Howes questioned the judiciousness of the Mexican War, and Samuel Gridley Howe ran unsuccessfully for Congress in 1846 as an opponent of slavery. Later, the Howes worked together to edit a free-soil publication called *Commonwealth*, which eventually failed financially. In 1859 Samuel Gridley Howe was among those New Englanders who contributed to John Brown's war chest. Despite their many instances of antislavery activity, the Howes were not entirely consistent in their beliefs. In 1859, while traveling in Cuba, they met and befriended Mr. and

Mrs. Wade Hampton II. This Southern family owned hundreds of slaves, and the Howes enjoyed the Hamptons' hospitality for several weeks at Millwood plantation near Columbia, South Carolina.[6]

Like many abolitionists, Julia Ward Howe had serious reservations about Lincoln. In November 1861, accompanied by her husband, she met the president in a White House drawing room. Their meeting was arranged by Governor John Andrew of Massachusetts, a close friend of the Howes and an unwavering Lincoln supporter. Years later she recalled the encounter. "None of us knew then—how could we have known?—how deeply God's wisdom had touched and inspired that devout and patient soul."[7]

The immediate circumstances under which Howe wrote "Battle Hymn of the Republic" are well known. Shortly after her meeting with the president, she attended a military review some miles from the nation's capital. Members of her party sang patriotic songs to pass the time on the bumpy trip, including "John Brown's body lies a-mouldering in the ground; / His soul is marching on." A member of the group, aware of her literary bent, suggested that she write a new set of lyrics for the popular hymn. That night she awoke from a sound sleep in her room at Willard's Hotel and scratched out a draft of "Battle Hymn," barely legible, in the darkness of her room.[8]

Early in December 1861 Howe asked James T. Fields, editor of *Atlantic Monthly,* if he would print her poem. Fields complied, paying five dollars for the piece. "Battle Hymn" was not immediately popular, but the lyrics gradually caught on with Union troops. Soldiers began to sing the stirring anthem as they marched into battle. Public acclaim followed the military response, and Howe later wrote proudly to her sister that "Battle Hymn" was "sung all over the country." President Lincoln, upon hearing the song in Washington for the first time, allegedly called out, "Sing it again!"[9]

Magazines and newspapers printed thousands of patriotic verses during the Civil War, but Julia Ward Howe's poem was special in that "Battle Hymn" clearly touched a responsive chord among so many Americans. As the Confederacy reached its military height in 1862, as the Union armies went down to defeat after defeat, many Northerners were moved by Howe's stirring words. On one level, the poem was a patriotic national anthem. "He has sounded forth the trumpet that shall never call retreat." Howe touched her readers with more than mere patriotic sentiment. Her words were filled with millennial vision. "Mine eyes have seen the glory of the coming of the Lord." She spoke of a vengeful God, an unmerciful

Creator demanding justice. Like many abolitionists, Howe believed that the war was both a punishment for the nation and a means of spiritual renewal through the emancipation of the slaves. "He is sifting out the hearts of men before his judgment seat!"[10]

"Battle Hymn" was also an abolitionist anthem.

> In the beauty of the lilies Christ was born across the sea,
> With a glory in his bosom that transfigures you and me:
> As he died to make men holy, let us die to make men free,
> While God is marching on.

Thousands upon thousands of Union soldiers now marched to the most inspirational abolitionist words ever written. While Howe's poem may not have made abolitionists of them all, "Battle Hymn" certainly gave them a collective rallying cry which included at least tacit acknowledgment of emancipation. Since "Battle Hymn" also was sung at patriotic gatherings across the North, the verses became an important abolitionist poem. It was reprinted in the *National Anti-Slavery Standard.* Howe continued to write and publish patriotic poetry, yet none of her other Civil War poems approached the eloquence of "Battle Hymn."[11]

Other abolitionist women joined Howe in writing essays and giving lectures supporting emancipation, arguing that immediate abolition was necessary, both to give justice to the slave and to give meaning and purpose to the bloody and destructive war. "This nation must be electrified, until one purpose pulsates every heart," Elizabeth Cady Stanton said in a speech to the New York State Anti-Slavery Convention. Susan Anthony echoed these sentiments. "*Stern necessity,*" she warned, "political, military, and most imperative, *moral necessity,* demands *immediate emancipation.*"[12]

Lydia Maria Child addressed a letter to President Lincoln in which she insisted that abolition must be granted in order to give direction to the Union war effort. Apologizing for the possible impropriety of writing a letter to the chief executive, Child contended that Union soldiers needed a philosophical reason for fighting. "Men," she wrote, "even the bravest, do not go resolutely and cheerfully to death in the name of diplomacy and strategy." While complimenting Lincoln on his concern for constitutional obligations, the abolitionist writer nevertheless maintained that God and the people favored emancipation. Child's rather naive belief that most Americans wanted immediate emancipation was one she shared with many abolitionists. "Did not the people, from press & pulpit, send up one simultaneous shout of joy, when Fremont's proclamation first trembled over the wires?" Susan Anthony asked in a Fourth of July address at Framingham, Massachusetts.[13]

Like Abraham Lincoln, the abolitionists thought the Civil War was part of America's continuing revolution. The founding fathers were men who believed in liberty and freedom; America must build on the foundation of 1776. In his Gettysburg Address, 19 November 1863, Lincoln spoke of "a new birth of freedom." Susan Anthony anticipated these sentiments when she wrote in 1862 of America's duty to abolish slavery. Once emancipation for all was achieved, "then might we boast the just government for which the Fathers of seventy-six fought & bled & died; *but, failed to live.*" Lydia Maria Child analyzed the war in the context of American history, as had Susan Anthony, but she also examined the conflict in a world perspective. Writing to a member of Congress, she said that if the Union was restored with slavery, "our terrible struggle will be invested with no moral dignity, and it will have no moral value as a historical lesson for the human race."[14] For these abolitionists, any form of compromise with the South was a violation of African Americans' basic human rights and denied America's democratic destiny.

Abolitionist women in the West also were active in delivering speeches and writing letters. Prudence Crandall Philleo, who had been the subject of much abolitionist publicity in the 1830s, now lived in LaSalle County, Illinois, and diligently distributed antislavery tracts from her home. As a young Quaker schoolteacher, she had enraged white townspeople in Canterbury, Connecticut, by admitting a black girl to her boarding school and then, in the face of public protest, running the school exclusively for black girls. Local opposition led to her arrest, and the night she spent in a jail cell previously occupied by a murderer gave enormous publicity to the antislavery cause. Her subsequent marriage to a Baptist minister led to her residence in Illinois.[15]

Hannah Tracy Cutler embarked on an extensive lecture tour of Illinois in the spring of 1862, finding ample evidence of antislavery sentiment. When she spoke in the town of Lexington, her audience responded favorably to a lecture on "The Christian Policy of Emancipation." Whereas the good people of Lexington had been only moderate Republicans in previous years, they were now "as radical as the *Liberator* itself." Though she was asked to give additional lectures in Lexington, Cutler's schedule forced her to move on. She was pleased by her reception in Peoria and Jacksonville, towns previously noted for their intolerance toward both abolitionists and female lecturers. Although the Peoria *Transcript* reported Cutler's speech sympathetically, Jacksonville's local newspaper did not. The *Sentinel* described her speech as "an abolition harangue of the Wendell Phillips style." At the town of Henry, Cutler encountered an enthusiastic audience, though a few hooligans threw rotten eggs at the home where she was staying. Still, her spirits soared, and she declared, in numerous letters to the *Liberator,* that "never was there a time when the people were so ready to hear the truth, and the whole truth." In the course of six weeks, Cutler spoke in numerous towns in Livingston, McLean, Woodford, Peoria, Fulton, Marshall, and Morgan counties.[16]

Cutler's Ohio colleague Frances D. Gage reported to the *Liberator* about her lectures in Columbus and Cleveland. Ohioans, according to Gage, were increasingly disturbed by the "masterly inactivity" of the United States government in failing both to prosecute the war more vigorously and to make abolition a war aim. Gage worked with freedmen's relief in addition to her abolition activities. In October 1862 she journeyed to the South Carolina Sea Islands, where she took charge of five hundred freed blacks on Parris Island. Later she turned to lecturing and fund-raising on behalf of the freedmen.[17]

Whether or not these abolitionists were exaggerating the growth in public antislavery sentiment, Congress began to act. In April 1862 slavery was abolished in the District of Columbia, with compensation to slaveholders. Lydia Maria Child expressed both thanks to God and a modicum of cynicism when she wrote to her niece following the congressional legislation. "After thirty years of arguing, and remonstrating, and pleading, and petitioning, and hoping, and fearing, and well nigh despairing, Slavery is *at last* abolished in ten miles square." The Philadelphia Female Anti-Slavery Society passed a resolution praising the congressional measure as "ample recompense for our thirty years of anti-slavery labor." Slavery in the territories, once so bitterly debated in Congress, was abolished in June 1862.[18]

The Second Confiscation Act, which became law with the president's signature in July 1862, enabled the Union army to free all slaves of Confederate masters once they escaped behind Union lines. Many abolitionists saw this measure as another hopeful sign, yet another example of "the reaping from our many years of sowing." But abolitionists were quick to see the limitations of this bill. Maria Weston Chapman described the act as "an Emancipation bill with clogs on." Only the slaves of rebel masters could be freed, and their safety was contingent upon the whim of Union generals who might or might not allow their escape behind Union lines. Lincoln, with his serious reservations about the legality of the bill, did not intend to enforce it. In short, the Second Confiscation Act was far from the comprehensive emancipation bill that the abolitionists had long desired.[19]

Ever mindful of the need to balance such considerations as border-state threats to secede, English and French threats to recognize the Confederacy, political threats of the radical Republicans in Congress, and his own philosophical feelings about slavery, Lincoln decided in March 1862 to act. In a message to Congress he proposed compensation for slave-holders in any state which would voluntarily abolish slavery. When border-state legislators rejected the plan in July, Lincoln sent a preliminary emancipation decree to members of his cabinet. It was announced publicly after the battle of Antietam. The Emancipation Proclamation would go into effect 1 January 1863 and would free all slaves in areas still in rebellion against the Union.[20]

Abolitionists looked upon the proclamation as an important step forward. Maria Weston Chapman wrote to Abby Hopper Gibbons: "Hurrah! Hosanna! Hallelujah! Laudamus! Nunc dimittis! Jubilate! Amen!" The Philadelphia Female Anti-Slavery Society passed a resolution hailing "with unutterable joy and gratitude, the Day of Jubilee which has dawned on the American nation." William Lloyd Garrison was much more circumspect, commenting to daughter Fanny, "The President's Proclamation is certainly a matter for great rejoicing, . . . but it leaves slavery, as a system or practice, still to exist in all the so-called loyal Slave States." The abolitionist press responded in a similar fashion. The *Liberator* questioned Lincoln's three-month grace period, arguing that the proclamation should take effect immediately. The *Standard* protested its limitations, while the *Independent* predicted that despite its shortcomings the Emancipation Proclamation would unite the people of the North against slavery.[21]

Some abolitionists were clearly skeptical of the measure. Here was no sweeping emancipation bill. Slaves in the Confederacy were freed in theory; in fact, Lincoln had no control over such slaves. Amy Post summarized the views of many when she wrote that the proclamation was "more than I feared but much less than I hoped." Abolitionists also complained about Lincoln's motives. Lydia Maria Child wrote about the proclamation unenthusiastically, concluding that it was issued "reluctantly and stintedly . . . merely a war-measure."[22] Again and again the abolitionists failed to recognize the limitations on the president's war power. Instead, they focused on Lincoln's motives, which they perceived to be purely political rather than humanitarian.

Another reason for abolitionist disillusion was the failure of the proclamation to arouse public enthusiasm. Many had optimistically predicted that when emancipation became an official war aim, Northerners would embrace abolition and the war would end quickly. This did not happen. "The War does not seem to end, with the *1st* of Jan.," Ellen Wright complained in a letter to her cousin. "How great has been the punishment which we must bear, for Slavery!"[23]

A group of women abolitionists decided the national crisis called for a greater degree of female activism. While individual abolitionist women had aided the cause through their speeches, fund-raising, and letter writing, their wartime efforts had not yet been collectively organized. Many women, such as young Ellen Wright, felt a sense of frustration at their seeming inability to aid the cause in an active way. Elizabeth Cady Stanton and Susan B. Anthony, who had demonstrated their organizational abilities in the prewar feminist movement and the abolition crusade, seized the initiative in organizing women against slavery. Through their efforts, they hoped the American people would be inspired to send a clear message to Congress and the president demanding immediate emancipation for all slaves in all slave states.

In 1862 Elizabeth Cady Stanton and her children had moved from rural Seneca Falls to New York City, where Henry Stanton had been deputy collector of the Customs House since the previous year. On 16 January 1863 he wrote a gloomy letter to Susan Anthony from Washington despairing about the antislavery conflict. "The country was never so badly off as at this moment. . . . You have no idea how dark the cloud is which hangs over us." Fully aware of the talents of his wife and her comrade, Stanton continued: "We must not lay the flattering unction to our souls that the proclamation will be of any use if we are beaten and have a dissolution of the Union. Here then is work for you. Susan, put on your armor and go forth!"[24]

It was not an easy proposition. Women, Elizabeth Cady Stanton recalled in her memoirs, were accustomed to doing charitable work. Before the war they had participated widely in religious revivals, in Bible and tract societies, in charity fund-raising on behalf of orphaned children and fallen women, even in temperance agitation. Only a very small number had been active in antislavery or feminist societies. When the war broke out, this pattern began to repeat itself as women quickly joined local soldier's aid societies, many of them affiliated with the United States Sanitary Commission. But the organization Stanton and Anthony envisioned would not call upon women to knit socks, roll bandages, or make jams and jellies for the wounded soldiers. Instead, it would be an organization dedicated to a radical principle—the abolition of slavery—and would be based on the idea of female participation in the political sphere. Stanton and Anthony decided to call their organization the Woman's National Loyal League. After lengthy consultations with William Lloyd Garrison, Horace Greeley, Massachusetts governor John Andrew, Robert Dale Owen, and others, they determined that their goal would be a mammoth petition to Congress carrying signatures from every state in the Union.[25] This document would provide senators and congressmen with irrefutable proof that Americans favored the complete and immediate abolition of slavery.

Stanton and Anthony had several precedents from which to work. Women had proved their effectiveness as petition collectors during the 1830s, and several wartime antislavery petitions had already been introduced into Congress by abolitionist Senator Charles Sumner of Massachusetts. On 16 April 1862 Sumner presented a petition, some seven hundred feet long, signed by 15,200 women. The next day he introduced another petition signed by women of Wilmington, Delaware, and in May he introduced yet another petition signed by 8,000 women. Senator Edgar Cowan of Pennsylvania presented a similar document signed by members of the Fallowfield Monthly Meeting of Women Friends. Little is known about these petitions except for the gender of their signers. The *Times* of London found the petitions newsworthy enough to report their introduction.[26] The existing network of antislavery societies, founded in the thirty years preceding the war, could be called upon for assistance with the league's petition.

Union League clubs were another precedent. These male groups served as booster clubs for the Republican party and as pressure groups specifically aimed at refuting Copperhead or peace sentiment. Publication societies in New York and Boston reprinted and distributed speeches espousing patriotism, abolition, and military victory. Female versions of the Union League clubs, often called Loyal Leagues, had cropped up in a variety of locations, including Manchester, Rockville, East Windsor Hill, and Hartford, Connecticut; Stevensville, Pennsylvania; Richwood, and Wilmington, Ohio; Tazewell County, Illinois; and Madison, Wisconsin, whose group claimed to be the first such organization. Members of these organizations, like their male counterparts, urged support for the Union war effort.[27]

In spite of these regional precedents, the Loyal League would become a new type of organization, a national abolitionist network run by women from a decidedly feminist perspective. Prewar reform women formed local antislavery societies and held national conventions. After the Seneca Falls meeting, woman's rights advocates staged annual conventions as well; but a national feminist abolitionist network was something else entirely.

Important though it would become, the Loyal League has received very little attention from historians. Gerda Lerner alluded to the league's importance when, in assessing the history of female abolition efforts, she wrote, "The final surge of women's antislavery political activity came in 1863 when the Women's Loyal National League was formed." In her book on nineteenth-century women's participation in the public sphere, Mary Ryan alluded to Stanton's use of the league as a means through which to inject "a feminist perspective into the central political debates of the Civil War period."[28] Ellen DuBois traced the development of the woman's rights movement from its origins at Seneca Falls to the feminist schism of 1869 in her insightful book *Feminism and Suffrage*, but she did not focus on the Loyal League's impact on that movement. Nor has the league received the thorough analysis it deserves in any of the biographies of Stanton and Anthony. And yet this organization would make an important contribution to the wartime antislavery movement, would emphasize new ideas about women's role in the political realm, and would help to shape the leadership and agenda of the feminist movement in the postwar era.

Elizabeth Cady Stanton's appeal "To the Women of the Republic" was printed in antislavery journals and in several other newspapers as well. Hoping to reach many more women than those already involved in antislavery or reform societies, Stanton wanted to arouse a nationwide surge of support for abolition, equality, and "pure democracy." Her argument was based on several premises. First, she appealed to the patriotic feelings of Northern women. Confederate women, she claimed, "see and feel the horrors of the war; the foe is at their firesides; while we, in peace and plenty, live and move as heretofore." Second, she attempted to reach women on terms they would find acceptable by invoking the doctrine of separate spheres. Northern women must work actively for emancipation, she argued, because the women of the nation were traditionally the moral and religious teachers of the family. Slavery was a moral issue, and therefore it fell within women's rightful sphere to discuss it. Stanton defined the role of women in times of national crisis by recalling another traditional concept, republican motherhood, which emphasized women's duty to instill in their children the moral fiber, sense of duty, and patriotism that would make them good citizens. She reminded her readers that even in the era of the American Revolution against British tyranny, republican mothers such as Abigail Adams voiced their opinions on the subject of freedom and liberty. Now was the time to speak out against slavery.[29]

The convention of the Woman's National Loyal League took place on 14 May 1863 at the Church of the Puritans in New York. Convention officers included Lucy Stone, who presided; Elizabeth Cady Stanton, Angelina Grimké Weld, Fannie Willard, Mary Cabot, Mary White, Mrs. E. O. Sampson Hoyt, Eliza Farnham, and Mrs. H. C. Ingersol, vice presidents; Martha Wright and Lucy Colman, secretaries; and Susan Anthony, Ernestine Rose, Antoinette Brown Blackwell, Amy Post, and Annie Mumford, who composed the business committee. These officers represented the states of New York, New Jersey, Pennsylvania, Connecticut, Massachusetts, Maine, Wisconsin, and California.[30]

In the opening speech of the convention, Elizabeth Cady Stanton asked women to recall that the motto which defined true patriotism was not "*Our Country Right or Wrong*" but rather "*Freedom and Our Country.*" As the moral arbiters of the home, women must instruct their children on the evils of slavery, while instilling in them a love of republican government. Susan Anthony later expanded on this theme when she declared that the exigencies of the hour dictated that woman must cease to be "the passive recipient of whatever morals and religion the trade and politics of the nation may decree . . . and make herself what she is clearly designed to be, the educator of the race."[31]

Several speakers invoked the natural rights philosophy of the Declaration of Independence to justify the abolition of slavery. "Government derives its just power from the consent of the governed," Lucy Stone reminded the audience, adding, "All human beings have equal rights." When the patriots of 1776 were denied their right of self-government, they went to war to redress this grievance, Antoinette Brown Blackwell declared in comparing the present situation to that noble conflict. Elizabeth Cady Stanton and Susan B. Anthony also invoked the theme of America's continuing revolution, with Stanton optimistically predicting the "true Republic that will surely rise from this shattered Union."[32]

Angelina Grimké Weld reached new heights of eloquence when she addressed the convention. After blaming the Southern slavery interests for causing the war, she declared, "My heart is full, my country is bleeding, my people are perishing around me." But, she said, "I feel as a South Carolinian, I am bound to tell the North, Go on! Go on! Never falter, never abandon the principles which you have now adopted." In her address, Elizabeth Cady Stanton had suggested that Copperheads might be deported to colonize Liberia. Angelina Weld continued the satire by suggesting that Liberia was a freedom-loving country which did not deserve to be saddled with Copperhead traitors; rather, Copperheads should be deported to England where they would find sympathetic company. Lucy Stone, carrying the argument one step further, stated that Copperheads might wish to join the editorial staff of the *Times* of London. [33]

Susan Anthony then read a series of resolutions prepared by the business committee. The committee praised President Lincoln's Emancipation Proclamation, while urging him to initiate a more comprehensive abolition decree. Another resolution emphasized the principle of self-government as an inalienable right of the American people, and another demanded civil and political equality for all Americans regardless of race or gender. This resolution, with its inclusion of gender equality, passed only after heated discussion. [34]

Mrs. E. O. Sampson Hoyt of Wisconsin spoke for those delegates who opposed the inclusion of woman's rights at the convention. Arguing that "Woman's Rights as an *ism* has not been received with entire favor by the women of the country," she claimed that thousands of Northern women would refuse to participate in league activities if feminism was associated with the organization. Invoking the American Revolution as had so many previous speakers, she claimed that patriot women had assisted their government without setting forth "in any theoretical or clamorous way their right to equal suffrage." In fact, while insisting that she favored emancipation of the slaves, Hoyt nevertheless objected to the inclusion of abolition, temperance, or any other extraneous issue. The league's "principal object should be to help maintain . . . the integrity of our Government," she concluded. [35]

Hoyt did not win support from the majority of the convention delegates. Lucy Colman, declaring that "I recognize for myself no narrow sphere," saw a comparison between the issue at hand and the struggle within the American Anti-Slavery Society over Abby Kelley's 1840 appointment to the business committee. Woman's rightists did not back down then, and they should not do so now. Lucy Stone pointed out that "if justice to the negro and to woman is right, it cannot hurt our loyalty to the country and the Union." Delegates applauded Ernestine Rose when she rebutted Hoyt declaring that "if it had not been for Woman's Rights, that lady would not have had the courage to stand here and say what she did."[36] Feminism would remain an integral part of the Woman's National Loyal League.

In the evening session of the Loyal League convention, an address to President Lincoln written by Elizabeth Cady Stanton was presented for its approval. The letter was supportive in tone. "We come not to criticize or complain. . . . We come to strengthen you with earnest words of sympathy and encouragement." After congratulating the president on his issuance of the Emancipation Proclamation, Stanton declared that further action must be taken in order to free the slaves. At no time in the nation's history was the time more propitious for rectifying the one mistake made by the founding fathers. Finally, Stanton admonished the president to give free rein to the abolitionist generals. "Your proclamation gives you immortality," she wrote. "Be just, and share your glory with men like these who wait to execute your will." After the reading of Stanton's address, Ernestine Rose spoke boldly in favor of immediate emancipation of the border-state slaves, urging the administration to "do its whole duty to freedom and humanity." The convention ended on a conciliatory note as it approved Stanton's draft to President Lincoln. After providing for a permanent league office in New York City's Cooper Institute, the convention adjourned.[37]

By founding a national women's organization with political aims, Stanton and Anthony were taking yet another step away from the emphasis on moral suasion that had characterized so much antebellum reform sentiment. Lori Ginzberg has emphasized that the shift toward seeking political solutions to social problems had begun in the 1850s. As moral suasion failed to eliminate intemperance and other sins, reformers looked increasingly to governmental solutions to America's ills. Hence political rights took on a new significance, and an increasing number of women began to think of securing these rights for themselves along with freedom and enfranchisement for the slave.[38]

Creation of the Loyal League marked another turning point in the history of women's involvement in abolitionism, because it signaled the passing of leadership to a younger generation of women. By 1863 Maria Weston Chapman, founder of the Boston Female Anti-Slavery Society, had completely disassociated herself from abolition work, including the annual fund-raising events that she had once organized so adeptly. Believing that the American Anti-Slavery Society had already accomplished its goal in achieving a war to eliminate slavery, Chapman wrote in 1862: "It had done its work. It had borne the Lord to Jerusalem." Helen Benson

Garrison quietly took over the burden of arranging what by then were called Subscription Anniversaries, staged primarily to raise money for the financially strapped *National Anti-Slavery Standard.* In a letter to Elizabeth Cady Stanton after the Loyal League convention, Chapman also expressed doubt about the efficacy of antislavery petitions but added, "It *cant* do any harm . . . be of good cheer about the country—the cause—whether the petition be numerously signed or not." To her daughter, Chapman admitted: "Our lectures of 30 years standing do not put the case nearly so squarely & effectually as the rising generation. . . . We were trained to a preparatory work, & well we have performed it but that work is no longer needed."[39]

The Philadelphia Female Anti-Slavery Society also curtailed its activities. Led by Lucretia Mott and Mary Grew, the Philadelphia women's group staged its twenty-fifth and final fund-raiser in December 1861. Their decision to discontinue the fairs was based on logic similar to that of Chapman, the belief that "our *peculiar mission,* as pioneers, as agitators, as 'jungle-cleavers,'" was over. Nevertheless, they argued that the national and state antislavery agencies must continue to operate until slavery was completely eradicated.[40]

Although she continued to be one of abolition's most important philosophers, Lydia Maria Child seemed to be losing her enthusiasm for organized abolition work. She ceased to attend the Annual Subscription Anniversaries and declined to participate in the Loyal League convention, citing age, health, and family commitments.[41] The withdrawal of Maria Weston Chapman, Lucretia Mott, and to some extent Lydia Maria Child was surprising given their previous commitment to emancipation. All three had been speaking, organizing, and writing on behalf of the slave since the early 1830s, and yet this longevity helps to explain their shortsightedness in deemphasizing abolition work at the very time when it seemed most important. In 1866 Lucretia Mott wrote to Wendell Phillips that "people dread the infliction of the *old* when younger speakers are present."[42] Mott was exaggerating, but she, Chapman, and Child were all in their late fifties or sixties during the Civil War, and with talented, energetic, and ambitious younger women such as Elizabeth Cady Stanton and Susan B. Anthony ready to assume leadership in a national organization, the older generation stepped aside.

The accession of Stanton and Anthony ensured a clear feminist bias for the Loyal League. At the beginning of the war, women activists had declared their intention to forgo woman's rights conventions, but as Elisabeth Griffith has pointed out, Stanton had a lengthy track record of turning organizations in which she participated into forums for feminism. In 1852 she had been elected president of New York's Woman's State Temperance Society, while Anthony served as secretary. By combining temperance with feminism, Stanton had alienated conservatives, who proceeded to vote her out of office in 1853.[43] Determined that this should not happen again, she squelched the conservative attempt to vote down the equality resolution at the May 1863 convention of the Loyal League.

Stanton may have overcome Mrs. Hoyt's objection, but the Wisconsin delegate represented the views of a substantial number of women. Indeed, the majority of letters sent in support of the league and included in the published *Proceedings* were from women who wanted to "stand by" the government against the Southern traitors, stamp out disloyalty in the North, and, as one woman from Indiana expressed it, "arouse the smoldering fires of patriotism." Some of these correspondents indicated antislavery beliefs, but only a fraction revealed feminist inclinations, such as the Massachusetts woman who spoke of performing righteous works "in our legitimate sphere and *out of it* if needs be."[44]

Stanton's feminism evoked protest even from some of abolition's strongest supporters. William Lloyd Garrison, who traditionally defended the inclusion of woman's rights at antislavery conventions, wrote a letter to his wife in which he protested vehemently the meeting's "resolving itself, in fact, into a Woman's Rights Convention." Also complaining that the meeting was badly managed and the speakers' voices did not carry in the Church of the Puritans, Garrison concluded that the convention was a failure.[45]

In order to bolster the league's feminist-abolitionist credentials, Stanton turned for support to women who had, for one reason or another, been inactive for years. She enlisted the help of Angelina Grimké Weld, who had lived in virtual retirement from public speaking for several decades. Weld attended the league's founding convention on her twenty-fifth wedding anniversary and agreed to serve as a vice president. In addition to giving speeches, she went from door to door near her New Jersey home armed with petitions. Lucy Stone also rejoined the public abolition movement after years of devoting herself to family responsibilities, and her sister-in-law, the noted minister Antoinette Brown Blackwell, became a league secretary. Amelia Bloomer, who had once edited a reform newspaper called *The Lily*, had moved west in the 1850s but sent a letter in support of the league from her Council Bluffs, Iowa, home.[46]

Following the May convention, Stanton and Anthony began the arduous task of organizing the league. Although Lucy Stone had served as presiding officer of the convention—her prewar success as a speaker having made her an attractive candidate for such a position—Stanton assumed the presidency of this organization. She had no intention of relinquishing control to another. After years of living in rural Seneca Falls with child-care responsibilities monopolizing her time, Stanton relished her new urban life and the freedom to devote more time to reform activities. The league would afford her unprecedented opportunities to sharpen her skills as a writer, speaker, and leader.

Within a short time, the league had a new set of officers and an organizational structure for mailing petitions, collecting and recording signatures, and requesting contributions. Voting membership was bestowed upon any woman who contributed one dollar or more; honorary members could make any donation they chose. League members often wore a breast pin which depicted a slave breaking his chains and bore the league motto, "In Emancipation is national unity." Each petition collector would obtain contributions of a penny or more from every signer of the petition. Members would ask for help from their clergymen and from local teachers in disseminating information about the project. Stanton also urged women to form auxiliary leagues in every state of the North in order to facilitate the petitioning process. Ultimately league members hoped to obtain at least one million signatures on what they referred to as their "mammoth petition."[47] Clearly Stanton hoped to exceed the level of antislavery petitioning that women had achieved in the 1830s.

The petition itself was worded simply. Addressed to the "Honourable Senate and House of Representatives of the United States," it stated: "The undersigned, Women of the United States above the age of eighteen years, earnestly pray that your honourable body will pass, at the earliest practicable day, an Act emancipating all persons of African descent held to involuntary service or labor in the United States." Stanton, who believed in utilizing every human resource available to her, enlisted the help of her children in the petitioning process and urged others to do the same. Although girls and boys under the age of eighteen could not sign the petition, any child who collected at least fifty names and fifty cents earned a badge and membership in the league. In a letter to Garrison's two youngest children, Stanton claimed that her son Theodore spent two or three hours every day sorting and rolling petitions as they arrived in New York.[48]

From its inception the Woman's National Loyal League received support from sympathetic men. Senator Charles Sumner of Massachusetts allowed league members the use of his franking privilege in sending out the petitions. Robert Dale Owen, head of the National Freedmen's Relief Association, became a trusted adviser. Although leadership in the organization was to remain female, the membership voted on 11 June 1863 to allow male signatures on their antislavery petitions. Male and female signatures were tabulated separately to encourage a friendly gender rivalry, and the states were encouraged to compete for signatures as well.[49]

Although African Americans certainly were eligible for membership, there is no evidence that a large number of blacks joined. Before the war, leadership of the national antislavery movement fell almost entirely to white men and women. This pattern was repeated in the Woman's National Loyal League, for there is no indication that Stanton and Anthony actively recruited black members or officers. Frederick Douglass, the nation's most prominent former slave, did give lectures on behalf of the league; but on balance, black participation in this essentially white, middle-class organization appears to have been minimal.

Elizabeth Cady Stanton and Susan Anthony, who had worked so well together before the war, once again demonstrated their organizational abilities through the Woman's National Loyal League. Anthony acted as the chief financier and strategist, while Stanton provided the philosophical base for the organization. Because she devoted her full efforts to the league and because she had no means of financial support, Susan Anthony became a paid agent of the league, receiving a weekly salary of twelve dollars. Only by boarding with the Stanton family could she survive on such a pittance, but the living arrangement appears to have been mutually satisfactory, especially in that it facilitated consultation on league affairs.[50]

With her usual single-minded devotion to the cause, Anthony worked very hard on behalf of the Loyal League. In September 1863 she wrote confidently to Samuel May that "we, the League, are *alive* and planning a most vigorous prosecution of *our war* of *ideas*—not bullets & bayonets." When one male league member sent her a completed set of petitions containing more than two hundred names, Anthony congratulated the gentleman and then admonished him that "it will not do for the friends of freedom to slacken in any of their efforts." Ellen Wright, who had complained about women's limited role in the war to her friend Lucy McKim, was also drawn into league activities by Susan Anthony. "Women as well as men must take up their packs & wander & work for their country," Ellen wrote to her mother on 21 May 1863. Her mother was put to work as well after Anthony sent her "half an acre of petitions" in June 1863.[51]

Fund-raising occupied a good deal of Susan Anthony's time. Requesting a small contribution from each signer of the petition, Anthony saw to it that the *National Anti-Slavery Standard* printed lists of these contributors. Americans from all across the Northern states made contributions ranging from a penny up to one hundred dollars, though most contributions were below two dollars. The small size of these contributions and the geographical range of the communities indicates that Stanton and Anthony were succeeding in their plan to establish a broadly based organization.[52]

Susan Anthony also appealed to the leadership of the American Anti-Slavery Society and to others for help in fund-raising. The Hovey Fund, an abolitionist charity, paid Susan Anthony's salary. Henry Ward Beecher collected $200 from his parishioners at Plymouth Church in Brooklyn. Ticknor and Fields, the Boston publishers of Harriet Beecher Stowe, Julia Ward Howe, and others, agreed to allow a league contribution box in their offices. Gerrit Smith, Elizabeth Cady Stanton's well-heeled cousin, sent a generous donation, and Jessie Benton Frémont delighted abolitionist admirers of her husband by sending $50 to the league.[53]

In their speeches and writing, league officers emphasized several important themes. Elizabeth Cady Stanton wanted to refute those who argued that the president's issuance of the Emancipation Proclamation effectively ended the slavery question. On the contrary, Stanton declared, the battle was far from over. This radical abolitionist, who had once argued vehemently in favor of secession from the Union, now assumed a flag-waving patriotic stance. The league president even spoke of the sanctity of the Union when she declared: "There is no geographical division strong enough to sunder a people bound together as we are by one political & religious faith."[54]

Stanton also appealed to women's desire for peace by alleging that slavery not only had caused the present war but indeed had been the cause of "every national difficulty since the formation of the government." Specifically she pointed to the military action involved in the acquisition of Florida from Spain, the war with Mexico, the difficulties involving Kansas statehood, even the panics of 1837 and 1857.[55]

In speaking about the slaves, league members invoked traditional abolitionist arguments about the immorality of the institution, giving special emphasis to the plight of women and children. Lydia Maria Child was never more persuasive than when she spoke of "wives polluted" and "children sold." Abolitionists frequently emphasized the readiness of slaves for freedom by publicizing their contributions as cooks, guides, and messengers in the Union army. In addition, they tried to dispel fears about the presence of newly freed slaves in the North by comparing their situation to that of recently arrived immigrants. The solution, Susan Anthony suggested, was education coupled with jobs.[56]

Not above using fear tactics, Anthony also predicted the dire consequences that might result if slaves were not freed. "Insurrection," she insisted, "fearful & bloody would surely follow any & every attempt to subject those heroic freedmen to the old regime of the lash." If the North lost the war, Lydia Maria Child predicted ominously, the South would spread its undemocratic principles northward. Elizabeth Cady Stanton tried to stir up partisan fervor by comparing Northern culture to that of the South. How many authors and poets, artists, inventors, and orators had the South produced in the last century, she asked in an address before the Loyal League. What female writers of the South could be compared with Harriet Beecher Stowe and Lydia Maria Child?[57]

League officers also emphasized the philosophical principles underlying the Union war effort. Stanton continued to argue that the Civil War was a democratic struggle. The "Slave Power" had long dominated American government by corrupting the political parties, by threatening churches and schools as well. The Southern slavocracy must be crushed so as to eliminate "the hateful principle of caste and class." A government with "slavery for its cornerstone, cannot live on the same continent with a pure democracy."[58] Susan Anthony agreed with these sentiments. Throughout history, she argued, slavery had brought down nations from the time of the pharaohs to Abraham Lincoln. Only when slavery was eliminated could "all the Magna Carta of human rights . . . be restored to us; and for the first time in our national existence, might we try the experiment of a pure democracy." Sarah Grimké's optimism about the future was evident when she wrote to Garrison in November 1863, "This blessed war is working out the salvation of the Anglo-Saxon as well as of the African race."[59]

Angelina Grimké Weld added her views in an "Address of the Woman's National Loyal League to the Soldiers of Our Second Revolution." Having argued since the beginning of the war that soldiers and civilians needed to understand its philosophical basis, league members designated Weld's address as their official statement to soldiers in the field. After congratulating the troops on their courage and encouraging them to reenlist for the duration of the crisis, Weld turned to the subject at hand. In the present conflict, she argued, black men were the immediate victims, but working-men of every color were also threatened by the Southern slavocracy. "The nation is in a death-struggle—it must either become one vast slaveocracy of petty tyrants, or wholly the land of the free." The Civil War was not a war of races, as the South contended. Instead, Weld argued, the war was a conflict of principles, a struggle in which all who favored freedom of speech, freedom of suffrage, freedom to work, and freedom of education were "driven to do battle in defense of these or to fall with them, victims of the same violence that for two centuries has held the black man a prisoner of war."[60]

Lydia Maria Child wrote her own treatise on the philosophy of the war, for her nephew served in the Union army and she felt the need to see that he understood what was at stake. "This is a war to decide whether this is a free country," she wrote, "where working-men elect their own rulers, and where free schools give all an equal chance for education, or whether we are to live under despotic institutions, which will divide society into two classes, rulers and servants."[61]

Other league members viewed the war in similarly grandiose terms. "This is no rebellion to be put down at Gen. Mc[Cl]ellan's elegant leisure, but a *grand Revolution*," Susan Anthony declared in a Fourth of July oration. Elizabeth Cady Stanton liked to recall the Hungarian freedom fighter Louis Kossuth, whose sister had claimed that all Hungarian no-blewomen gave up their jewelry to the public treasury, wearing only iron bands as a symbolic ornament. Stanton, alluding to the cries of many Northerners who encouraged fashion economy during the war, contended that only through similar self-sacrifice and suffering could America be redeemed.[62] Although she praised Hungary's fight for freedom, Stanton and other league members also emphasized America's unique position in the world as distinct from and superior to European nations. She likened the Southern planter class to Europe's aristocracy, dismissing both. After characterizing the United States as the "one spot on this green earth where manhood & labor was dignified," the league president urged women to "concentrate every energy of your being to save our free institutions from the wreck that threatens them." America's free institutions made this country superior to Old World governments, she concluded, adding, "This is a war of the people & they must plan it & fight in it." Just as the nation faced threats to free institutions posed by a possible Southern victory, so too the nation was threatened by foreign nations, which were following the Civil War with great interest and, Stanton believed, "plotting our downfall."[63]

Stanton, Anthony, Grimké, Child, Weld, and others proved themselves to be gifted thinkers and rhetoricians, and also adept politicians. They donned the mantle of patriotism by blaming the South for starting what had become an expensive and deadly war. They appealed to women's maternal instincts by invoking the special suffering of slave women and children. They discussed the philosophy of the "grand Revolution" and at the same time raised women's household economy to the level of patriotism. Just as they made it seem logical to eschew frivolous dress, so too they implied that signing a petition toward the political goal of emancipation was equally patriotic. In short, they discussed political issues from the traditionally masculine sphere while at the same time appealing to women through the rhetoric of true womanhood.

In addition to giving speeches themselves, officers of the Woman's National Loyal League sponsored lectures by prominent Americans from the ranks of government, journalism, and reform. New York league members organized one such lecture series in the fall of 1863. At the first meeting Henry Bellows, head of the United States Sanitary Commission, addressed the group at Cooper Institute. Horace Greeley also delivered a brief address, as did Frances D. Gage, who had begun to work with freedmen in South Carolina. Congressman William D. Kelley of Philadelphia spoke to the league on 21 November; Frederick Douglass, Theodore Weld, and Wendell Phillips each spoke before the league in the ensuing months. Although Anna Dickinson was far too independent and self-centered to participate in any organized movement, league members did persuade her to speak before the group. Elizabeth Cady Stanton and Susan B. Anthony admired Dickinson greatly. When they wrote their monumental *History of Woman Suffrage* after the war, they included Dickinson's photograph as the frontispiece of the volume that included the Civil War years. Because of Dickinson's eloquence and dramatic power, they compared her to the young Fanny Kemble.[64]

The abolitionist press encouraged the Loyal League by giving favorable coverage to the league's petitioning activities and public lectures. The *Liberator*, the *National Anti-Slavery Standard*, and the *Independent* published detailed articles about the group's activities. The *Commonwealth*, edited by the well-known abolitionist minister Moncure Conway, offered these words of encouragement in October 1863: "God speed these patriotic women in their labor of love."[65]

Even when, as in New York, attendance at league meetings fluctuated greatly, the general press accorded the women considerable coverage. The New York *World* was always critical, accusing league members of behaving in an unwomanly fashion. Women, who were traditionally the moral teachers of the family, should not stoop to the level of advocating emancipation by force. This paper had labeled the league's founding convention "a genuine 'witches Sabbath,'" while the Springfield, Massachusetts, *Republican* questioned the constitutionality of the league petitions and the femininity of the women who disseminated them. "All the maiden philanthropists, of whatever age or sex, may find all the employment they need in . . . works of charity and mercy," one reporter wrote in January 1864. "But they should also be told, if they do not already know it, that by asking the government to violate the Constitution in order to manifest a sacred animosity to slavery, they are really doing injury to the cause of the Union." Even the *Times* of London took note of the Loyal League, which it criticized as containing "female ranters like Miss Dickinson."[66]

The New York *Times* and the *Tribune* reported news of league activities in a more sympathetic manner. Horace Greeley's *Tribune* applauded the Loyal League for "undertaking to do what never has been done in the world before, to obtain one million of names to a petition." At the same time, the *Tribune*'s editor may have been slightly nervous about Stanton and Anthony's tendency to interject feminism into the league, for the newspaper offered this cautious praise in one article: "The Women of the Loyal League have shown great practical wisdom in restricting their efforts to one object." After recording in April 1864 that the league had fifteen thousand petitions in circulation, Greeley's newspaper strongly urged its readers to sign and return the documents without delay.[67]

The tenor of these newspaper comments—support for the league's antislavery stance but uneasiness with its feminism—reflected the dual purpose of the league. Woman's rights and abolitionism were inseparable. Increasingly, Elizabeth Cady Stanton acted as the principal philosopher of the league, showing her continuing adeptness in appealing to women through the rhetoric of true womanhood and at the same time conveying an activist image. While being careful to avoid offending religiously devout women, she cautioned them to supplement daily prayers by writing and speaking against slavery. They must also urge husbands, fathers, and brothers to vote in favor of an emancipation bill. While praising women for their work on behalf of the sanitary and freedmen's organizations, she urged them not to restrict their reform activities to benevolent societies. By the winter of 1863, Stanton, recalling the appeals of prewar feminists and abolitionists, began urging women to join the league's petition drive because the right to petition was the only political right given to women under the Constitution.[68]

Stanton knew that prewar petitioning had encouraged female assertiveness and propelled women toward activism in the public sphere. In a series of letters printed in the *National Anti-Slavery Standard,* she hammered away at the significance of the new petition campaign, reminding women of the importance of the war and the necessity of their active political participation in it. "Let it not be said that the women of the Republic, absorbed in ministering to the outward alone, saw not the philosophy of the revolution through which they passed; understood not the moral struggle that convulsed the nation—the irrepressible conflict between liberty and slavery. Remember the angels of mercy and justice are twin sisters, and ever walk hand in hand."[69]

Stanton was moving beyond the mere inspiration for women to become politically active during the national crisis. By early 1864 she was placing ever greater emphasis on "the inauguration of the moral power of woman to be recognized in the politics of the nation." She was clearly looking forward to the resumption of overtly feminist agitation after the war when she wrote, "By our earnestness and zeal in the exercise of this one right [to petition], let us prove ourselves worthy to make larger demands in the readjustment of the new government."[70] Just as the newly arrived freedmen living in Washington's refugee camps were demonstrating their ability to live quietly and respectably, just as black men were proving their manliness and courage by volunteering for duty in the Union army, so women could prove their readiness for enfranchisement by patriotically supporting the war effort, by becoming informed on political questions, and by exercising their political right of petition on behalf of the slave.

Though Stanton and Anthony made a concerted effort to appeal to women on terms they would find acceptable, the feminist bias of the league was undeniable, and it probably hampered recruitment. Whether Stanton liked it or not, American women were more interested in tending sick soldiers and singing patriotic anthems than they were in participating in an organization devoted to emancipating slaves and women.

Rochester, New York, provides a case in point. Amy Post, who was appointed to the league's business committee at the May convention, spearheaded the petition campaign in that city. A committed feminist and abolitionist, she galvanized Rochester's radical—or "ultraist" reformers as Nancy Hewitt calls them—for the league. Although Post and her co-workers were successful in convincing a large number of Rochesterians to sign the mammoth petition, their success was never matched by the degree of public support for the local Soldier's Aid Society, which was, Hewitt wrote, "deemed more respectable to work for than the feminist-tainted Loyal League."[71]

The women's periodical press provides another illustration. During the war, women's magazines had a combined circulation of approximately 250,000. Few of these periodicals mentioned political issues in any depth, issues such as nationalism and states' rights, slavery and freedom, Republican versus Democrat. In its January 1863 issue, the most popular magazine of them all, *Godey's Lady's Book,* expressed the wish for peace, which would afford "leisure for mental improvement" and a "wide range of benevolent interest." *Godey's* failed even to mention that the Emancipation Proclamation had gone into effect. Although women's magazines did not ignore the war, most of them limited their treatment of this delicate subject to sentimental stories and poems with titles such as "The Bereaved Mother," "The Dead Soldier's Ring," and "Woman the Soldier's Friend." Magazine editors also urged women to participate in nursing as well as charitable activities and to avoid "reckless extravagance" in dress. Only a few of the more religious and reform-oriented journals—those with rather limited circulation—went so far as to urge the abolition of slavery. Women's magazines apparently found the Loyal League's platform too radical, for no journal endorsed or even mentioned the activities of the Woman's National Loyal League.[72]

Abolitionist women were not deterred by challenges. Even though they were aware that many women would not consider joining a noncharitable organization, they continued their attempts to recruit from all classes. Nor were they deterred by threats of physical danger, as they had already demonstrated during the secession crisis. When in July 1863 draft riots brought normal life in New York to a halt, Abby Hopper Gibbons, who was caring for wounded soldiers at Point Lookout, Maryland, learned that her home had been gutted. The Gibbons' residence was known to be a gathering place for abolitionists; as such, it was a logical target for the rioters.[73]

More serious was the burning of the Colored Orphan Asylum. The

home of Henry and Elizabeth Stanton, just two blocks from the orphanage, was also threatened. Neil Stanton, their son, was seized by a
mob, who suspected him of being a "three-hundred-dollar fellow" who
had bought himself out of the draft. Showing some presence of mind, Neil
steered the ringleaders into a saloon, where he acquiesced in their demands to offer three cheers for Jeff Davis. His mother showed more idealism but somewhat less practical wisdom. Home alone with the younger
children, she hurried them out onto the roof, then decided she could fend
off any possible intruders by composing a speech emphasizing patriotism
and republican pride. Fortunately, the police and two companies of soldiers arrived on the scene and reestablished order; Stanton did not have to
deliver her speech. Susan Anthony, prevented by mob activity from get-
ting to the league office in the Cooper Institute, took refuge in the home of
a cousin.[74]

Several days later, members of the Woman's National Loyal League
gathered in the Cooper Institute. Discussing the riots and their significance, the women concluded that the recent mob action was yet
another example of the dangers threatening all black Americans and
further proof of the need to grant citizenship in addition to emancipation
for all blacks.[75]

While Elizabeth Cady Stanton and Susan B. Anthony organized league
events from their headquarters in New York City, their designated agents
directed activities in the West. Hannah Tracy Cutler, who had lectured
extensively in Illinois, and Josephine Griffing, an Ohio activist, became
paid agents of the Woman's National Loyal League in the summer of 1863.
In August the *Standard* announced that Griffing would begin an extensive
tour of Michigan and northern Illinois. Josephine Griffing worked for
freedmen's relief in addition to her league lecturing. Because of her labor
on behalf of destitute black men and women, she was appointed general
agent of the National Freedmen's Relief Association in Washington. In
this capacity she distributed food and opened three schools where black
women received vocational training. These labors, which earned Griffing
the admiration of Senator Charles Sumner, also helped to inspire formation of the Freedmen's Bureau in 1865.[76]

The state of Illinois proved to be fertile ground for the Woman's National Loyal League. The Galesburg *Free Democrat* urged its readers to sign
the league's "mammoth petition." In Chicago every Methodist minister in
the city pledged to circulate the Loyal League petitions and to preach a
sermon on the duty of Congress to pass an antislavery amendment. When

Frederick Douglass gave a benefit lecture for the league in Chicago, the *Tribune* reported that "Bryan Hall was crowded with a large and appreciative audience." Douglass reiterated the abolitionist plea that the antislavery fight was far from over and argued persuasively in favor of granting the vote to black men.[77]

In December 1863 the American Anti-Slavery Society met in Philadelphia for its third decade meeting. It was a time for looking back and for assessing the future. Samuel May recalled that women had not been allowed to sign the original Declaration of Sentiments in 1833, though Garrison was quick to point out that the society had passed a resolution encouraging women to form auxiliary societies. Mary Grew read a brief report outlining the history of women's antislavery societies. Lucretia Mott remembered the World's Anti-Slavery Convention in 1840, a meeting which had done so much to bring about an organized woman's rights movement in America. Abby Kelley Foster, stern and uncompromising as ever, warned the assembled crowd not to be overconfident, not to dwell too much on past glories when the antislavery crusade was not yet over.[78]

Susan Anthony spoke on behalf of the Woman's National Loyal League. While Anthony acknowledged the importance of sanitary commission and freedmen's relief work, she insisted, as had Elizabeth Cady Stanton on numerous occasions, that the political question of emancipation was the most pressing issue of the day. Women were uniquely suited to work in the league's petition drive "because as women we could have no voice as to what should be the basis of reconstruction of this government, save through the one right which the nation has left to us, the right of petition." Like Abby Kelley Foster, Anthony was dismayed by the number of people who believed the president's Emancipation Proclamation effectively freed the slaves. Such complacence must not be tolerated. However, Anthony was encouraged by the success of the petition drive. One recent mail had brought close to 5,000 signatures. Lucy Stone added her voice to that of her colleague. "We are not allowed to vote," Stone declared, "but we may petition, and by and by they will hear."[79]

The American Anti-Slavery Society passed a resolution at its third decade meeting to petition Congress for a constitutional amendment freeing the slaves. The Loyal League's petition was a more general one asking Congress to abolish slavery. Antislavery advocates could, of course, sign both petitions, but the society's actions angered Elizabeth Cady Stanton. She wrote Garrison a letter, later printed in the *Liberator,* in which she complained about the "bad policy of all specific petitioning."[80]

In all probability Stanton's chief concern was that Garrison's new petition drive would upstage the league's efforts. After February 1864 Stanton
and Anthony included the specific demand for a constitutional amendment in their own petitions, an action which brought them the endorsement of Abby Kelley Foster. The Worcester, Massachusetts, abolitionist had previously withheld her support from the league, claiming the
organization was not radical enough. Stanton and Anthony need not
have worried about being upstaged by Garrison. Their petition drive had
brought in more than 100,000 signatures by February 1864, and they were
ready, through the auspices of Charles Sumner, to present the first installment to the Senate.[81]

The first 6,000 petition forms, bearing 100,000 signatures, were glued
end to end, rolled into a bundle, and mailed to Sumner in a trunk. "These
signatures represent, mothers wives sisters & daughters of honest men
who have fought and died for our country," Stanton and Anthony said.
"Through you they now ask that the cause be made worthy [of] their
terrible sacrifice." Furthermore, the women emphasized that since "the
'Right of Petition' is woman's only political right under our government, it
is the sacred duty of her representatives to give this petition earnest careful
consideration."[82]

On 9 February 1864 two black men entered the Senate chamber and
carried the first installment of league petitions to the desk of Charles
Sumner. The senior senator from Massachusetts stood to address his colleagues. "This petition is signed by one hundred thousand men and
women," he declared, "who unite in this unparalleled number to support
its prayer. . . . They are from the families of the educated and uneducated,
rich and poor." "Here they are," he said, "a mighty army, one hundred
thousand strong, without arms or banners, the advance guard of a yet
larger army."[83]

The women of the Loyal League were fully aware that slavery was the
root of the present war and that this "monster," this "*national enemy*" must
be destroyed. While Sumner was careful to make clear that the league
petitions included signatures of both women and men, he emphasized the
female origins when he stated: "There is no reason so strong as the reason
of the heart. Do not all great thoughts come from the heart?" At the
conclusion of his speech, which became known as the "Prayer of One
Hundred Thousand," Sumner asked that the petition be referred to his
select committee on slavery and freedmen, created at his request in January 1864. He was anticipating a plethora of petitions in the new year,

Table 1. Signatures on Woman's National Loyal League petitions, February 1864

State	Men	Women	Total
New York	6,519	11,187	17,706
Illinois	6,382	8,998	15,380
Massachusetts	4,248	7,392	11,641
Pennsylvania	2,259	6,366	8,625
Ohio	3,670	4,674	8,330
Michigan	1,741	4,441	6,182
Iowa	2,025	4,014	6,039
Maine	1,225	4,362	5,587
Wisconsin	1,639	2,391	4,030
Indiana	1,075	2,591	3,666
New Hampshire	393	2,261	2,654
New Jersey	824	1,709	2,533
Rhode Island	827	1,451	2,278
Vermont	375	1,183	1,558
Connecticut	393	1,162	1,555
Minnesota	396	1,094	1,490
West Virginia	82	100	182
Maryland	115	50	165
Kansas	84	74	158
Delaware	67	70	137
Nebraska	13	20	33
Kentucky	21	—	21
Louisiana (New Orleans)	—	14	14
Citizens of the U.S. living in New Brunswick	19	17	36
Total	34,399	65,601	100,000

Source: Elizabeth Cady Stanton, Susan B. Anthony, and Matilda Joslyn Gage, eds., *History of Woman Suffrage*, 3 vols., 2d ed. (Rochester, N.Y.: Charles Mann, 1889), 2:79.

notably those of the Loyal League, and wanted a forum from which to advertise them. "I hope very soon to report . . . an amendment of the Constitution abolishing slavery throughout the U. States," Sumner wrote confidently to the duchess of Argyll the day before introducing the league's petitions.[84]

New York and Illinois vied for the most signatures (table 1). As late as 29 January the president's home state was in the lead, but the Empire State eventually exceeded Illinois's total. The Chicago *Tribune* reflected this state rivalry in its story on the petition totals, printing Illinois's total first and burying New York's higher total in the middle of the column.[85]

The degree of league organization in the individual states varied greatly. New York, which produced the greatest number of signatures, included strong efforts in New York City and Rochester, thanks to Amy Post's support. Because local organization in Illinois was good, that state produced a high proportion of signatures despite its relatively small population. Massachusetts, long a center for antislavery agitation, contributed more than 11,000 signatures. The Philadelphia Female Anti-Slavery Society, now led by Sarah Pugh and Abby Kimber, had ceased to hold fundraising fairs but did respond enthusiastically to the league petition campaign. Their efforts produced several thousand signatures.[86]

Sometimes individual efforts were successful. Tiny New Hampshire had no formal league organization, but two Concord women initiated a petition drive. New Hampshire contributed more than 2,500 signatures. One widow from rural Wisconsin, whose husband and two sons had died in the war, collected 1,800 signatures on league petitions. Furthermore, the feisty woman recorded all the names of those who refused to sign the petitions, so that "they may be handed over to the future scorn they so well deserve." More than 40,000 signatures came from the states of the Old Northwest, indicating the league had been successful in spreading an essentially eastern organization into the western states. Of the total signers, roughly two-thirds were female. Despite the invaluable help that Stanton and Anthony received from men, their organization remained a female operation.[87]

By February 1864 the Woman's National Loyal League had an active membership of 5,000, had circulated 12,000 petitions, and had collected more than 100,000 signatures. Abolitionist senators Charles Sumner and Henry Wilson assured the women that the petitions constituted the bulwark of their drive for legislative action to end slavery.[88] But the battle was not over. The league was still far from its goal of obtaining one million signatures, and Congress had not yet passed an emancipation amendment. As the winter of 1863–64 gave way to spring, Elizabeth Cady Stanton and Susan B. Anthony began to look ahead to the presidential election.

The Presidential Election of 1864

The day has passed for making Providence the scape-goat for all our
ignorance and folly. . . . We do not propose to leave the next
Presidency to chance.
—Elizabeth Cady Stanton to Caroline Healey Dall, 3 June 1864

Abolitionists had been sharply critical of President Lincoln ever since his
inauguration in March 1861. They were infuriated by his revocation of the
Frémont and Hunter edicts, and they regarded his Emancipation Proclamation as too little, too late. They also criticized Lincoln's appointees,
notably Secretary of State William Seward, whom Lydia Maria Child
dismissed as a "crooked and selfish hypocrite" because he had pandered to
the Southern states during the secession crisis. They condemned a wide
array of Union generals, including George B. McClellan. Even the president's wife became an abolitionist target. Mary Todd Lincoln was looked
upon with suspicion in large part because of her Kentucky background.
She also aggravated many because of her well-known penchant for expensive clothing. "So *this* is what the people are taxed for!" huffed Lydia Maria
Child upon reading in the newspaper of Mrs. Lincoln's latest purchases.
"To deck out this vulgar doll with foreign frippery" was inexcusable to
Child, who had written *The Frugal Housewife* and donated all her extra
savings to freedmen's relief.[1]

When in December 1863 Abraham Lincoln announced his lenient "10
percent plan" for Reconstruction, members of the American Anti-Slavery
Society were sharply divided in their responses. Some abolitionists, including Wendell Phillips, Elizabeth Cady Stanton, and Susan Anthony,
were growing increasingly impatient with a president who had seemed so
slow in freeing the slaves and yet appeared so compassionate toward the
Confederates, offering amnesty for military officers except those of the
highest rank. Other abolitionists, led by William Lloyd Garrison, became
increasingly respectful of the president. These abolitionists believed the
president was slowly leading the people to accept the notion of emancipation. Warning Oliver Johnson, editor of the *Standard*, that "breakers
are ahead," Garrison correctly predicted that "our society is to be rent

ʊ asunder."[2] Debate over presidential politics would lead to an abolitionist schism on a scale not seen since 1840. This schism also had important consequences in the presidential election of 1864.

The first important abolitionist debate over Lincoln's Reconstruction policy came in January 1864, when Wendell Phillips and William Lloyd Garrison faced one another at the annual meeting of the Massachusetts Anti-Slavery Society. Phillips introduced a resolution stating that "the Government, in its haste, is ready to sacrifice the interest and honor of the North to secure a sham peace . . . leaving the freedmen and the Southern States under the control of the late slaveholders." While Phillips conceded that the president had made significant strides to emancipate the black man, he charged that Lincoln showed no interest in the elevation of the freedmen's political or social status.[3]

William Lloyd Garrison, by contrast, criticized some of Lincoln's policies while believing the president to be well-meaning. The Emancipation Proclamation was a clear example of Lincoln's sincerity regarding emancipation. "The President must be judged by his possibilities," Garrison said, "rather than by our wishes or by the highest abstract moral standard. In my judgment the re-election of Abraham Lincoln . . . would be the safest and wisest course." Phillips won the debate when his resolution passed the convention by a few votes. Phillips was able to carry both the American Anti-Slavery Society and the New England Anti-Slavery Society with him in condemning Lincoln's Reconstruction policies. In each instance Garrison defended the president.[4]

With Lincoln's record under fire, radicals sought an alternative candidate for the presidency in 1864. Secretary of the Treasury Salmon P. Chase with his close ties to the abolition movement was one possibility. But when Senator Samuel C. Pomeroy of Kansas circulated a letter promoting Chase's candidacy, the action failed. Republicans across the North united behind Lincoln, forcing the treasury secretary to withdraw his name. General John C. Frémont was another possibility, an attractive candidate in the eyes of many abolitionists because of his attempt to free slaves in his Missouri military district. By 1863 Frémont had begun to encourage his political supporters, as had his equally ambitious wife, Jessie.[5]

On 16 January 1864 Anna Dickinson made her views on the presidential question known. For some time, friends of the young abolitionist, notably Congressman William Kelley of Philadelphia, had hoped to make arrangements for Dickinson to speak before Congress. The plans were finally completed, and Dickinson received a formal invitation on 16 December 1863. Among the signers of this unprecedented invitation were Schuyler Colfax, Owen Lovejoy, George Julian, and Thaddeus Stevens of the House of Representatives and Charles Sumner and Henry Wilson of the Senate.[6]

Never before had a woman been asked to speak in the halls of Congress. "Who would have thought five years ago that it was possible that a woman would deliver an anti-slavery lecture in the Hall of Representatives," marveled the New York *Independent*. Tickets went on sale two days before the lecture and sold out quickly. Fully aware of her popularity as a speaker, Dickinson had hoped to pocket the proceeds from her speech, but Congressman Kelley assured his friend that personal remuneration from a congressional lecture was out of the question, whereupon Dickinson agreed to donate the proceeds to freedmen's relief. The evening before her historic lecture, Speaker Colfax hosted a reception attended by high-ranking members of Congress and the cabinet; Congressman Kelley escorted Miss Dickinson, who was the center of attention.[7]

At half past seven on 16 January, Anna Dickinson entered the Hall of Representatives. She was escorted by Vice President Hannibal Hamlin, who introduced her by alluding to the Maid of Orleans. Seated before the twenty-one-year-old speaker was the most distinguished audience in the country. Members of the Senate and House, the Supreme Court, the Lincoln cabinet, and the vice president of the United States honored the young Quaker woman with enthusiastic cheers. Her speech "Words for the Hour" was in large part a stinging rebuke of President Lincoln for his lenient Reconstruction program. In future speeches Dickinson would demand that Southern land be confiscated and redistributed to the freedmen. She was especially angered that the president would consider granting amnesty to any rebel leaders.[8]

At eight o'clock, in the midst of Dickinson's vituperative remarks, President and Mrs. Lincoln arrived at the House of Representatives. Dickinson continued to condemn the president's policies. "Mr. Lincoln sat with his head bowed, rarely looking Miss Dickinson in the face," one reporter wrote. Later Dickinson admitted that the arrival of the Lincolns had shocked her, but the young orator gave no visible hint of this reaction during her speech.[9]

Suddenly she changed her tone. "This was pre-eminently a people's war," she said; "it was guided by a man of the people. . . . Granted that we had much yet to do, we had the man to complete the grand and glorious work, *and that work was left for his second term of office*." The audience, initially caught off guard by this seemingly abrupt about-face, eventually rejoiced with "volleys of cheers." There were calls for the president to speak, but he slipped out a side door after telling the vice president, teasingly, that he was far too embarrassed to address the audience. Hamlin conveyed this sentiment to the crowd, which responded with laughter. [10]

The speech in Washington was the high point of Anna Dickinson's career. "Joan of Arc never was grander," announced one Washington newspaper. Charles Dudley Warner, the flamboyant Connecticut newspaperman, wrote to his friend: "You have conquered Washington—you have taken the capital. . . . I only wish you could take Richmond as easily. . . . To see Uncle Abraham at your feet, and Mrs. Abe at your head, and to bring down the House the way you did." Dickinson's speech received attention from newspapers all across the United States, from Washington and Philadelphia to Cincinnati, St. Louis, and Detroit. Predictably, the Democrats in Congress objected to Dickinson's speech. One representative went so far as to introduce a resolution stating "that we disapprove of such a use of this hall for political purposes, and regard it as disrespectful to the minority of this House." The resolution was dismissed by Speaker Colfax who could point to Dickinson's philanthropic role. Her speech netted $1031 for freedmen's relief. [11]

Now at the peak of her popularity, Anna Dickinson received invitations to speak before the legislatures of Pennsylvania, Ohio, and New York. In late January she repeated her "Words for the Hour" lecture to a capacity crowd at the Philadelphia Academy of Music. Her endorsement of Lincoln received enthusiastic applause. On 2 February 1864 she repeated the address again at the Cooper Institute in New York, where the doors were shut and guarded an hour before her lecture to prevent additional people from attempting to push their way into the packed hall. Speeches in Brooklyn and Boston followed. Dickinson continued to have her critics, however. The New York *World* complained about the "absurd adulation" the young orator attracted, while declining to cover Dickinson's Cooper Institute speech. [12]

Anna Dickinson's support for President Lincoln's reelection was short-lived. Indeed, her sudden endorsement of a second Lincoln term is difficult to comprehend given her radical beliefs about punishing rebel leaders and confiscating their land. Lincoln's moderate views on Reconstruction were far too lenient to suit her. In all probability, Dickinson's decision to endorse the president in her speech before Congress came as a result of her shock upon seeing him enter the Hall of Representatives, coupled with her flair for the dramatic. Her style of oratory derived much of its effectiveness from her use of immoderate statements. Castigating the president for his Reconstruction policies, then suddenly endorsing his reelection created just the sort of climactic scene for which Anna Dickinson had become famous.

Although Samuel Pomeroy of Kansas tried to woo Dickinson into the Chase camp, the Quaker orator showed no interest. But neither did she continue to endorse Abraham Lincoln for a second term. Embarking on a midwestern tour in February 1864, Dickinson spoke to audiences in Cincinnati, Indianapolis, St. Louis, Chicago, Toledo, Cleveland, Erie, and finally upstate New York, where she gave several lectures and spoke before the New York legislature. In no instance did newspapers covering her speeches report a presidential endorsement. Instead, she continued to argue that the South must be punished for the crime of slavery. In several instances the audiences were less than enthusiastic toward Dickinson's Reconstruction views. [13]

Whitelaw Reid, a journalist, friend, and confidant of Anna Dickinson, urged her not to criticize the president so vehemently. "It can do no good now for you to get tangled in the strifes of personal politics," he wrote in April 1864, "& it may do much harm. Mr. Lincoln's popularity with the masses is established, by what means it no longer does good to inquire, & attacks on him only serve to influence the ardor of his friends." Reid, who supported Chase, hoped the Republican convention might be postponed. Radical Republicans could then unite behind an alternative candidate such as Chase or Benjamin Butler and perhaps swing the Republican convention behind them. [14]

Dickinson ignored Reid's advice. The Confederate massacre of black troops at Fort Pillow, Tennessee, soldiers who might have been taken prisoner, added more anti-Southern rhetoric to her invective. Such an act of barbarism appalled the radicals, many of whom regarded the incident as all the more reason to punish the South. Dickinson's speeches in the spring of 1864 emphasized the Fort Pillow massacre. At Cooper Union on 19 April, the New York *Times* reported, Dickinson, in recalling the Fort Pillow massacre, "inquired, with great earnestness, is this a time to offer amnesty and pardon?" [15]

Increasingly angered by the president's Reconstruction policies, Dickinson went to Washington sometime in late March or early April, and Lincoln consented to an interview. In the course of their discussion, the president interjected, "That reminds me of a little story," upon which the twenty-one-year-old abolitionist quickly interrupted: "I didn't come to hear stories." Furthermore, she told Lincoln that his lenient Reconstruction plan was "all wrong; as radically bad as can be." President Lincoln ended the conversation, according to Dickinson, by saying, "All I can say is, if the radicals want me to lead, let them get out of the way and let me lead." Dickinson left the interview remarking to a friend, "I have spoken my last word to President Lincoln."[16]

Congressman Kelley of Philadelphia accompanied the young woman on her interview with the president. His version of the story was significantly different. "In that interview A. E. D. said but very few words," Kelley recalled. "What she did say was 'fool'ish according to her own acknowledgment at the time. She burst into tears—struck an attitude and begged Mr. L. to excuse her for coming there to make a fool of herself. The President was paternally kind and considerate in what he said to her, and her requital is most—inexcusable."[17]

Lincoln himself never commented in any extant letters about the meeting. In all probability, both Dickinson's and Kelley's versions contained elements of the truth. Dickinson was known as one who spoke her mind, and she undoubtedly told the president what was wrong with his Reconstruction policy. Although Kelley was clearly a Lincoln supporter and Dickinson's anti-Lincoln speeches may have made him somewhat biased in retelling the incident, it is entirely possible that Dickinson lost her composure during the meeting. Her volatile temperament was well known among the abolitionists, some of whom had witnessed her emotional outbursts firsthand. Garrison was one who had. Because he had played a pivotal role in the young woman's rise to prominence and continued to act as a father figure, she respected him and even depended on him for help in preparing lecture material. In a letter to his wife, Garrison described a dinner party hosted by James and Lucretia Mott and attended by Miller McKim, Theodore and Elizabeth Tilton, Dickinson, and himself. The conversation centered around Lincoln's policies, which Garrison supported. Without elaborating, Garrison commented, "I hurt Anna's feelings so much that she left the room to give vent to her feelings" but later returned.[18] At least one aspect of Dickinson's version was correct, however, for she never again spoke to the president. After her meeting with Lincoln, she did not endorse his reelection.

Supporters of the president, well aware of Anna Dickinson's popularity on the lecture circuit, were dismayed by the young woman's election-year criticism of Lincoln. Copperhead Democrats, on the other hand, were so impressed by Anna Dickinson's success that they introduced a woman speaker of their own. Emma Webb was a New York actress who lectured on at least a few occasions for the proslavery, procompromise cause. Born in New Orleans in 1843, Webb was eight months younger than her abolitionist rival. She made her theatrical debut in New Orleans, later joining her sister in a joint premiere at New York's Bowery Theater 10 January 1860. The Webb sisters were pretty and talented enough to ensure their continued success on the New York stage.[19] In appearance Emma Webb was very different from Anna Dickinson. The abolitionist orator with her shoulder-length curls and short stature looked young and innocent. Webb, on the other hand, had a long face and aquiline nose. Her hair was pulled back into a bun, giving her a more mature, sophisticated appearance.

Lecturing to an audience of four hundred at the Cooper Institute 6 April 1864, Webb complained about Anna Dickinson's contention that the present war was "holy." This was a most unwomanly attitude, according to Webb, who sidestepped the possible impropriety of a Copperhead woman on the lecture platform by claiming that "this cruel and fratricidal war" had forced her to speak out. By supporting the war, Dickinson was actually encouraging violence and bloodshed. Insisting that slavery was the natural condition of the black man, Webb challenged the abolitionists to name one place in the world where free blacks were civilized and contented. She also adopted a typical Copperhead approach by emphasizing the abolitionists' belief in racial equality. Anna Dickinson "says we are fighting for a flag," Webb declared; "yes, a flag half African and half white—not American. This country should be called New Africa." The New York actress never lost an opportunity to praise General McClellan for his military talents and his sound judgment. She also lauded two other "staunch men of truth," Democrat Thomas Seymour of Connecticut and Copperhead Clement Vallandigham of Ohio.[20]

Everywhere she went, Webb directly attacked Anna Dickinson's popular lecture "Words for the Hour" by lecturing on "Lessons for the Hour" and "Delusions of the Hour." In Cincinnati the *Enquirer* announced that Webb would "reply to Miss Anna Dickinson's Abolition harangue." In Brooklyn, reiterating her theme that emancipation could bring only turmoil, she pointed to the example of the West Indies. These former slave colonies were now desolate, and the freed slaves had become heathens. "Wherever the negro is subordinate," Webb insisted, "he is useful and happy." She claimed that slaves served the same purpose as greenbacks in America; they were legal tender. Finally, the Copperhead orator charged that the abolition movement bore the responsibility for the Civil War, adding, "the Constitution or Abolitionism must die."[21]

Emma Webb's approach to oratory was in many ways similar to Dickinson's. Both capitalized on a delicate and feminine appearance and on the public's wartime fascination with Joan of Arc imagery; both discussed complex issues in very simple terms; both cultivated a sense of the dramatic and appealed to the patriotism of their listeners; both defied traditional views about woman's sphere in aspiring to fame, fortune, and independence. If Webb dreamed of matching Dickinson's success, she was sorely disappointed. Offended that the New York *Tribune* accused her of "repeating some Copperhead's lecture," Webb wrote Horace Greeley claiming to have a "patriotic mission to perform."[22]

There were other Dickinson rivals as well. A Democratic orator named Teresa Esmonde spoke out against Dickinson's "rampant abolitionism and abuse of McClellan" in 1863, proposing a "public discussion" with her. Cordelia Phillips, a Republican orator, gave at least a few speeches in support of Lincoln's reelection in 1864, while another speaker, Emma Hardinge, delivered a Cooper Union address in March 1865. *Frank Leslie's Illustrated Newspaper* announced Hardinge's forthcoming lecture while noting that "female lecturers are on the increase." Democratic socialite Maria Daly complained in her diary about the number of orators Dickinson had inspired, women she believed to be motivated by vanity and monetary gain. The New York diarist dismissed these female orators by concluding, "What fools people are to go and listen." Although Dickinson had nothing to fear from her rivals—their speeches never generated anything close to the degree of attention her own activities received—she was certainly aware of at least some of them. Dickinson's Civil War scrapbook contains newspaper clippings of Webb's speeches, and Emma Webb, like Teresa Esmonde, challenged her to a public debate.[23] She either refused or ignored these requests, no doubt because she did not wish to share the limelight and risk losing her popularity to another.

By the spring of 1864, abolitionists were clearly divided in their political loyalties. Wendell Phillips threw his considerable influence behind the presidential candidacy of John C. Frémont, while William Lloyd Garrison supported the reelection of President Lincoln. With Phillips firmly in control of the American Anti-Slavery Society, Garrison's interest in the organization he helped found waned as did his friendship with his old colleague. But if Phillips had eclipsed Garrison in leadership of the anti-slavery societies, Garrison still controlled the antislavery journals. On

18 March 1864 Garrison's *Liberator* issued a ringing endorsement of Lincoln's reelection. While admitting that Lincoln had made numerous mistakes as president, Garrison felt that his issuance of the Emancipation Proclamation was ample reason to vote him in for another term. Garrison's colleague Oliver Johnson of the *National Anti-Slavery Standard* used the pages of his own journal to endorse the president.[24]

Elizabeth Cady Stanton and Susan B. Anthony had their own political agenda. The two women already had broadened the Loyal League's philosophical appeal unmistakably, calling for women's increased activism during the national crisis and beyond. By early 1864 they began emphasizing the need for female participation in present and future electoral contests. By demonstrating that women were active participants in the presidential campaign, they could show that women both wanted and deserved to be granted the right to vote after the war, along with the former slaves. But first they had to convince women that presidential politics was a logical step beyond petitioning for a political purpose.

Both women were early supporters of John C. Frémont. The Missouri general had proved his commitment to emancipation most notably by his attempt to liberate the slaves in Missouri. In contrast with Lincoln, Frémont seemed to be uncompromising in his advocacy of immediate abolition, a true humanitarian whose beliefs made him morally superior to the incumbent president. "It seems to me that [the] Liberator and Standard are gone '*Stark Mad*' in their echo of the Politicians cry—'Save the Union,'" Susan Anthony wrote to Anna Dickinson, adding, "to profess confidence in Lincoln would be a lie in me."[25]

The incipient Frémont movement also appealed to Stanton and Anthony because it seemed to represent a genuine democratic uprising. Frémont organizers in New York issued a call for supporters to meet at Cleveland in late May, where they planned to nominate Frémont and initiate a massive popular uprising before the Republican convention convened in Baltimore on 7 June. Stanton and Anthony both endorsed the convention. "It is time to inaugurate an entirely new mode of making Presidents," Elizabeth Cady Stanton wrote to Jessie Frémont, 4 May 1864. "Let the people place men before the nation and in mass convention make known their choice." Political candidates should be chosen by the people and not by the political power brokers. Furthermore, in a democracy, one four-year term was long enough for any man to serve as chief executive.[26]

Elizabeth Cady Stanton also had personal reasons for disliking the Lincoln administration. Henry Stanton, having campaigned actively for

Lincoln in 1860, was rewarded with an appointment as deputy collector of the Customs House in New York. It was his responsibility to oversee the procuring of refundable bonds for domestic and foreign shipments, a kind of insurance for the government against ships carrying contraband to the Confederacy. Neil Stanton, eldest son of Henry and Elizabeth, worked as a clerk in his father's office. Unbeknownst to his parents, Neil accepted bribes and forged Henry's signature on documents enabling certain ships to sail without bonds. When an informant's tip made the ruse public, Henry Stanton was relieved of his job in December 1863. The Customs House scandal was a terrible embarrassment to the Stanton family.[27]

Elizabeth Cady Stanton blindly refused to acknowledge her son's culpability in the scandal and instead blamed her husband's enemies in the Lincoln administration. Letters to her abolitionist friends in 1864 were peppered with sarcastic comments about "Dishonest Abe," "the utter rottenness of the present administration" and "let Abe finish up his jokes in Springfield."[28] Clearly, she had private reasons for opposing the president's reelection; nevertheless, her radicalism and the influence of Wendell Phillips make it likely that she would have opposed a second term even if the scandal had not occurred.

Firmly committed to Frémont's candidacy, Stanton and Anthony were faced with an important decision. The first anniversary of the Woman's National Loyal League would be observed in a few weeks. Having created a national network with several thousand members, Stanton and Anthony might use its influence as a propaganda force in the election. Should the league endorse Frémont? Garrison and others were certainly afraid of this possibility. In printed circulars advertising the anniversary meeting, Stanton and Anthony appealed to the "women of the Republic to make themselves a *Power for Freedom* in the coming Presidential Campaign." They went so far as to ask Jessie Benton Frémont to preside at the May meeting, but Mrs. Frémont, citing a recent change of residence, declined.[29]

Caroline Dall, a Boston feminist, responded to the league advertisement by writing a lengthy letter to Stanton which was eventually published in the *Liberator*. While endorsing Stanton's notion that women might "interest" themselves in political questions, they should not "dictate"; indeed, they should limit their interest to the "moral aspects of government." Dall urged the league president not to turn the anniversary meeting into an "electioneering caucus"; she admitted great personal admiration for the president, whom God had led to the White House, and she found Stanton's objections to the two-term principle to be invalid. Dall urged the league president to continue carrying out the original goal of the league, namely, to educate the people about the importance of emancipation. "As a convention of women, stand on this high ground," she wrote. "Do not commit yourselves to unlimited laudation of any man—nominate no candidate, whether it be Lincoln or another—but teach the nation what to demand of either or both." If the league became a partisan political body, it might easily risk losing many of the supporters who saw the league's role to be antislavery advocacy.[30]

In her reply to Dall, also published in the *Liberator,* Stanton assured her Boston colleague that the league was not responsible for her private letters. However, she did take issue with Dall on several points. One of the earliest feminists to acknowledge the importance of seeking legislative solutions to problems of injustice and inequality, Stanton had called for woman suffrage in 1848. She pointed out to Dall that the year-old Loyal League was the first and the only organization of women committed to a political purpose. Through its petitioning, the league was dedicated to democracy and human rights. Much was at stake in the 1864 election, she claimed, and women must not wait for an invitation before participating in the political arena, for "aristocracy never seeks to share its privileges."[31]

Stanton ridiculed Dall's notion that Abraham Lincoln was sent to the executive chair by the Almighty. Believing that too many women failed to interest themselves in political questions because of a fear of involvement in what was believed to be the work of God and mortal men, Stanton questioned whether Franklin Pierce and James Buchanan were also divinely appointed. Did God change political parties every four years? To bring God into the "'muddy pool of politics' would be far worse than for the daughters of the Pilgrims . . . to share all the dangers and difficulties of this earthly sphere." Stanton then recalled women's participation in the "Tippecanoe and Tyler too" campaign of 1840 and the recent electoral speeches of Anna Dickinson in Connecticut and Pennsylvania as examples of women's political interests and abilities.[32]

The league's anniversary convention would not dissolve into an "electioneering caucus or political cabal," Stanton assured Caroline Dall, but what better forum in which to debate the important issues of presidential politics? For the last thirty years, antislavery conventions had served as the "nation's school," where "our most liberal Christians, clearest logicians, earnest orators" have debated, learned, and then instructed the American public through the lecture circuit. Stanton anticipated a similar role for the forthcoming Loyal League convention. "The day has passed for making Providence the scape-goat for all our ignorance and folly," she declared; "we do not propose to leave the next Presidency to chance." Susan B. Anthony shared Stanton's anticipation about the coming convention. In a letter asking Charles Sumner to address the anniversary meeting, Anthony noted that the league's activities to date had centered largely around the antislavery petition and alluded to a desire for women to expand their political role in the coming year.[33]

If Stanton was not swayed by the opinion of Caroline Dall, she was influenced by that of Wendell Phillips. In response to an invitation from Susan Anthony, Phillips agreed to address the anniversary convention in a fifteen-minute speech, but he cautioned Stanton against endorsing Frémont. The general's name should be placed in nomination at the Cleveland convention on 31 May and not before; furthermore, Stanton should not "turn into a partisan machine something meant for a specific definite object." Although Phillips's letter was affectionate and witty, he warned Stanton that if she ignored his advice, he would not address the league anniversary meeting. Stanton acceded to his terms, but she was not pleased about his attitude and, in thanking him for agreeing to speak, added a sarcastic note about being "ladylike . . . in our convention."[34]

Stanton hoped William Lloyd Garrison might address the league anniversary meeting as well, but only if he took the proper attitude toward the presidential campaign. Urging him to "put the name of Fremont at the heart of your Liberator," Stanton questioned whether the nation could last another four years under "Lincoln's dynasty." Garrison was clearly concerned about the possibility of Stanton and Anthony turning the Loyal League anniversary into a Frémont political rally, while leading a vehement attack on Lincoln's presidency. He regretted the timing of Caroline Dall's broadside, although he agreed with her sentiments and hoped it would carry some weight with the league officers. "They mean well," he said of Stanton and Anthony, "but their vision is limited." Though he remained friendly toward both women, Garrison did not address the Loyal League convention.[35]

The anniversary meeting of the Woman's National Loyal League convened 12 May 1864 at the Church of the Puritans in New York. Charlotte Wilbur, recording secretary, read the report of the executive committee. The league could boast a successful year. With a membership of 5,000, the Loyal League's 2,000 active petition collectors had rolled up 265,314 names on 20,000 petitions in the past year. In addition, they had printed numerous copies of Sumner's "Prayer of One Hundred Thousand" speech for distribution across the country. League-sponsored lectures helped to educate the people about the importance of immediate emancipation. Josephine Griffing of Ohio and Hannah Tracy Cutler of Illinois remained paid lecturing agents of the league.[36]

The English abolitionist George Thompson gave a speech, as did Wendell Phillips, Lucretia Mott, and Ernestine Rose. Phillips applauded league members for their efforts in educating the American people about the importance of antislavery, and he singled out Anna Dickinson for special commendation. Phillips also endorsed female suffrage, arguing that women should contribute their "moral power" to American politics. Charles Sumner, who claimed that senatorial duties precluded his attendance, sent a letter of support which was read by Susan Anthony. It contained no reference to feminist issues but focused on the petition. "I am grateful to your Association for what you have done to arouse the country," Sumner said. "Now is the time to strike and no effort should be spared."[37]

With or without male abolitionist support, Stanton and Anthony gave the anniversary meeting a more overtly feminist tone than that of the first convention. In circulating the "mammoth petition," league members had complained that women occasionally refused to sign because they believed that slavery and other weighty matters should be debated only by Congress. Stanton and Anthony were especially anxious to dispel this notion of deference toward elected officials, a belief strong among so many women. They argued that the national crisis called for a new type of woman, one who would continue to aid the sanitary and freedmen's organizations but also would be an active participant in the political sphere. By lifting politics into the "sphere of morals and religion . . . it is the duty of women to be co-workers [with men] . . . in giving immortal life to the NEW nation."[38]

Clearly, Stanton and Anthony still found it expedient to use the rhetoric of patriotism and true womanhood. They did not equivocate, however, in discussing the specific issue of pay equity. The convention members passed a resolution demanding that female nurses who had received formal medical training should be paid on the same scale as male medical personnel. They passed another resolution demanding the vote for all citizens who fought for their country or paid taxes for its support. Although not explicitly stated, the latter group would encompass some women. If these groups were not enfranchised, a "true republic" would never be achieved. The feminist bias of these resolutions almost certainly alienated some conservative women. Although several hundred thousand women would sign the petitions, only five thousand would join the organization.[39]

In her research on antebellum female abolitionists in upstate New York, Judith Wellman found a decline in the number of female signatures on antislavery petitions between the late 1830s and the mid-1850s. She attributed this decline to the trend toward the petitions focusing on political issues rather than moral ones.[40] The creation of the Loyal League with its national membership of five thousand and its petition campaign reaching hundreds of thousands would seem to indicate that while petitioning for a political aim had become acceptable for thousands of women, membership in a feminist political organization had not.

Even if the league's feminism alienated some women, its five thousand members represented a national abolitionist and feminist movement, inspiring activists from Maine to California.[41] While encouraging male participation, the league was organized and directed by women. Its creation, therefore, was a development of tremendous significance in the history of the woman's rights movement. Although this important organization dissolved at the end of the war, it would serve as a precedent for later feminist efforts in terms of philosophy, leadership, and tactics.

Despite their personal endorsement of John C. Frémont's presidential candidacy, Stanton and Anthony did not commit the league to any candidate. The only mention of Frémont's name came when Susan Anthony read the letters of league supporters who were unable to attend the convention. Emile Pretorius, a German-American from St. Louis, congratulated the league on its patriotic work, signing his letter, "Yours for Fremont and Freedom."[42]

If Stanton and Anthony restrained the impulse to endorse Frémont, they made little attempt to hide their antipathy toward President Lincoln. Gone was the conciliatory spirit of last year's convention, as resolution after resolution of the Loyal League condemned the present administration. The league stated emphatically that the United States government "*still* upholds slavery by military as well as civil power." League members demanded for black soldiers, sailors, and laborers pay equal to that of their white counterparts and the right of suffrage as well. Like Anna Dickinson, Stanton and Anthony reserved their harshest words for the government's failure to protect black soldiers from the rebel atrocities perpetrated at Port Hudson, Milliken's Bend, Olustee, and Fort Pillow. These outrages were additional proof of the "*heartless character* or *utter incapacity*" of the Lincoln administration to conduct the war.[43]

Garrison was so pleased by Stanton and Anthony's decision to withhold a Frémont endorsement that he did not complain about their discussion of feminist issues, which had angered him the previous year. "I did not attend the meeting of the Women's League," he wrote to Helen Garrison, "but it was addressed by Phillips, Thompson and others, and went off very satisfactorily." Horace Greeley's *Tribune* also offered cautious praise to the league for having attracted a "respectable audience." However, Stanton and Anthony did use the league to help the Frémont movement in other ways. With political backers of the general who were openly courting abolitionist support, they helped organize the first Freedom and Frémont Club, which opened for business in the Cooper Institute offices of the Woman's National Loyal League. "The movement we inaugurated in our little room was the first plainly spoken protest against the present situation," Elizabeth Cady Stanton later recalled. Eventually, similar clubs were started all across the Northern states, often organized by German-Americans who tended to be sympathetic to the radical antislavery position and by those abolitionists who followed the leadership of Phillips, Stanton, and Anthony.[44]

Four hundred supporters of General Frémont gathered in Cleveland on 31 May to nominate their candidate for president on the Radical Democratic party ticket. A number of War Democrats joined the German-American radicals and Phillips-style abolitionists in calling for an enlightened alternative to Abraham Lincoln. The Frémont platform included several demands that Stanton and Anthony regarded as vitally important: a constitutional amendment freeing the slaves in all the states, a congressional Reconstruction program which would protect the rights of the newly freed slaves, confiscation and redistribution of rebel lands, and a one-term presidency. Susan Anthony, visiting family members in Rochester, New York, commented that she was somewhat disappointed by Frémont's acceptance letter. "It did not electrify as I had expected it would," she wrote. "These men don't see the right way to express themselves." Specifically, Anthony was concerned by Frémont's contention that slavery was dead. Such a sentiment must be qualified, Anthony believed, by the notion that slavery was in the process of dying. Not until the last Southern slave had been freed would she cease to labor for universal emancipation.[45]

Initially unconcerned by the third-party candidacy of John C. Frémont, supporters of the president became increasingly alarmed as the Frémont movement gained momentum. Exactly twenty years earlier, the votes gained by antislavery advocate and Liberty party candidate James G.

Birney had contributed to the defeat of Lincoln's hero Henry Clay. Republican strategists now feared a similar occurrence. Furthermore, no president since Jackson had been elected to a second term. Elizabeth Cady Stanton distributed Frémont tracts from her New York home, enjoying both the summer heat and the political heat of the presidential campaign. "Well, Susan, the Lincoln stock is running down rapidly," she wrote 22 August 1864. To Wendell Phillips, she speculated that Lincoln's reelection campaign was effectively dead, and, she added sarcastically, "I shall not wear crepe at the funeral."[46]

When Abraham Lincoln gave a pocket veto to the Wade-Davis bill on Reconstruction, he further alienated many radicals, including Elizabeth Cady Stanton, who engaged in a newspaper debate on the subject with her influential cousin Gerrit Smith. In early August, Smith wrote a letter to Wade and Davis protesting their criticism of Abraham Lincoln and endorsing the president's reelection. As a radical, Smith found many of the president's policies to be objectionable. Indeed, Lincoln had committed "grave errors" during his first term in office. He had been overly concerned with the wishes of the border states and the peace Democrats. His amnesty proclamation was a questionable use of presidential power. But the suppression of the present rebellion was the vital question of the day, Smith argued, and all loyal Americans should support Lincoln's reelection. "Though it may be at the expense of passing by our favorite candidate," he concluded, "we should nevertheless all feel ourselves urged by the strongest possible motives to cast our votes . . . to defeat the compromising or sham Peace Candidate."[47]

Elizabeth Cady Stanton challenged Smith in the pages of the *National Anti-Slavery Standard.* Stanton insisted that her cousin, who had introduced her as a young girl to the horrors of slavery, had become far too compromising. While conceding that Lincoln might indeed be an "honest" chief executive, she nevertheless insisted that honesty alone was not enough for such a vitally important job. "We need leaders to galvanize the virtue and patriotism of the nation into life," she wrote, "and concentrate thought and action in the right directions." Smith's overriding emphasis on putting down the rebellion was all well and good, but what of the rebel atrocities perpetrated against black soldiers? What of the president's failure to free all the slaves? In defeating the rebels, she asked, "may we not need something more than soldiers on the banks of the Potomac?" Oliver Johnson, pro-Lincoln editor of the *Standard,* added his own remarks after reprinting the Smith-Stanton debate. "It strikes us that Mrs. Stanton fails to break the force of Mr. Smith's argument," he wrote, "and succeeds only in showing that skill with which she can befog a plain question."[48]

Stanton and Anthony were no more successful in convincing their female abolitionist colleagues to support John C. Frémont's candidacy. Most women abolitionists endorsed Lincoln, whose 1864 platform called for a constitutional amendment to end slavery. Harriet Beecher Stowe was unabashedly enthusiastic in her support for Lincoln. Living quietly in Hartford with her retired husband, Stowe, who had scrupulously avoided political statements since her "Reply to 'The Affectionate and Christian Address'" of the previous year, now broke her silence. Once again her strong moral convictions overcame her traditional view of woman's sphere, and she wrote an article about the war and Lincoln's leadership.

The Civil War was more than a "mere local convulsion," Stowe argued, for at stake were the rights of common men everywhere. The war had changed her attitude toward England. In the 1850s she had defended Britain's class system, attributing the country's social problems to intemperance. Now she emphasized democracy, claiming the working classes of Europe supported the North, while the "privileged classes" admired the aristocratic South. Abraham Lincoln, she declared boldly, was the servant of God. A genuine man of the working classes, Lincoln was honest, energetic, and shrewd, and he was "firmly and from principle an enemy of slavery." Stowe defended the president's suspension of habeas corpus, calling it a military necessity and insisting that the Constitution was safe in Lincoln's hands. She concluded that Lincoln's "clearness of vision" would lead ultimately to the "promised land of freedom which is to be the patrimony of all men, black and white." Stowe's article, which originally appeared in *The Watchman and Reflector*, a national Baptist newspaper, was later reprinted in the popular weekly *Littell's Living Age*.[49]

Other women abolitionists praised Lincoln with slightly less enthusiasm. Maria Weston Chapman endorsed the president "because to a progressive domestic policy, he adds a friendly foreign one." Josephine Griffing, the Loyal League lecturing agent from Ohio, wrote confidently, "*I know* that the People of the *West* are *safe* with Mr. Lincoln in the chair." Lincoln might not be the type of inspirational leader for whom many abolitionists hoped, but he was a known commodity and had demonstrated a fundamental desire to end slavery. Mary Grew and Sarah Pugh of Philadelphia were not entirely satisfied with the president's record, but they were inclined to believe that no one would do a better job. Grew hoped that with the election behind him, Lincoln might become "more bold &

uncompromising." Elizabeth Buffum Chace, a Rhode Island abolitionist, criticized Lincoln for his slowness in emancipating the slaves but admitted he was gradually moving in the proper direction. Like Grew, Elizabeth Chace would rather trust the presidency to Lincoln than to an untested leader.[50]

Even Mary Lincoln had become less of a target. The well-known Minnesota abolitionist and journalist Jane Grey Swisshelm met the Lincolns at a White House reception in 1863 and found the president's wife to be charming. Mrs. Lincoln's cordiality toward Swisshelm was something of a surprise to the Minnesotan. Later she learned that Mrs. Lincoln had become an antislavery advocate herself. The Kentucky-born Mary Todd Lincoln was influenced by her husband's antislavery sentiments, by the stories of slave brutality which she heard from her mulatto dressmaker and confidante, Elizabeth Keckley, and by her close friendship with Charles Sumner. At Keckley's urging, she helped to raise money for the Contraband Relief Association.[51]

Many abolitionists supported Lincoln's reelection because they disliked or distrusted Frémont. In an attempt to win backing from a wide variety of Lincoln's foes, Frémont organizers accepted support from any anti-Lincoln group. Oliver Johnson alleged that Copperhead money funded the *New Nation,* a newspaper dedicated to promoting Frémont's candidacy and edited by G. P. Cluseret, a radical general who had served on Frémont's staff. Cluseret actively recruited Democrats, but the extent of Copperhead involvement in the Frémont campaign remains questionable.[52]

Convinced that Frémont was in league with the Copperheads, Lydia Maria Child commented to John Greenleaf Whittier: "I am exceedingly sorry for the course Wendell Phillips is pursuing. . . . Since Frémont has written a letter, so obviously courting the Copperheads, I don't see how he *can* stand by him." Lincoln, on the other hand, deserved his reputation as an honest politician, though admittedly the president should be able to empathize with the freedmen to a greater degree than he had demonstrated thus far. With the exception of Charles Sumner, Lydia Maria Child could think of no other candidate who could better serve the nation than the Illinois Republican.[53]

Lucy Stone was also suspicious of John C. Frémont and his Democratic supporters. The platform of the Cleveland convention was far too vague in her eyes. "I expected the largest antislavery utterance instead of the announcement that slavery is dead," she wrote to Anthony in July 1864.

Furthermore, Stone was outraged by Frémont's choice of Colonel John Cochrane as a running mate. Cochrane had cast ballots for Pierce in 1852, for Buchanan in 1856, and for Breckinridge in 1860. Stone questioned, with justification, the degree of commitment such a man could have for abolition. "Bad as Mr. Lincoln is," Stone concluded, "a union with him and his supporters, seems to me *less bad* than a union with peace Democrats."[54]

Susan Anthony and Elizabeth Cady Stanton did not comment publicly on the subject of Frémont's Democratic support or his repudiation of the Cleveland platform plank on confiscation of Southern land. Wendell Phillips did write to Stanton in August, "I wish I had more influence with F[rémont] & that some of his men had less." Phillips added, "But I believe in *him*."[55] These three abolitionists seemed to be philosophically committed to the candidacy of the Missouri general, and no amount of criticism from their peers would alter their views.

By summer's end, the Democrats had nominated George B. McClellan to be their presidential standard-bearer. Their platform called for a return to the original war aim of the Union: reunion with the slave states and attempts to bring about a negotiated peace. In order to appeal to a broad range of voters, the Democrats chose Ohio peace advocate Congressman George H. Pendleton to be McClellan's running mate. Abolitionists despised McClellan. Lydia Maria Child, complaining about her husband's sanguine attitude toward the election, declared vehemently, "If such an awful thing *should* happen as having McClellan for President, I should feel like quitting the country."[56]

Abolitionists continued to debate the presidential question. Many of those who were dissatisfied with Garrison's approach canceled their subscriptions to the *Liberator*, often after twenty years of faithful reading. Elizabeth Pease Nichol, an ardent abolitionist and supporter of Garrison, sent a generous contribution to the Boston newspaper when she learned that cancellations were threatening the paper's continuation. Lydia Maria Child bemoaned the abolitionist schism, commenting to a friend, "I am afraid we may wreck our vessel on the rock of disunion among ourselves."[57]

To avert just such a calamity, abolitionist and radical leaders met in New York. They planned a political convention to meet in Cincinnati on 28 September 1864. Its purpose would be the nomination of a presidential candidate behind whom the supporters of both Frémont and Lincoln could unite. Frémont pledged to withdraw his presidential candidacy in deference to a compromise candidate providing that candidate endorsed a platform based on universal emancipation and Lincoln agreed to withdraw from the contest.[58]

Events beyond Frémont's control quickly ended his presidential aspirations. On 3 September General William T. Sherman captured Atlanta, ending months of military stalemate, sending thousands of Northerners into the streets to celebrate, and causing many to view Abraham Lincoln with new respect. Plans for a Cincinnati convention were dropped, and two weeks after the Atlanta breakthrough, Frémont withdrew as a presidential contender. Most of Frémont's backers had urged him to take this course of action in order to unify the Republican party. Wendell Phillips was the notable exception. The uncompromising Bostonian believed Frémont should remain as a candidate in order to symbolize opposition to the Lincoln administration.[59]

Nor did Stanton and Anthony soften their attitudes toward the president. Complaining of the number of abolitionists who were supporting Lincoln's reelection, Stanton wrote to Anthony, "One by one our giants are being swept down with the current." Stanton was not impressed by the Republicans' momentum, commenting that all the talk about the need for party unity was "the merest twaddle." She continued to believe that one term in office was long enough for any president. Wendell Phillips wrote to Stanton on 27 September 1864, assuring her that he had no intention of speaking on the Republicans' behalf. "I would cut off both hands before doing any thing to aid Mac's election," he said, and "I would cut off my right hand before doing any thing to aid A. L.'s election."[60]

The supporters of both Frémont and Lincoln had actively courted Anna Dickinson. After her anti-Lincoln diatribes in April and May, the Quaker orator ceased to speak on the presidential question, lecturing instead on "the condition of women," a favorite topic and a speech which Garrison described as "the best and most eloquent I have ever heard from her lips." Susan Anthony tried to interest her in the Frémont campaign, urging that she speak the "absolute truth" and not cater to the "popular cry of the multitude." Anthony hoped to organize a northern lecture tour, providing a format for Wendell Phillips and perhaps Anna Dickinson and Frederick Douglass to promote Frémont's campaign. But Dickinson had serious doubts about Frémont. Even though she had admired him for his attempt to free the Missouri slaves, his relationship with the Copperheads and the vagueness of the Cleveland platform bothered her.[61]

Many of Dickinson's friends pressured her to support the president. "You are so incurably wrong-headed on the Lincoln question," Whitelaw Reid wrote from Baltimore 6 June 1864. Theodore Tilton, editor of the New York *Independent,* had opposed Lincoln's nomination, but he contended it was now time for all patriotic Americans to unite in opposition to the Democrats. Lincoln was not the ideal candidate, Tilton said, but he was without doubt the choice of nine-tenths of the Republican party. Benjamin Prescott shared these views. The New Hampshire Republican chairman expressed disappointment that she would not be campaigning in his state, but he urged his former protégé not to sit out the campaign. "Your talents should not be idle and your voice should not be silent in times like these," he wrote, after gently chiding Anna. "You don't like Lincoln. I see many things in him I could improve, but can we do better?"[62]

Although Dickinson complained about the pressure that friends were exerting, their persistence combined with the Union victory at Atlanta convinced her to take action. In a letter dated 3 September 1864, printed in the abolitionist press, she reaffirmed her commitment to abolition and endorsed, after a fashion, the reelection of Abraham Lincoln.[63]

Declaring that "my love for the dear cause is as great as ever" and reiterating her independence of party ties, Dickinson denied ever having supported the Cleveland convention or its candidate. She did, however, admit to having favored a postponement of the Republican convention in the hopes that it would select an alternative candidate to Abraham Lincoln. With two short months left before the election, what remained to be done? Dickinson pledged her total support for the Republican party "from this moment till election morning!" The alternatives seemed clear. Either the party of Lincoln must win, or the nation would be led into a "deceitful peace," the Union crushed. Her dislike for the president was demonstrated by her assertion that "I shall not work for Abraham Lincoln; I shall work for the salvation of my country's life . . . for the defeat of this disloyal peace party."[64]

Theodore Tilton immediately wrote to Dickinson, relieved, no doubt, that she had chosen to take his advice. Whitelaw Reid also wrote in support of her actions, as did Oliver Johnson. The editor of the *National Anti-Slavery Standard* lamented that many radicals had "wasted their power in foolish, factious and abortive ways, so that they will not have their due influence over Lincoln during his last term." At least one of Dickinson's friends was not pleased by her decision to campaign for the Republican ticket. Lillie Chace, the daughter of Elizabeth Buffum Chace, was a close friend. "Do not I entreat thee let support become endorsement," she wrote

19 September. "If thee must swallow the bitter pill, don't conceal the fact that it is bitter."[65]

Because of a sore throat, Anna Dickinson did not begin campaigning in earnest until October. Returning to the scene of her earlier triumphs, she spoke to attentive crowds in Middletown and Hartford, Connecticut. In Boston on 25 October she "excited great enthusiasm" at Music Hall. Dickinson's address at New York's Cooper Institute, entitled "The Chicago Platform and the Last Ditch," was indicative of her campaign style.[66]

With her sarcastic manner in peak form, Dickinson discussed the Democratic candidates. Vice-presidential hopeful Congressman George H. Pendleton had an abysmal record in Congress, having voted against every single government-sponsored measure to aid the Union war effort. But Dickinson's harshest invective was saved for General George B. McClellan, a favorite target long before he sought the presidential nomination. Dickinson criticized his military record, blaming him for the disastrous Peninsular campaign and claiming that the credit for Antietam lay with generals Hooker and Burnside. Then she told an anecdote. A little old lady summarized McClellan's generalship appropriately when she said, "Why, my dear, what are these people attacking poor little General McClellan for. I am sure that he never attacked anybody." This story evoked laughter and cheers from the audience.[67]

Dickinson's campaign speeches always centered around the slavery theme. In discussing emancipation, her sarcasm often gave way to empathy, and she spoke with logic and conviction. Under the peace plan of the Democrats, what was to become of the three and a half million slaves, some of them already freed under Lincoln's Emancipation Proclamation? What of the black men currently serving their country in the Union army? "Shall they be sent back to slavery? We answer, never." McClellan's peace plan was a sham, Dickinson concluded, for "there is no use in trying to heal the wounds of the Union without extracting the bullet that made them—slavery."[68]

In her native Philadelphia on 2 November, Dickinson continued her condemnation of McClellan and Pendleton. Every seat in National Hall was taken; within half an hour before her speech, all standing room had been filled as well. After criticizing McClellan's military record with great vigor, Dickinson told her audience that they must not be frightened into favoring compromise with the South. The North stood for liberty, truth, and freedom. God was watching over the country. "What is compromise?" she asked. "It is a torn and divided banner, with one-half trampled under foot and the other reft of its power and pride. It is national insolvency. It is continual and incessant war. It is European recognition and intervention; it is worse than fifty years of war; we will have no compromise." Here was Anna Dickinson at her best. Her appeal was direct and logical, her words movingly patriotic. The audience interrupted her frequently with applause.[69]

Abraham Lincoln was reelected by a comfortable margin on 8 November 1864. Anna Dickinson probably entered the campaign too late to play a decisive role in the election returns, yet her influence should not be overlooked. Her speeches late in the campaign drew audiences in the thousands; many people were turned away for lack of space. Her addresses were accorded extensive coverage in the local press. In two of the states where Dickinson campaigned, Connecticut and New York, the vote was a close one. Abraham Lincoln's Union ticket carried Connecticut by fewer than twenty-five hundred votes. In New York the final tally was 368,726 to McClellan's 361,986.[70] Perhaps the young Quaker's eleventh-hour campaigning contributed to Republican momentum in those states.

Most women abolitionists reacted to Lincoln's reelection with relief and rejoicing. "I am a happy woman since the election," wrote Lydia Maria Child. "It makes me feel that our republican form of government rests on more secure foundations." While Child found many points on which to fault the president, she had "constantly gone on liking him better and better." Other abolitionists shared this sentiment. Lucy Stone commented to a friend, "How glad I am, that Mr. Lincoln [in] spite of his short comings, is re-elected." Even the Frémont supporters appear to have viewed the election results philosophically. Gerrit Smith wrote to his cousin Elizabeth Cady Stanton on 19 November offering assurances that their friendship had not been tarnished by their disagreement over presidential politics.[71]

Late in life, Stanton admitted she had misjudged the president. Writing in her diary on Lincoln's birthday in 1901, she recalled her only meeting with the president, which occurred before the Loyal League's founding convention. She had arrived feeling prejudiced toward Lincoln and left feeling much the same way. In hindsight, "my conscience pricks me now when I recall how I worked and prayed in 1864 for the defeat of Lincoln's re-election." She realized that Lincoln's slow and deliberate course, gradually leading public opinion toward the idea of emancipation, was a wise policy. Every year on Lincoln's birthday, Stanton commented wryly, "I celebrate it somewhat in sackcloth and ashes."[72]

In a letter dated 20 November 1864, Wendell Phillips urged Elizabeth Cady Stanton to carry on the antislavery fight, for the battle was not yet over. "Now our common duty is to throw all *personal* matters behind us," he wrote, "& rally together to claim of the Repub. party the performance of their pledge." Specifically, Phillips was referring to the constitutional amendment to free the slaves.[73]

Phillips need not have admonished Stanton, for the presidential contest did not slow her efforts regarding the "mammoth petition." In fact, the women of the Loyal League had carried on their petitioning activities with renewed vigor ever since Sumner's "Prayer of One Hundred Thousand" speech in February 1864. In March, Susan Anthony had sent out 25,000 petitions forms, thanks to New York printers who donated both paper and services free of charge. The accompanying broadsides emphasized the league's position that slavery was a sin, with war its just retribution, and further declared the "*Constitutional right of the Government*" and the "*moral duty of the people* to abolish slavery."[74]

The league petitions now bore a new statement including the call for a constitutional amendment:

> *To the Senate and House of Representatives of the United States, in Congress assembled:*
> The undersigned, citizen of —— believing slavery the great cause of the present rebellion, and an institution fatal to the life of Republican government, earnestly pray your honorable bodies to immediately abolish it throughout the United States; and to adopt measures for so amending the Constitution, as forever to prohibit its existence in any portion of our common country.

The league continued to tally the male and female signatures and to separate the petitions by state.[75]

The Thirteenth Amendment freeing the slaves was passed by the Senate on 8 April 1864. Immediately, the Woman's National Loyal League sent out an additional 15,000 petition forms to be returned directly to the Senate's select committee on slavery and freedmen.[76] They hoped to build on the momentum created by the Senate's action, but their strategy did not produce the desired effect, for, month after month, the House failed to approve the antislavery amendment.

Senator Sumner of Massachusetts continued to be the Loyal League's chief congressional sponsor. Although Sumner was arguably the senator most closely associated with the antislavery cause, he had little direct influence in writing the Thirteenth Amendment. Lyman Trumbull and the Judiciary Committee drafted the bill, which Sumner found to be painfully inadequate. Sumner firmly believed that the concept of "equality before the law" should be included. However, the bill did emancipate the slaves, and Sumner eventually lent his support to the measure.[77]

With each new batch of petitions from the Woman's National Loyal League, Sumner had an opportunity to raise the slavery question before the Congress. By presenting these petitions on at least a bimonthly basis throughout the winter, spring, and summer of 1864, Sumner kept hammering at the point that emancipation by constitutional amendment was the will of the American people. After presenting the first installment of league petitions on 9 February 1864, the senior senator from Massachusetts followed with more petitions on 11 February, 15 and 23 March, 14, 15, 25, 27 April, and 9 May. By June he was presenting petitions at a rapid rate, on 1, 2, 6, 7, 14, 15, 16, 20, 22, 23, 24, 27 June and 1 July. In a speech on 15 April introducing 41,218 names, Sumner read the newly worded petition. On 25 April, another 12,276 names were added. By 7 June, after Stanton had mailed another 85,000 signatures, the total climbed to 300,000, many of them, Sumner was proud to report, from the working classes. The state of Illinois led all states by 2,000 signatures. By the time Congress recessed for the summer, league petition totals neared 400,000.[78]

The House of Representatives finally passed the Thirteenth Amendment in January 1865. Ratification of the amendment was accomplished by the end of the year. Although members of the Woman's National Loyal League had fallen far short of their goal to obtain one million signatures on the "mammoth petition," the achievement was nevertheless a notable one.

On the local and state levels, the women had inspired antislavery sentiment in an unprecedented way. While antislavery petitioning was hardly new, a grassroots campaign encompassing every Northern free state was a significant achievement. By coordinating antislavery efforts, the women could address Congress with a far stronger voice than abolitionist groups had been able to do before the war. The Loyal League also galvanized a group of people—women—who did not traditionally attempt to influence congressional legislation and who were now doing so in large numbers.

On the national level, the league operated as an effective pressure group. While many people, including some abolitionists, believed the

Emancipation Proclamation ended the abolition controversy, the Loyal League pushed incessantly for stronger measures to secure universal emancipation on a constitutional basis. When the Senate ratified the Thirteenth Amendment in April, league members did not assume the battle was over. Instead, they stepped up pressure on Congress through Senator Sumner's frequent introduction of petitions. The total of close to 400,000 signatures represented the largest number of signatures ever introduced on a congressional petition up to that time. [79]

According to the 1860 census, the white adult population of the Northern free states was approximately nine and one-half million. Roughly one in twenty-four of these Americans living in the free Northern states signed an abolition petition circulated by the Woman's National Loyal League. [80] It was quite an accomplishment for the two women of vision and energy who, along with their supporters, had embarked on the project in the spring of 1863. Although Charles Sumner ceased to introduce antislavery petitions after the summer recess of 1864, league activity did not stop. Elizabeth Cady Stanton commented in a letter to Susan Anthony on 8 December 1864 that she had recently organized two local leagues, in addition to distributing tracts and making speeches. [81] League activists probably exerted pressure on their state legislatures to ratify the Thirteenth Amendment.

The Loyal League played an important role in the development of nineteenth-century women's activism. Its formation by Stanton and Anthony signaled the passing of leadership to a second generation of abolitionist women, a generation as dedicated to feminism as they were to antislavery. The league marked an organizational transition as well. Whereas prewar women had formed regional antislavery, woman's rights, benevolent, and temperance societies, the league was a national feminist-abolitionist movement.

The league's tactics also marked a transition. Women reformers in the early decades of the nineteenth century had emphasized moral suasion. By the time of the Civil War, some abolitionists had already broken with Garrison's approach, to advocate a political solution to the slavery question. The Woman's National Loyal League with its emphasis on political petitioning and its leaders' involvement in the philosophical issues of the 1864 presidential campaign demonstrated the continuing shift from the moral suasion of antebellum reform to the electoral and constitutional issues that would dominate the Reconstruction era.

Indeed, the significant degree of interest in the issues of the 1864 campaign was an indication that activist women increasingly viewed electoral contests as relevant to their interests. Elizabeth Cady Stanton failed to persuade most abolitionist women to support Frémont. But her admonition to promote the "power of women to be recognized in the politics of the nation," while not yet fully realized, was taken to heart by a growing number of activist women who thought, wrote, and spoke about presidential politics in 1864.

Thousands more attended Anna Dickinson's lectures. In both the state and national campaigns in which she participated, women attended her speeches in large numbers, so large they were sometimes numerically dominant and occasionally were asked to stay home in order to leave seats for voting males. Abolitionist women encouraged Dickinson, and her speeches received wide coverage in the press. The New York *Tribune*, for example, began a report of one Dickinson campaign speech during the 1864 contest by noting the presence of "an immense audience, including many ladies."[82] With hundreds of such stories—Dickinson's scrapbooks provide ample evidence of this—women across the nation heard about this gifted orator, grasped her political message, and learned that with so many women attending her speeches, perhaps it was worthwhile for true women to interest themselves in national affairs. Dickinson's invitation to speak before a joint session of Congress was an honor never before accorded an American woman. Her address with its national press coverage further enhanced her visibility, but more importantly it represented another breakthrough for women. If a woman could address the Congress on questions relating to presidential politics and Reconstruction, could not the political role of all American women be broadened?

The success of the Woman's National Loyal League as a feminist network was limited by its newness and its radicalism, which undoubtedly threatened many middle-class women. Its success was also restricted by the fact that it was introduced during a period of unprecedented turmoil, destruction, and death, a time when many Americans were not inclined to grapple with issues of civil rights and feminism. But its creation was an important step and one that would serve as a philosophical and organizational precedent for the postwar woman's rights movement.

Within a few weeks of his second inauguration, Abraham Lincoln was assassinated by a Southern sympathizer. Abolitionists mourned the nation's loss. Fanny Kemble learned of the news at the London offices of the *Spectator*, where she had gone to offer her poem about the American war. Overcome with grief, she had to be helped into a cab. Julia Ward Howe lamented that except for the death of her beloved son, "nothing has happened that has given me so much personal pain as this event . . . we can only work on, and trust in God." Like many religious Americans, Lydia Maria Child saw the hand of God at work. Although she was "shocked and distressed" by the assassination, Child wondered if "kind-hearted Abraham, was certainly in danger of making too easy terms with the rebels."[83]

In the wake of Lincoln's assassination, many abolitionists in addition to Child began to contemplate the newly defined issues of Reconstruction. Members of the Woman's National Loyal League began to contemplate the future of the woman's rights movement. For four years women had subjugated their own hopes and aspirations to the good of their country. They had ceased to hold woman's rights conventions. Instead, they had nursed the wounded soldiers, they had raised money to help the freedmen, and they had worked hard to promote universal emancipation of the slaves. Now, many woman's rights advocates believed the country should reward their philanthropic efforts and acknowledge their growing political sophistication by granting to women the rights of citizenship and suffrage.

The Postwar Feminist Movement

> Our Fathers declared all men equal, then placed the power in the
> hands of the few. . . . They declared taxation without representation
> tyranny then taxed all these disfranchised classes. . . . From the
> baptism of this second revolution, with a century of added experience
> shall we repeat the blunder of the Fathers & build again on the old
> foundation whose corner stone is class & caste[?]
> —Elizabeth Cady Stanton, undated "Speech on Reconstruction"

With the war over, the South defeated, and the slaves liberated, national
attention turned toward the question of black male suffrage. Radical
Republicans in Congress, intent upon directing the course of Reconstruction, favored black enfranchisement for both humanitarian and tactical
reasons. They needed the votes of Southern blacks to ensure their domi-
nance in the South and their national political hegemony. The Fourteenth
Amendment, introduced late in 1865, defined national citizenship. It also
stipulated that states of the Confederate South, before being readmitted to
the Union, must grant the vote to black men or lose congressional repre-
sentation proportionately. The Fourteenth Amendment made no provision for woman suffrage.[1]

Not only did Radical Republicans in Congress support the Fourteenth
Amendment, but many abolitionists praised the measure, which was written by no less a figure than the league's former sponsor Charles Sumner. In
1866 abolitionists and feminists joined ranks to found the American Equal
Rights Association, an organization dedicated to furthering the political
rights of blacks and women. Ellen DuBois believes this organization represented "the culmination of the abolitionist phase of American feminism."
With Wendell Phillips, Gerrit Smith, and Horace Greeley in leadership
positions, support for the Fourteenth Amendment became inevitable.
These men might sympathize with the cause of universal suffrage, but
freedmen's rights must take precedence during the "Negro's Hour." Elizabeth Cady Stanton, furious with her longtime ally Wendell Phillips,
wrote to him testily, "Do you believe the African race is composed entirely
of males?"[2]

The congressional action angered Susan Anthony and confirmed her
worst fears. Almost alone among feminists, she had argued in favor of
holding wartime woman's rights conventions, only to be overruled by

Stanton, who believed that such overtly feminist agitation would be inappropriate. According to Elisabeth Griffith, the debate over this question was the first serious tactical dispute between the two feminists. Although Anthony's strategy of holding conventions during the Civil War would have alienated many, Stanton's strategy was clearly a failure. She had insisted that women would be compensated for their wartime abolition work by congressional support for woman's rights in the postwar period. Now aware that her plan had been naive, Stanton reacted with bitterness. To Charles Sumner she wrote, "The question of woman's suffrage to us who have labored for that purpose over twenty years, has the same importance that negro suffrage has to you, no more, no less."[3]

Worst of all, with the American Equal Rights Association supporting the Fourteenth Amendment, radical feminists had no organizational vehicle through which to protest the congressional action, for the Woman's National Loyal League had disbanded with ratification of the Thirteenth Amendment. Never ones to give up without a fight, Stanton and Anthony decided to do what they could to stop the Fourteenth Amendment from excluding women. In a letter to the *National Anti-Slavery Standard,* 2 January 1866, Stanton reminded women that the federal Constitution in its present form did not limit the right of suffrage to any sex or class. "This attempt to turn the wheels of civilization backward, on the part of Republicans claiming to be *the* liberal party," she declared, "should rouse every woman in the nation to a prompt exercise of the only right she has in the Government, the right of petition."[4]

With Anthony's help, she drafted just such a petition to "prohibit the States from disfranchising any of their citizens on the ground of sex." It was the first woman suffrage petition presented to Congress instead of the state legislatures. Anthony organized the petition drive by holding planning sessions with many colleagues, including Martha Wright in Auburn, New York; Lydia Mott in Albany; Ernestine Rose and Abby Hopper Gibbons in New York City; Lucy Stone and Antoinette Brown Blackwell in New Jersey; Stephen and Abby Kelley Foster in Worcester, Massachusetts; and Caroline Dall, Wendell Phillips and William Lloyd Garrison in Boston. During the Christmas holidays of 1865 Anthony and Stanton wrote letters and broadsides to accompany their petition forms. By the end of the 1865–66 congressional session, they had collected 10,000 signatures on their woman suffrage petition, a notable achievement in a relatively short time, except when compared with the Loyal League's nearly 400,000 signatures on the antislavery petition. Clearly, Stanton, Anthony and their followers were flying in the face of public opinion. Indeed, Phillips and Garrison, while supporting the petition, endorsed the Fourteenth Amendment with or without a woman suffrage provision.[5]

Because Sumner had deserted them, Stanton and Anthony approached the Democrats for help. Senator Gratz Brown of Missouri spoke on their behalf in the Senate. In his speech Brown asked fellow senators and congressmen to grant women the vote. Throughout the war women made their needs secondary to the cause of the slave. Now, these women feared that "the same Constitutional amendment which may carry civil rights to the emancipated classes may prohibit those rights, either directly or by implication, to women." Although Anthony raved about "how splendidly" the Missouri senator had handled the presentation, Brown failed to persuade his colleagues.[6] Radical Republican support for the Fourteenth Amendment was unshakable, and the amendment was ratified in 1868. Anthony complained that "the Republicans are very cowardly," while Stanton feared the woman suffrage cause might be set back fully one hundred years because of passage of this amendment.[7]

Incapable of stopping the Fourteenth Amendment, Stanton forged ahead by contending that it did not prohibit women from holding elective office. To prove her point, she ran for the House of Representatives from New York City's Eighth District in 1866, the first woman to run for Congress. Announcing as an independent candidate whose "creed is free speech, free press, free men and free trade," and, of course, woman suffrage, Stanton garnered twenty-four votes and a host of newspaper articles, some sympathetic, most critical or satirical. Accepting her inevitable defeat with good humor, Stanton insisted that her only disappointment was that she had not "procure[d] photographs of her two dozen unknown friends."[8]

Feminists, including Stanton, faced several more defeats in 1866–67. Late in 1866 the Senate considered a proposal to grant black suffrage in the District of Columbia. An amendment which would have broadened the proposal to include women failed by a vote of thirty-seven to nine. Feminists were also active in New York, where the state constitutional convention debated and rejected woman suffrage, and in Kansas, where voters defeated a proposition which would have allowed women to vote. Elizabeth Cady Stanton, Susan B. Anthony, and Lucy Stone all journeyed to Kansas and gave numerous speeches in support of woman suffrage.[9]

The debate over woman's rights and Reconstruction politics caused deep divisions within the feminist ranks. During the Civil War, Elizabeth Cady

Stanton had become the most visible feminist leader. Moving from the village of Seneca Falls to New York City, where she was able to participate more widely in reform activities, she had founded the Woman's National Loyal League. It was the only national feminist organization of the war and afforded Stanton the opportunity to gain stature as a public speaker, acclaim as a patriotic organizer, and newspaper coverage in both capacities. Never lacking in ego, Stanton enjoyed the power and the prestige. She expected to retain her leadership position after the war, assuming she would continue to hold center stage as feminism's chief philosopher and orator.

But conservative feminists were increasingly dissatisfied with Stanton's leadership. Although her poise, determination, and speaking ability had won her praise as Loyal League president, postwar colleagues tended to see her as increasingly uncompromising, even doctrinaire. Tensions peaked at the May 1869 convention of the American Equal Rights Association. Elizabeth Cady Stanton's demand for a woman suffrage amendment to the Constitution divided the convention, prompting Stanton and Anthony to form their own splinter group, the National Woman Suffrage Association (NWSA).[10]

Ellen DuBois has written that the NWSA was "the first national feminist organization in the United States," a judgment which is accurate only in the context of DuBois's belief that the "National Loyal Women's League . . . provided a precedent for the organization of women primarily around the black man's emancipation and only secondarily around their own." Whether the Woman's National Loyal League or the National Woman Suffrage Association deserves the distinction of being first, there is no question about the fact that the Loyal League provided a model for the NWSA, which included among its members Lucretia Mott, Anna Dickinson, Martha Wright, Ernestine Rose, and Amy Post, all of whom had been affiliated with the Loyal League. The two organizations were similar in structure. All of the NWSA leaders and most of its members were female, just as the league had been. Noting that men had taken over leadership of the American Equal Rights Association, Stanton and Anthony were determined that this should not happen again. The National Woman Suffrage Association, like its wartime counterpart, held regular meetings in New York while coordinating activity in the states through designated emissaries. Finally, the two groups shared a radical perspective. While attempting to appeal to a wide spectrum of women, the NWSA would maintain its position as the left wing of the feminist movement in the late nineteenth century. The Loyal League had served a similar purpose during the war.[11]

Conservative feminists, led by Lucy Stone and her husband Henry Blackwell, promoted passage of the Fifteenth Amendment, which went one step further than the Fourteenth in guaranteeing suffrage for all adult males. Stone and Blackwell believed that the best hope for female suffrage lay with continued support of the powerful Republican party. Once the black man was enfranchised, the party might turn its attention toward woman's rights. These more moderate feminists founded the American Woman Suffrage Association (AWSA). An outgrowth of a regional organization called the New England Woman Suffrage Association, the AWSA included Abby and Stephen Foster, Mary Livermore, Henry Ward Beecher, and Julia Ward Howe among its leaders.[12]

The schism of 1869 was foreshadowed by events in the Civil War. During that time Elizabeth Cady Stanton and Susan B. Anthony moved ideologically to the left of many of their female colleagues, cementing a trend which had originated even before the war. The growing tension between Stanton/Anthony and more moderate feminists such as Lucy Stone may clearly be seen in the election of 1864, when Stanton and Anthony worked for Frémont, refusing to endorse Lincoln even after Frémont's withdrawal from the race. Stone, Livermore, and Howe all admired the president.

In many ways, the feminist division of 1869 was reminiscent of the abolitionist schism of 1840. Both involved questions of philosophy and tactics. Fed up with Elizabeth Cady Stanton, members of the AWSA believed that her radicalism threatened the whole movement. Like Garrison's opponents in 1840, the AWSA believed that feminists must remain orthodox on all issues except suffrage. The American Woman Suffrage Association's organ, the *Woman's Journal*, was designed to attract political moderates in support of suffrage for women.

Stanton and Anthony, like Garrison before them, believed that all barriers to human perfection should be removed. Refusing to concentrate solely on the question of the vote, these women promoted divorce reform, improved working conditions for factory women, even unionization. They incurred the wrath of many by accepting money from George Francis Train, a wealthy financier whose business dealings with the notorious Crédit Mobilier ended before the scandal became public. Train, who was a Democrat and reportedly had been a Copperhead, bankrolled *The Revolution*, a newspaper edited by Stanton and Anthony. Just as they had been willing to overlook John C. Frémont's Copperhead support during the Civil War, the two women scrupulously ignored the shadier side of their new backer. The *Woman's Journal* outlived *The Revolution*, a financial failure once Train abandoned the venture.[13]

Historians traditionally have argued that feminist activity ground to a halt during the period 1861–65.[14] Perhaps some of them have been influenced by the allegations of Stanton and Anthony in *The History of Woman Suffrage*, published in several volumes between 1881 and 1902, with two additional volumes appearing in 1922. Angered, no doubt, by women's exclusion from the Fourteenth and Fifteenth Amendments, they exaggerated the extent to which women had abandoned their feminist agenda during the war. "In 1861 came 'the war of the rebellion,' " they wrote. "The women who had so perseveringly labored for their own enfranchisement now gave all their time and thought to the nation's life."[15] Clearly this was not the case. Although the feminist conventions that had become an annual event after the Seneca Falls meeting were not held during the war, the Loyal League was implicitly feminist and afforded its leaders a national platform from which to espouse woman's rights. Stanton and Anthony encouraged female participation in the political process, and the nearly 400,000 signatures on the mammoth petition to Congress, the majority of them female, indicate they had succeeded. League leaders also urged women to think ahead to postwar possibilities for women and discussed specific issues such as the concept of gender equality, equal pay for equal work, even suffrage.

Throughout the war Anna Dickinson lectured on woman's rights. Her standard speech on the subject, usually titled "Rights and Wrongs of Women" or "A Plea for Woman," had helped to thrust her into the national limelight in 1860. Shortly before delivering a woman's rights lecture in Boston's Tremont Temple, 21 October 1862, Dickinson revealed her commitment to feminism in a letter to Abby Kelley Foster. "The cause," she wrote, "is nearer my heart than anything else on earth."[16]

Women's issues also received attention from the press during the Civil War. The New York *Independent* ran a series of articles in the spring of 1864 under the banner "Woman's Right to Labor." The New York *World*, a Democratic newspaper, printed a similar series in December 1863.[17] Though it was a subordinate concern to abolitionism, feminist activity was never totally eclipsed by the Civil War emphasis on African American rights.

The postwar period may, with some justification, be interpreted as the nadir of the nineteenth-century woman's rights movement. The Fourteenth and Fifteenth Amendments gave the vote to black men, in theory if not in fact. Women made no such gain. Many female activists, in addition to having participated in the wartime emancipation crusade, had labored for decades before that time on the slave's behalf, and yet citizenship's most treasured privilege still eluded them.

Angered by congressional action, Elizabeth Cady Stanton and others resorted to racist rhetoric. Increasingly they referred to blacks as "Sambo." In *The History of Woman Suffrage*, Stanton and Anthony lamented that "in the enfranchisement of the black man," women "saw another ignorant class of voters placed above their heads." This bigotry may have been more rhetorical than substantive. In 1866, during the intense debate over the Fourteenth Amendment, Elizabeth Cady Stanton invited the black abolitionist Sojourner Truth to be a guest in the Stanton home. Her invitation was accepted. Truth was one of several black women to support the NWSA, choosing to overlook its racist rhetoric and endorse its platform of support for both political and economic equality. Some of Stanton's white colleagues were less forgiving. Lucretia Mott was horrified by Stanton's racist rhetoric. William Lloyd Garrison became so disenchanted with Stanton that he dismissed her as a "female demagogue . . . untruthful, unscrupulous and selfishly ambitious."[18]

Even if their racist rhetoric was mere invective, it was an unfortunate change of tactics for a group of women who had worked tirelessly on behalf of the slave during the war years and one which set a very poor precedent. By the turn of the century, Southern suffragists had adopted an openly racist ideology in their campaign, emphasizing that the votes of white women were needed to offset black votes in the South. Some Northern feminists employed similar logic with regard to the immigrant vote.[19]

Increasingly, feminists would narrow their focus to white, middle-class issues, leaving aside their earlier altruistic rhetoric about justice and equality for all and their plans to reform the whole of American society. The tendency to move away from moral idealism and toward a narrowly defined set of political aims has been a common occurrence in the history of American reform movements. According to Lori Ginzberg, the postwar woman's rights movement, like Progressivism, civil rights, and feminism in the twentieth century, involved change from "what might loosely be called a moral transformation to a narrower concentration on electoral politics."[20]

The schism in the Equal Rights Association divided and therefore hurt the woman's rights movement. Although there had always been differences of opinion in the feminist ranks, the divisions produced by the debate over the Fourteenth and Fifteenth Amendments were deep and long lasting. Not until 1890 did the National and American Woman Suffrage Associations reunite, with Elizabeth Cady Stanton as president of the combined group.

There were gains as well. The schism of 1869 benefited the feminist movement in at least one way. In breaking their ties with the abolition movement and with the Republican party, Ellen DuBois has pointed out, Stanton and Anthony came to the realization that only through the agitation of women could female emancipation be achieved. Thereafter they carried out their suffrage activities independent of any political party or other reform group. Elizabeth Cady Stanton summarized the argument in a letter to Ann Greene Phillips. "American statesmen can be eloquent in denunciation of an aristocracy based on color, wealth, family, land, orders of nobility, but an aristocracy based on sex is a different question." Concentrating specifically on Reconstruction, she concluded, "Of course they would rather see the experiment of equality tried in a southern plantation than at their own firesides, in their own beds."[21]

One obvious gain that the Civil War brought to postwar feminism was the addition of new recruits. Julia Ward Howe had been critical of the woman's rights movement before the war, believing such activity to be unladylike. Civil War abolitionism helped to change her mind. "The women of the North had greatly helped to open the door which admitted him [the slave] to freedom and its safeguard, the ballot," she wrote after the war. "Was the door to be shut in their face?" Howe was an enormous asset to the suffrage cause, for she was a paragon of gentility. "Your mother's great importance to this cause," one blue-blooded Bostonian told Julia's daughters, "is that she forms a bridge between the world of society and the world of reform."[22]

Mary Livermore was another feminist convert who added respectability to the cause. This Chicago minister's wife was active both in sanitary commission work and abolition activities. It was Livermore who defended Anna Dickinson so staunchly during the young woman's controversial 1863 visit to the Chicago Sanitary Fair. In her autobiography Livermore remembered the prewar articles she wrote for her husband's Universalist newspaper on women's economic, educational, and legal disadvantages. It was not until after the war, however, that she embraced organized feminism. "During the war, and as the result of my own observations," she recalled, "I became aware that a large portion of the nation's work was badly done, or not done at all, because woman was not recognized as a factor in the political world." As an organizer for the American Woman Suffrage Association and especially as editor of the *Woman's Journal,* she made a considerable contribution to feminism.[23] Howe and Livermore were just two of the women who embraced the woman's suffrage movement after the war.

Anna Dickinson made a significant contribution as well. The Reverend Antoinette Brown Blackwell told a New York audience in January 1865 that "the respect and attention accorded to Miss Dickinson by the public was as much a pledge of the emancipation of woman, as was the Proclamation of Freedom a pledge for the liberation of the slave." Dickinson's popularity was not fleeting. Throughout the war, she attracted large and enthusiastic audiences composed of both males and females. Newspaper reporters covering her lectures often noted that there was "an immense audience, including many ladies," or that "the ladies were present in unusual numbers."[24]

Although she was too independent to be an active member of the National Woman Suffrage Association, Dickinson did sympathize with feminist issues, and her contribution to nineteenth-century woman's rights should not be overlooked. Ida Tarbell wrote at the turn of the century, "Anna Dickinson effectually ended popular opposition in the North to woman lecturers." Because of the Philadelphia Quaker's work for the Union cause, "the people began to feel that if a woman could render a patriotic service of this kind, the day had passed when there should be objection to her doing it." Mary Livermore wrote in her memoirs that the young woman "made it possible for any woman who had anything to say, and knew how to say it, to follow her on the platform."[25]

After the war Dickinson acted in plays and also joined the lyceum circuit. More often than not, her speeches related to women's political, social, and educational rights. Her speaking ability and popularity made her an important voice for woman's rights in the postwar period. By the 1870s Dickinson was earning $20,000 a year, an enormous sum by nineteenth-century standards. Her success helped to inspire a generation of young women to take elocution lessons in colleges and academies.[26]

Even Harriet Beecher Stowe, though uncomfortable with organized feminism, admitted to novelist Sara Parton in 1869 that she favored woman suffrage. "The more I think of it," she added, "the more absurd this whole government of men over women looks." She also dismissed the antifeminist argument that suffrage would unsex women, telling Parton, "Unsexed?—I should like to see what could make women other than women and more than men." Stowe's evolution was remarkable. Once skeptical of Garrisonian abolition and a follower of her sister Catharine's conservative interpretation of woman's sphere, she had won national attention by publishing her antislavery novel in 1852, issued a strongly worded manifesto to the English government in 1863, and publicly supported Abraham Lincoln's reelection in 1864. By the end of the decade she embraced woman's rights. Although at one point Stowe agreed to write articles for *The Revolution*, she backed out when Stanton and Anthony refused to change the name of their newspaper to "*True Republic* or some name equally satisfactory." Stowe did eventually write stories in which she voiced support for married woman's property reform and female guardianship of children, but she published them in more traditional journals. She justified her beliefs by insisting that woman's rights were necessary to enhance woman's duties as wife and mother.[27]

The image of reform women improved in the postwar period. Although feminists had given speeches and signed petitions for a variety of causes before the war, they were almost universally condemned as unladylike except by a small group of reform-minded citizens. The public response to the activities of the Loyal League, however, was frequently positive. "The leading journals vied with each other in praising the patience and prudence, the executive ability, the loyalty, and the patriotism of the women of the League," Elizabeth Cady Stanton recalled, exaggerating slightly. "And yet these were the same women who, when demanding civil and political rights . . . for themselves, had been uniformly denounced as 'unwise,' 'imprudent,' 'fanatical,' and 'impractical.'"[28] Undoubtedly this change in public opinion carried into the postbellum period. Abolitionist orators and writers such as Lucy Stone, Susan Anthony, Anna Dickinson, and Elizabeth Cady Stanton spoke on feminist concerns after the war. Even though they encountered public opposition to their views, they encountered far less opposition to the public expression of those views than had prewar feminist abolitionists.

Stanton herself helped to win respectability for women speakers. She became a successful lyceum lecturer, crisscrossing the country and addressing audiences on all manner of topics from child rearing to divorce reform. Stanton financed the college education of several of her children from the proceeds of her lectures.[29]

One key to her success was Stanton's ability to cloak her feminism in a mantle of motherhood and respectability. During the Civil War she frequently justified her political demands for women by invoking widely held notions about woman's "traditional" and "rightful" sphere. In her later years she relied on this same technique. As she aged, Stanton grew more and more rotund, yet her girth seemed to help her public persona. Elizabeth Cady Stanton looked like the quintessential grandmother, with her white hair arranged in sausage curls around her face, her plump figure always clothed tastefully in lace collar and cuffs. Stanton's rosy-cheeked face appeared in advertisements for women's facial soap. In her mid-seventies, according to the Washington *Star,* she looked "as if she should be the Lord Chief-Justice, with her white hair puffed all over her head, and her amiable and intellectual face marked with the lines of wisdom." Many other journals portrayed her as the "Grand Old Woman of America." Though Stanton had gained respectability as well as weight, her views were as radical as ever. She championed such causes as woman suffrage and divorce reform until her death at eighty-six in 1902.[30]

The postwar period was a negative one in many ways for women. They were not included in the Fourteenth and Fifteenth Amendments. And yet there were gains, albeit less tangible ones, which resulted from the Civil War and in part from women's abolition work during the war. Women had long been accepted as nurses and seamstresses and charity organizers. Their Civil War work in these areas, while significant, was not pathbreaking. The petitioning, public speaking, and political organizing that Northern women performed during the war helped to gain new acceptance for women in the public sphere after the war. In the 1830s women had been painfully insecure at the lecture podium, their early efforts meeting with overwhelming public hostility. By the 1870s they were increasingly confident as public figures and looked forward to women's greater political participation. Although suffrage would not be granted to women until the second decade of the twentieth century, woman's rights advocates in the postbellum period did not face the same degree of ridicule that they faced before the war. Becoming the champions of the slave and the patriotic supporters of the Union cause had clearly helped to give legitimacy to women speakers and political organizers. Elizabeth Cady Stanton, Susan B. Anthony, and their lieutenants had helped to win the war. In the years to come, they would continue to battle for woman's rights.

Abbreviations

Notes

Essay on Sources

Index

Abbreviations

AED   Anna Elizabeth Dickinson
ECS   Elizabeth Cady Stanton
HBS   Harriet Beecher Stowe
FAK   Frances Anne Kemble
SBA   Susan Brownell Anthony

AAS   American Antiquarian Society, Worcester, Mass.
BPL   Boston Public Library
CHS   Chicago Historical Society
CUB   Columbia University, Butler Library, New York
CUL   Cornell University Library, Ithaca, N.Y.
HH   Houghton Library, Harvard University, Cambridge, Mass.
HL   Henry E. Huntington Library, San Marino, Calif.
HWS   *History of Woman Suffrage*, ed. Elizabeth Cady Stanton, Susan B. Anthony, and Matilda Joslyn Gage, 3 vols., 2d ed. (Rochester: Charles Mann, 1889)
LC   Library of Congress, Washington, D.C.
MHS   Massachusetts Historical Society, Boston
NA   National Archives, Washington, D.C.
PHS   Historical Society of Pennsylvania, Philadelphia
RUL   Rochester University Library, Rochester, N.Y.
SDL   Stowe-Day Library, Hartford
SLR   Schlesinger Library, Radcliffe College, Cambridge, Mass.
SSC   Sophia Smith Collection, Smith College, Northampton, Mass.
UVA   Clifton Waller Barrett Library, University of Virginia Library, Charlottesville
VCL   Vassar College Library, Poughkeepsie, N.Y.
WNLL   Woman's National Loyal League

Notes

✫

Chapter 1

1. American Anti-Slavery Society, *Proceedings of the American Anti-Slavery Society at Its Third Decade* (New York, 1864; rept. New York: Arno Press and the New York *Times*, 1969), 74.

2. Alma Lutz, *Crusade for Freedom: Women of the Antislavery Movement* (Boston: Beacon Press, 1968), 8–10; Blanche Glassman Hersh, *The Slavery of Sex: Feminist Abolitionists in America* (Urbana: Univ. of Illinois Press, 1978), 7–9.

3. Merton L. Dillon, "Elizabeth Chandler and the Spread of Antislavery Sentiment to Michigan," *Michigan History* 39 (Dec. 1955): 484–92; Dwight Lowell Dumond, *Antislavery: The Crusade for Freedom in America* (Ann Arbor: Univ. of Michigan Press, 1961), 279; John L. Thomas, *The Liberator: William Lloyd Garrison* (Boston: Little, Brown, 1963), 101, 143–54; Lutz, *Crusade for Freedom*, 19.

4. See Barbara Welter, "The Cult of True Womanhood, 1820–1860," *American Quarterly* 18 (Summer 1966): 151–75; Linda K. Kerber, *Women of the Republic: Intellect and Ideology in Revolutionary America* (Chapel Hill: Univ. of North Carolina Press, 1980); and Nancy Cott, *The Bonds of Womanhood: "Woman's Sphere" in New England, 1780–1835* (New Haven: Yale Univ. Press, 1977), among others.

5. Lawrence Foster, *Religion and Sexuality: Three American Communal Experiments of the Nineteenth Century* (New York: Oxford Univ. Press, 1981), 229.

6. Keith E. Melder, *Beginnings of Sisterhood: The American Woman's Rights Movement, 1800–1850* (New York: Schocken Books, 1977), 56.

7. Hersh, *The Slavery of Sex*, 10–11.

8. Aileen S. Kraditor, *Means and Ends in American Abolitionism: Garrison and His Critics on Strategy and Tactics, 1834–1850* (New York: Pantheon Books, 1969), 4–6.

9. Lutz, *Crusade for Freedom*, 22.

10. Ibid., 23, 194; Jane H. Pease and William H. Pease, "The Role of Women in the Antislavery Movement," *Canadian Historical Association Historical Papers*, 1967–68, 179; Catherine Clinton, "Maria Weston Chapman,

1806–1885," in G. J. Barker-Benfield and Catherine Clinton, eds., *Portraits of American Women from Settlement to the Present* (New York: St. Martin's Press, 1991), 147–67; John Jay Chapman, *Memories and Milestones* (New York: Moffat, Yard, 1915), 210–11, 218–19.

11. ECS, *Eighty Years and More: Reminiscences of Elizabeth Cady Stanton* (New York: European Publishing Company, 1898), 129; Lutz, *Crusade for Freedom,* 190–91.

12. Lutz, *Crusade for Freedom,* 71.

13. Ibid., 58; Hersh, *The Slavery of Sex,* 11; Wendell Phillips Garrison, *William Lloyd Garrison, 1805–1879: The Story of His Life Told by His Children,* 4 vols. (New York: Century Company, 1885), 2:15–27.

14. Irving H. Bartlett, *Wendell and Ann Phillips: The Community of Reform, 1840–1880* (New York: W. W. Norton, 1979), 17–18, 40; Irving H. Bartlett, *Wendell Phillips: Brahmin Radical* (Boston: Beacon Press, 1961), 35–40.

15. Ira V. Brown, "Cradle of Feminism: The Philadelphia Female Anti-Slavery Society, 1833–1840," *Pennsylvania Magazine of History and Biography* 102 (April 1978): 144–47.

16. Anna Davis Hallowell, ed., *James and Lucretia Mott: Life and Letters* (Boston: Houghton, Mifflin, 1884), 18, 35, 62; Otelia Cromwell, *Lucretia Mott* (New York: Russell & Russell, 1971), 45; Margaret Hope Bacon, *Valiant Friend: The Life of Lucretia Mott* (New York: Walker, 1980), 37; Carleton Mabee, *Black Freedom: The Nonviolent Abolitionists from 1830 through the Civil War* (New York: Macmillan, 1970), 186–89.

17. Brown, "Cradle of Feminism," 149–53.

18. Gerda Lerner, "The Political Activities of Antislavery Women," in *The Majority Finds Its Past: Placing Women in History* (New York: Oxford Univ. Press, 1979), 116; Benjamin Quarles, *Black Abolitionists* (New York: Oxford Univ. Press, 1969), 27–29; Shirley Jo-ann Yee, "Black Women Abolitionists: A Study of Gender and Race in the American Antislavery Movement, 1828–1860" (Ph.D. diss., Ohio State Univ., 1987), 224–27.

19. Helene G. Baer, *The Heart Is Like Heaven: The Life of Lydia Maria Child* (Philadelphia: Univ. of Pennsylvania Press, 1964), 19, 40–45; Hersh, *The Slavery of Sex,* 12; Mabee, *Black Freedom,* 192.

20. Lydia Maria Child, *Appeal in Favor of That Class of Americans Called Africans* (New York: John S. Taylor, 1836), 20–21, 37, 76, 134.

21. John Greenleaf Whittier, ed., *Letters of Lydia Maria Child* (Boston: Houghton, Mifflin, 1884), ix; Baer, *The Heart Is Like Heaven,* 67–68; Samuel J. May, *Some Recollections of Our Antislavery Conflict* (Boston: Fields, Osgood, 1869), 99.

22. Lutz, *Crusade for Freedom,* 174–79, 186–89.

23. Gerda Lerner, *The Grimké Sisters from South Carolina: Pioneers for Woman's Rights and Abolition* (New York: Schocken Books, 1975), 13, 19–21, 24, 57–59, 82–86.

24. Ibid., 123–25; Katharine Du Pre Lumpkin, *The Emancipation of Angelina Grimké* (Chapel Hill: Univ. of North Carolina Press, 1974), 85–89.

25. Lerner, *The Grimké Sisters*, 138–39; Lumpkin, *The Emancipation of Angelina Grimké*, 91.

26. Lerner, *The Grimké Sisters*, 4; Lutz, *Crusade for Freedom*, 98.

27. Kraditor, *Means and Ends*, 42; Catherine H. Birney, *The Grimké Sisters: Sarah and Angelina Grimké* (Boston: Lee and Shepard, 1885), 189–90.

28. Lerner, *The Grimké Sisters*, 1–8.

29. Ibid.

30. Ibid., 238, 255; Lumpkin, *The Emancipation of Angelina Grimké*, 170.

31. Lerner, "The Political Activities of Antislavery Women," 123; Hersh, *The Slavery of Sex*, 24, 42–43; Lutz, *Crusade for Freedom*, 213; Pease and Pease, "The Role of Women in the Antislavery Movement," 175–76.

32. John White Chadwick, ed., *A Life for Liberty: Anti-Slavery and Other Letters of Sallie Holley* (New York: G. P. Putnam's Sons, 1899; rept. New York: Negro Univ. Press, 1969), 65, 99–100.

33. Elizabeth Shafer, "Sojourner Truth: 'A Self-Made Woman,'" *American History Illustrated* 8 (Jan. 1974): 34–38; May, *Some Recollections*, 405–6; Yee, "Black Women Abolitionists," 57–60.

34. Lutz, *Crusade for Freedom*, 101.

35. Ibid., 102; Lerner, *The Grimké Sisters*, 160, 241; Edward T. James, ed., *Notable American Women, 1607–1950*, 3 vols. (Cambridge: Belknap Press, 1982), 1:511–12; Quarles, *Black Abolitionists*, 28.

36. Lutz, *Crusade for Freedom*, 102–5; Hersh, *Slavery of Sex*, 16; Dumond, *Antislavery*, 278; Lerner, *The Grimké Sisters*, 374 n.; Angelina E. Grimké, *An Appeal to the Women of the Nominally Free States: Issued by an Anti-Slavery Convention of American Women and Held by Adjournment from the 9th to the 12th of May, 1837* (New York: W. S. Dorr, 1837).

37. Bacon, *Valiant Friend*, 76–79; Lutz, *Crusade for Freedom*, 137–43; Leonard L. Richards, *"Gentlemen of Property and Standing": Anti-Abolition Mobs in Jacksonian America* (New York: Oxford Univ. Press, 1970), 156.

38. Lerner, "The Political Activities of Antislavery Women," 116; Dumond, *Antislavery*, 245.

39. Gilbert Hobbs Barnes, *The Anti-Slavery Impulse, 1830–1844* (Washington, D.C.: American Historical Association, 1933; rept. Chicago: Harcourt, Brace & World, 1964), 144, 266; Judith Wellman, "Women and Radical Reform in Antebellum Upstate New York: A Profile of Grassroots Female Abolitionists," in Mabel E. Deutrich and Virginia C. Purdy, eds., *Clio Was a Woman: Studies in the History of American Women* (Washington, D.C.: Howard Univ. Press, 1980), 117–18.

40. Kraditor, *Means and Ends*, 54, 59–60.

41. Ibid.; Lewis Perry, *Radical Abolitionism: Anarchy and the Government of God in Antislavery Thought* (Ithaca, N.Y.: Cornell Univ. Press, 1973), 11. Other important discussions of the abolitionist rift may be found in Louis Filler, *The Crusade against Slavery, 1830–1860* (New York: Harper and Row, 1963), 131–36, and Gilbert Barnes, *The Anti-Slavery Impulse*, 153–60.

42. Kraditor, *Means and Ends*, 49–53; Lutz, *Crusade for Freedom*, 155–56;

Bertram Wyatt-Brown, *Lewis Tappan and the Evangelical War against Slavery* (Cleveland: Press of Case Western Reserve Univ., 1969), 197–98.

43. Lutz, *Crusade for Freedom*, 151–52; Ronald G. Walters, *The Antislavery Appeal: American Abolitionism after 1830* (New York: W. W. Norton, 1978), 4.

44. Paulina W. Davis, *A History of the National Woman's Rights Movement* (New York: Journeymen Printers' Co-Operative Association, 1871; rept. New York: Kraus, 1971), 11–12; Eleanor Flexner, *Century of Struggle: The Woman's Rights Movement in the United States* (New York: Atheneum, 1974), 71; Lutz, *Crusade for Freedom*, 159.

45. Hersh, *The Slavery of Sex*, 189–90; Ellen Carol DuBois, *Feminism and Suffrage: The Emergence of an Independent Women's Movement in America, 1848–1869* (Ithaca, N.Y.: Cornell Univ. Press, 1978), 51–52.

46. Hersh, *The Slavery of Sex*, 189.

47. Ibid., 82; Elinor Rice Hays, *Morning Star: A Biography of Lucy Stone, 1818–1893* (New York: Harcourt, Brace and World, 1961), 31–37, 65–66.

48. Hersh, *The Slavery of Sex*, 83, 86; Hays, *Morning Star*, 127.

49. ECS, *Eighty Years and More*, 2–3, 31–32, 35; *HWS* 1:471; Elisabeth Griffith, *In Her Own Right: The Life of Elizabeth Cady Stanton* (New York: Oxford Univ. Press, 1984), 3–5, 26–33, 82–83, 100–101; Alma Lutz, *Created Equal: A Biography of Elizabeth Cady Stanton, 1815–1902* (New York: John Day, 1940), 4.

50. Kathleen Barry, *Susan B. Anthony: A Biography of a Singular Feminist* (New York: New York Univ. Press, 1988), 9–10, 18, 51.

51. Ibid., 61, 65–66; Hersh, *The Slavery of Sex*, 113–14; Ida H. Harper, *Life and Work of Susan B. Anthony*, 2 vols. (Indianapolis: Bowen-Merrill, 1899), 1:63–64.

52. ECS to Elizabeth Smith Miller, 15 Nov. 1856, in Theodore Stanton and Harriot Stanton Blatch, eds., *Elizabeth Cady Stanton As Revealed in Her Letters, Diary, and Reminiscences*, 2 vols. (New York: Harper & Brothers, 1922), 2:69.

Chapter 2

1. Joel Bernard, "Authority, Autonomy, and Radical Commitment: Stephen and Abby Kelley Foster," *Proceedings of the American Antiquarian Society* 90 (1980): 379; Milton Meltzer, *Tongue of Flame: The Life of Lydia Maria Child* (New York: Thomas Y. Crowell, 1965), 126.

2. ECS to SBA, Dec. 1857, in Stanton and Blatch, *Elizabeth Cady Stanton* 2:71–72; Ellen Carol DuBois, ed., *Elizabeth Cady Stanton, Susan B. Anthony: Correspondence, Writings, Speeches* (New York: Schocken Books, 1981), 59.

3. Lutz, *Crusade for Freedom*, 261.

4. Stephen B. Oates, *To Purge This Land with Blood: A Biography of John Brown* (New York: Harper and Row, 1970), 224; David M. Potter, *The Impending Crisis, 1848–1861* (New York: Harper and Row, 1976), 363–64; Sarah

Hopper Emerson, ed., *Life of Abby Hopper Gibbons, Told Chiefly through Her Correspondence*, 2 vols. (New York: G. P. Putnam's Sons, 1897), 1:261.

5. Potter, *Impending Crisis*, 371, 376–79; Milton Meltzer and Patricia G. Holland, eds., *Lydia Maria Child: Selected Letters, 1817–1880* (Amherst: Univ. of Massachusetts Press, 1982), 323–33; Jean Fagan Yellin, *Women & Sisters: The Antislavery Feminists in American Culture* (New Haven: Yale Univ. Press, 1989), 62–64, 194.

6. *Liberator*, 31 Dec. 1859; Yellin, *Women and Sisters*, 62–64.

7. Meltzer, *Tongue of Flame*, 151; James M. McPherson, *The Struggle for Equality: Abolitionists and the Negro in the Civil War and Reconstruction* (Princeton, N.J.: Princeton Univ. Press, 1972), 14, 26–28; Wendell Phillips, *Speeches, Lectures, Letters*, 2 vols. (Boston: Walker, Wise, 1864), 1:294; Bartlett, *Wendell Phillips*, 222–23; *Independent*, 15 Nov. 1860.

8. Maria Weston Chapman to Mrs. Mitchell, Jan. 1861, Antislavery Collection, BPL.

9. McPherson, *Struggle for Equality*, 32–36.

10. *Liberator*, 30 Nov. 1860; Lydia Maria Child, *The Patriarchal Institution, As Described by Members of Its Own Family* (New York: American Anti-Slavery Society, 1860), 53; Lydia Maria Child, *The Right Way the Safe Way* (New York: n.p., 1862), 3–4, 94–96.

11. Harriet A. Jacobs, *Incidents in the Life of a Slave Girl, Written by Herself*, ed. L. Maria Child (Boston: Published for the Author, 1861; rept., ed. Jean Fagan Yellin, Cambridge: Harvard Univ. Press, 1987), 5–8, 27–29, 54–56, 95–104, 114–17, 156–58, 168–70, 223–25.

12. Ibid., 1, 54–57; Elizabeth Fox-Genovese, *Within the Plantation Household: Black and White Women of the Old South* (Chapel Hill: Univ. of North Carolina Press, 1988), 376.

13. Fox-Genovese, *Within the Plantation Household*, 392.

14. Jacobs, *Incidents*, xvii–xxiv, 223–25.

15. Lydia Maria Child to Henrietta Sargent, 9 Feb. 1861, to John Greenleaf Whittier, 4 April 1861, in Meltzer and Holland, *Lydia Maria Child: Selected Letters*, 374–75, 378; Child to [Whittier], 14 March 1861, Child Collection, LC; Whittier to Child, 1 April 1861, Microfiche doc. no. 1299 in *The Collected Correspondence of Lydia Maria Child, 1817–1880*, ed., Patricia G. Holland and Milton Meltzer (Millwood, N.Y.: Kraus-Thomson, 1979).

16. *Liberator*, 25 Jan. 1861.

17. See the *Liberator*, 10 April 1863; *National Anti-Slavery Standard* (hereafter cited as *Standard*), 18 April 1863, 16 April 1864.

18. [Mary Putnam], *Record of an Obscure Man* (Boston: Ticknor and Fields, 1861), 19, 55, 58–59, 62–63; *Liberator*, 29 Nov. 1861; McPherson, *Struggle for Equality*, 140–41.

19. McPherson, *Struggle for Equality*, 40–41.

20. ECS, *Eighty Years and More*, 210–11.

21. McPherson, *Struggle for Equality*, 41–42; Bartlett, *Wendell Phillips*, 226–34; Phillips, *Speeches, Lectures, and Letters* 1:355, 392.

22. SBA to William Lloyd Garrison, 14 Dec. 1860, 18 Jan. 1861, Antislav-

ery Collection, BPL; ECS to Martha Wright, 22 Dec. 1861, Stanton Collection, LC; Harper, *Life and Work of Susan B. Anthony* 1:208.

23. ECS, *The Slave's Appeal* (Albany: Weed, Parsons, 1860), Garrison Family Papers, SSC; Lydia Mott to ECS, 28 Nov. 1860, Stanton Collection, LC.

24. ECS, "Speech on Slavery," [1860?], Stanton Collection, LC. One Northern senator, Charles Sumner, was "struck dumb in his seat" by South Carolina congressman Preston Brooks in 1856.

25. ECS, "Speech on Slavery," 1861, Stanton Collection, LC.

26. Ibid.

27. SBA, "What Is American Slavery," 1861, "The No Union with Slaveholders Campaign," 1861, "Judge Taney," 1861, Anthony Collection, LC.

28. Buffalo *Commercial Advertiser*, 4 Jan. 1861, reprinted in *Liberator*, 18 Jan. 1861; *Twenty-eighth Annual Report of the American Anti-Slavery Society for the Year Ending May 1, 1861* (New York: American Anti-Slavery Society, 1861; rept. New York: Kraus, 1972), 182 (hereafter cited as *28th Report . . . AASS*). This was the last annual report of the American Anti-Slavery Society.

29. *Liberator*, 18 Jan. 1861; *Standard*, 5 Jan. 1861.

30. Rochester *Evening Express*, 12 Jan. 1861, reprinted in *Liberator*, 25 Jan. 1861; *28th Report . . . AASS*, 182–83.

31. Henry B. Stanton to ECS, 12 Jan. 1861, and [1861], Stanton Collection, LC.

32. Utica *Herald*, 15 Jan. 1861, reprinted in *Liberator*, 1 Feb. 1861; *28th Report . . . AASS*, 183–84; New York *Times*, 15 Jan. 1861; SBA to ECS, 15 Jan. 1861, Stanton Collection, LC; *Liberator*, 8 Feb. 1861.

33. Syracuse *Courier and Union*, 30 Jan. 1861, reprinted in *Liberator*, 15 Feb. 1861; Syracuse *Daily Journal*, 31 Jan. 1861, reprinted in *Standard*, 16 Feb. 1861; *28th Report . . . AASS*, 184–87.

34. Syracuse *Onondaga Standard*, 6 Feb. 1861, reprinted in *Liberator*, 15 Feb. 1861; Lucy Stone to Antoinette Blackwell, 19 Jan. 1861, Blackwell Family Collection, LC.

35. ECS, "Free Speech," 4th Annual New York State Anti-Slavery Convention, 4–5 Feb. 1861, VCL; ECS, "Speech in Orleans County," 1861, Stanton Collection, LC; *Standard*, 23 Feb. 1861; *Liberator*, 15 Feb. 1861; *28th Report . . . AASS*, 187–88.

36. Cleveland *Weekly Review*, 16 March 1861, reprinted in *Standard*, 6 April 1861.

37. *Michigan State News*, 29 Jan. 1861, reprinted in *Liberator*, 15 Feb. 1861; *28th Report . . . AASS*, 188–91. Josephine Griffing's letter of 6 Feb. 1861 was printed in the *Liberator* on 15 Feb. 1861.

38. Josephine Griffing's letter of 25 May 1861 printed in the *Standard*, 1 June 1861; James, *Notable American Women* 2:92–94.

39. Josephine Griffing's letters of 16 Dec. 1860 and 20 June 1861 printed in the *Liberator* on 1 Feb. and 28 June 1861; Shafer, "Sojourner Truth," 38; James, *Notable American Women* 3:480–81.

40. Phillip S. Paludan, "The American Civil War Considered as a Crisis in Law and Order," *American Historical Review* 77 (Oct. 1972): 1027–34.

41. Ibid.; Syracuse *Courier and Union*, 30 Jan. 1861, reprinted in *Liberator*, 15 Feb. 1861.

42. McPherson, *Struggle for Equality*, 49–51; Bartlett, *Wendell Phillips*, 237–39; Mabee, *Black Freedom*, 343–45, 360.

43. SBA to Wendell Phillips, 28 April 1861, Anthony Collection, HH; Hersh, *The Slavery of Sex*, 107.

44. Hallowell, *James and Lucretia Mott*, 406–7. Charles Weld was not a consistent pacifist, for he considered traveling to Mexico to aid the cause of Maximilian (Mabee, *Black Freedom*, 348).

45. Lydia Maria Child to John Greenleaf Whittier, 21 Jan. 1862, Child Collection, LC.

46. McPherson, *Struggle for Equality*, 35, 60–61.

47. Stephen B. Oates, *With Malice toward None: The Life of Abraham Lincoln* (New York: Mentor, 1978), 280–84.

48. Martha Wright to Ellen Wright, 16 Sept. 1861, Garrison Family Papers, SSC; Lydia Maria Child to John Greenleaf Whittier, 22 Sept. 1861, Child Collection, LC; *Liberator*, 20 Sept. 1861.

49. Tubman later served as a nurse in a Virginia freedmen's hospital. See James, *Notable American Women* 3:481–83.

50. McPherson, *Struggle for Equality*, 102–3; Lydia Maria Child to Jessie Frémont, in *Liberator*, 11 Oct. 1861; Amy Post to Isaac Post, 16 Aug. 1862, Post Family Papers, RUL.

Chapter 3

1. See James Harvey Young, "Anna Elizabeth Dickinson and the Civil War" (Ph.D. diss., Univ. of Illinois at Urbana-Champaign, 1941; hereafter cited as "Anna Elizabeth Dickinson"), and "Anna Elizabeth Dickinson and the Civil War: For and Against Lincoln" *Mississippi Valley Historical Review* 31 (June 1944): 59–80 (hereafter cited as "Anna Elizabeth Dickinson and the Civil War"). See also Giraud Chester, *Embattled Maiden: The Life of Anna Dickinson* (New York: G. P. Putnam's Sons, 1951).

2. Young, "Anna Elizabeth Dickinson," 2–3.

3. Ibid., 3–4; Chester, *Embattled Maiden*, 13–14.

4. Chester, *Embattled Maiden*, 15.

5. Young, "Anna Elizabeth Dickinson," 6–7; Catherine Clinton, *The Other Civil War: American Women in the Nineteenth Century* (New York: Hill and Wang, 1984), 90.

6. Lucretia Mott to Lydia Mott, 22 Jan. 1861, Stanton Collection, LC; *HWS* 2:41; Young, "Anna Elizabeth Dickinson," 22–23, including quotation from the Philadelphia *Press*, 28 Feb. 1861; Chester, *Embattled Maiden*, 23–25.

7. *Standard*, 2 Nov. 1861.

8. *HWS* 3:42; Young, "Anna Elizabeth Dickinson," 28–29.

9. *Liberator,* 28 March 1862.

10. AED to William Lloyd Garrison, 16 March 1862, Garrison to AED, 22 March, 3 April 1862, Dickinson Collection, LC; AED to [Garrison], 25 March 1862, Antislavery Collection, BPL; *Liberator,* 18 April 1862, including reprints from the Fall River *Press* and the Providence *Press,* n.d.

11. William Lloyd Garrison to AED, 27 March 1862, AED to Susan Dickinson, 28 April 1862, Dickinson Collection, LC.

12. Samuel May, Jr., to Elizabeth Buffum Chace, 27 April 1862, in Lillie Buffum Chace Wyman and Arthur Crawford Wyman, eds., *Elizabeth Buffum Chace, 1806–1899: Her Life and Its Environment,* 2 vols. (Boston: W. B. Clarke, 1914), 1:236–37; Young, "Anna Elizabeth Dickinson," 42.

13. AED to Susan Dickinson, 28 April 1862, Dickinson Collection, LC; Boston *Post,* 21 April 1862, quoted in Young, "Anna Elizabeth Dickinson," 43.

14. *Standard,* 17 May 1862.

15. Ibid.

16. Ibid.; AED, *What Answer* (Boston: Ticknor & Fields, 1868).

17. *Home Journal,* n.d., quoted in *Frank Leslie's Illustrated Newspaper,* 23 May 1863. Dickinson kept scrapbooks of newspaper clippings describing her lectures; her Civil War clippings include several hundred newspaper articles, many undated and some from unidentified newspapers. See Philadelphia *Press,* 26 March 1862, and Providence *Press,* n.d., Dickinson Scrapbooks, LC; Young, "Anna Elizabeth Dickinson and the Civil War," 61.

18. See AED to William Lloyd Garrison, 27 March 1863, Antislavery Collection, BPL; AED to Caroline Dall, 13 Aug. 1862, Dall Collection, MHS.

19. *Liberator,* 6 June 1862; *Standard,* 17 May 1862.

20. New York *Times,* and New York *Tribune,* n.d., quoted in *Liberator,* 8 May 1863, 3 Feb. 1864.

21. Wendell Phillips quoted in HWS 2:42; William Lloyd Garrison to Oliver Johnson, 5 May 1863, Antislavery Collection, BPL.

22. AED to Susan Dickinson, 27 May 1862, Dickinson Collection, LC.

23. HWS 2:42–43; Young, "Anna Elizabeth Dickinson," 68–69.

24. Charles W. Slack to AED, 14 May 1862, Dickinson Collection, LC; *Standard,* 22 Nov. 1862.

25. Young, "Anna Elizabeth Dickinson," 70–75.

26. *Independent,* 8 Jan. 1863; *Liberator,* 16 Jan. 1863.

27. Fall River, Mass., *Daily Evening News,* 8 Jan. 1863, Dickinson Scrapbooks, LC.

28. William B. Hesseltine, *Lincoln and the War Governors* (New York: Alfred A. Knopf, 1948), 308; James M. McPherson, *Ordeal by Fire: The Civil War and Reconstruction* (New York: Alfred A. Knopf, 1982), 348.

29. Benjamin F. Prescott to AED, 12, 24 Feb. 1863 (see also his letters to her on 22 Jan., 18 Feb., 25 March, 2 April, 11 May 1863), Dickinson Collection, LC; Claremont, N.H., *National Eagle,* 10 March 1863, Claremont *Northern Advocate,* 10 March 1863, *Granite State Free Press,* 14 March

1863, and undated clippings, Dickinson Scrapbooks, LC; McPherson, *Ordeal by Fire*, 348; *HWS* 2:43–44. See also Everett S. Stackpole, *History of New Hampshire*, 4 vols. (New York: American Historical Society, 1916), 4:87.

30. Benjamin Prescott to AED, 22 Jan., 12 Feb. 1863, Dickinson Collection, LC; Hartford *Daily Times*, 2 April 1863; Young, "Anna Elizabeth Dickinson," 136; Young, "Anna Elizabeth Dickinson and the Civil War," 63, 67.

31. Hartford *Daily Times*, 24, 25, 27, 28, 30, 31 March, 2 April 1863; Hartford *Connecticut Courant*, 28 March 1863; Hartford *Press*, n.d., reprinted in *Liberator*, 8 May 1863.

32. Hartford *Connecticut Courant*, 11 April 1863.

33. Young, "Anna Elizabeth Dickinson," 137–40; Chester, *Embattled Maiden*, 70.

34. Young, "Anna Elizabeth Dickinson," 137–40; Judith Anderson, "Anna Dickinson, Antislavery Radical," *Pennsylvania History* 3 (July 1936): 147–63; William Hay to AED, 16 Oct. 1863, Dickinson Collection, LC.

35. Hartford *Connecticut Courant*, 11 April 1863; Portland, Maine, *Transcript*, reprinted in *Liberator*, 3 March 1865.

36. Hartford *Connecticut Courant*, 4 April 1863; Hartford *Press*, n.d., quoted in *Standard*, 11 April 1863; J. Robert Lane, "A Political History of Connecticut during the Civil War" (Ph.D. diss., Catholic Univ., 1941), 233.

37. For an analysis of the Connecticut campaign, see Lane, "A Political History of Connecticut," 236–38. On Pennsylvania politics, see Erwin Stanley Bradley, *The Triumph of Military Republicanism: A Study of Pennsylvania and Presidential Politics, 1860–1872* (Philadelphia: Univ. of Pennsylvania Press, 1964), 162–78. Regarding New York, see Young, "Anna Elizabeth Dickinson," 142–43, and undated clipping in Dickinson's Scrapbooks, LC. For all campaigns, see Hesseltine, *Lincoln and the War Governors*, 320, 327–29, 333–35, 337.

38. In a letter dated 27 April 1862, abolitionist Samuel May, Jr., discussed Dickinson's personal problems with Elizabeth Buffum Chace (Wyman and Wyman, *Elizabeth Buffum Chace* 1:236–37).

39. Anderson, "Anna Dickinson, Antislavery Radical," 158; Chicago *Evening Post*, 1 April 1891.

40. Benjamin F. Prescott to AED, 25 March, 11 May 1863, James W. Batterson to AED, 9 April 1863, Dickinson Collection, LC; Batterson, "Letter to a gentleman in New York," *Standard*, 25 April 1863; Young, "Anna Elizabeth Dickinson," 141–43; Chester, *Embattled Maiden*, 70–73.

41. *Standard*, 25 April 1863. Wendell Phillips quoted in Joseph Ricketson to AED, 30 May 1863, Dickinson Collection, LC; ECS to Martha Wright, 22 April 1863, Stanton Collection, LC; Young, "Anna Elizabeth Dickinson," 142–43; undated clipping in Dickinson Scrapbooks, LC.

42. Springfield, Mass., *Republican*, 22 April 1863, and New York[?] *Mercury*, 3 May 1863, in Dickinson Scrapbooks, LC; New York *Times*, 3 May 1863; New York *Tribune*, 2, 4 May 1863; New York *Herald*, 3 May 1863; *Liberator*, 8 May 1863.

43. New York *Times*, 3, 24 May 1863.

44. New York *Times* and New York *Tribune* quoted in *Liberator*, 8 May 1863; *Independent*, 23 April 1863; *Standard*, 16 May 1863.

45. New York *World*, n.d., reprinted in *Standard*, 2 May 1863.

46. Geneva, N.Y., *Gazette*, n.d., reprinted in *Standard*, 2 April 1864.

47. Mary Livermore to AED, 17 Aug., 1 Oct. 1863, Dickinson Collection, LC.

48. Mary A. Livermore, *My Story of the War: A Woman's Narrative of Four Years of Personal Experience* (Hartford: A. D. Worthington, 1890), 446; Chicago *Tribune*, 4, 5 Nov. 1863.

49. Chicago *Tribune*, 11 Nov. 1863.

50. Livermore, *My Story of the War*, 447.

51. Chicago *Tribune*, 18 Nov. 1863.

52. Hartford *Connecticut Courant*, 28 Nov. 1863; Hartford *Daily Times*, 18 Nov. 1863; New York *Tribune*, 20 Nov. 1863; New York *World*, 19 Nov. 1863; Portland, Maine, *Argus* and Portland *Press*, n.d., reprinted in *Standard*, 16 Jan. 1864; undated clippings, Dickinson Scrapbooks, LC.

53. Chicago *Tribune*, 4 Nov. 1863.

54. Chester, *Embattled Maiden*, 73.

55. *Standard*, 5 March 1864; New York *Herald*, 30 Oct. 1864; *Liberator*, 3 March 1865; Ellen Eakin to AED, 8 June 1863, Dickinson Collection, LC; Chester, *Embattled Maiden*, 65–66.

56. *HWS* 2:44; *Liberator*, 8 May 1863; New York *Herald*, 30 Oct. 1864.

57. *Arthur's Home Magazine* 18 (Nov. 1861): 262–63; *Frank Leslie's Illustrated Newspaper*, 23 May 1863.

58. Portland, Maine, *Transcript*, reprinted in *Liberator*, 3 March 1865.

59. Stephen S. Foster to Alla W. Foster, 1 Jan. 1864, Abigail Kelley Foster Collection, AAS.

60. Ida M. Tarbell, "The American Woman: How She Met the Experience of War," *American Magazine* 69 (April 1910): 809.

Chapter 4

1. Joseph M. Hernon, Jr., "British Sympathies in the American Civil War: A Reconsideration," *Journal of Southern History* 33 (Aug. 1967): 359–61, 364–65; Jasper Ridley, *Lord Palmerston* (New York: E. P. Dutton, 1971), 549–50; Robert L. Reid, "William E. Gladstone's 'Insincere Neutrality' during the Civil War," *Civil War History* 15 (Dec. 1969): 293–307; D. P. Crook, *The North, the South, and the Powers, 1861–1865* (New York: John Wiley and Sons, 1974), 77.

2. Autobiography of Hannah Tracy Cutler in *Woman's Journal*, 19, 26 Sept., 3, 10 Oct. 1896. In 1869, at the age of fifty-three, Cutler received her M.D. degree from Women's Medical College in Cleveland. She was active in the crusade for woman suffrage after the war (James, *Notable American Women* 1:426–27; Jeriah Bonham, *Fifty Years Recollections* [Peoria, Ill.: J. W. Franks and Sons, 1883], 22–47).

3. Hannah Tracy Cutler, *Letter from an American Woman to His Lordship Viscount Lord Palmerston,* dated Dwight, Livingston County, Ill., 9 July 1862 (n.p.), 2, CHS; Clinton, *The Other Civil War,* 86–87.

4. Cutler, *Letter from an American Woman,* 1–4.

5. Ruth Bogin, "Sarah Parker Remond: Black Abolitionist from Salem," *Essex Institute Historical Collections* 110 (1973): 121–29; Dorothy B. Porter, "Sarah Parker Remond, Abolitionist and Physician," *Journal of Negro History* 20 (July 1935): 287–93.

6. Bogin, "Sarah Parker Remond," 131; Benjamin Quarles, "Ministers without Portfolio," *Journal of Negro History* 39 (Jan. 1954): 30–31; *Notable American Women* 3:136–37.

7. According to Jean Fagan Yellin, Jacobs's English edition was published by W. Tweedie under the title *The Deeper Wrong: Or, Incidents in the Life of a Slave Girl* (Jacobs, *Incidents,* xxiv).

8. Sarah P. Remond, "The Negroes in the United States of America," *Journal of Negro History* 27 (April 1942): 216–18; *Standard,* 16 Nov. 1860, 11 May 1861.

9. Lyman Beecher, *Autobiography, Correspondence, Etc., of Lyman Beecher, D.D.,* ed. Charles Beecher, 2 vols. (New York: Harper & Brothers, 1866), 1:525–26; Charles Edward Stowe, *A Life of Harriet Beecher Stowe Compiled from Her Letters and Journals* (Boston: Houghton, Mifflin, 1891), 1–2, 34–35; Lyman Beecher Stowe, *Saints, Sinners, and Beechers* (New York: Blue Ribbon Books, 1937), 156; Maria Caskey, *Chariot of Fire: Religion and the Beecher Family* (New Haven: Yale Univ. Press, 1978), 169–71.

10. Edward Wagenknecht, *Harriet Beecher Stowe: The Known and the Unknown* (New York: Oxford Univ. Press, 1965), 12–13; James, *Notable American Women* 1:121–23.

11. Forrest Wilson, *Crusader in Crinoline: The Life of Harriet Beecher Stowe* (New York: J. B. Lippincott, 1941), 123–25; Louis L. Tucker, "The Semi-Colon Club of Cincinnati," *Ohio History* 73 (Winter 1964): 16–19; Mary Kelley, *Private Woman, Public Stage: Literary Domesticity in Nineteenth-Century America* (New York: Oxford Univ. Press, 1984), viii–xi.

12. Stowe, *Life of Harriet Beecher Stowe,* 198; Stowe, *Saints, Sinners, and Beechers,* 164; Kelley, *Private Woman, Public Stage,* 170.

13. Beecher, *Autobiography* 1:137; Lutz, *Crusade for Freedom,* 246; HBS to Calvin Ellis Stowe, 1837, in Stowe, *Life of Harriet Beecher Stowe,* 87–88; Wilson, *Crusader in Crinoline,* 37–38.

14. Wilson, *Crusader in Crinoline,* 188–90; Lutz, *Crusade for Freedom,* 247.

15. Wilson, *Crusader in Crinoline,* 251–54; Lutz, *Crusade for Freedom,* 247–49; Stowe, *Life of Harriet Beecher Stowe,* 144–45.

16. Edmund Wilson, *Patriotic Gore: Studies in the Literature of the American Civil War* (New York: Oxford Univ. Press, 1962), 5, 8–9; Eric J. Sundquist, ed., *New Essays on Uncle Tom's Cabin* (New York: Cambridge Univ. Press, 1986), 18.

17. Stowe, *Saints, Sinners, and Beechers,* 184–85; Jane Tompkins, *Sensational Designs: The Cultural Work of American Fiction, 1790–1860* (New York:

Oxford Univ. Press, 1985), 124–25. Ralph Ulveling, Detroit Public Library, estimated to Lyman Beecher Stowe that *Uncle Tom* was translated into forty languages (Ulveling to Stowe, 10 Feb. 1909, Stowe Collection, SLR).

18. Annie Fields, ed., *Life and Letters of Harriet Beecher Stowe* (Boston: Houghton, Mifflin, 1897), 158–59; Annie Fields, *Authors and Friends* (Boston: Houghton, Mifflin, 1896), 170; Wilson, *Crusader in Crinoline*, 341–43; HBS, "Tribute of a Loving Friend to the Memory of a Noble Woman," *Atlantic Monthly* 23 (Feb. 1869): 242–50; HBS, *Sunny Memories of Foreign Lands*, 2 vols. (Boston: Phillips, Sampson, 1854), 1:287–300. Today the twenty-six leather-bound volumes are housed at the Stowe-Day Library, Hartford. The library staff hopes someday to quantify and categorize by occupation the signers of this important English document.

19. HBS, *Sunny Memories* 2:19; Frank J. Klingberg, "Harriet Beecher Stowe and Social Reform in England," *American Historical Review* 43 (April 1938): 548, 551.

20. Fields, *Life and Letters*, 210–12.

21. HBS to Frederick Douglass, 9 July 1851, in Stowe, *Life of Harriet Beecher Stowe*, 149–51; Wilson, *Crusader in Crinoline*, 394–95.

22. HBS to Anne Weston (a sister of Maria Weston Chapman), n.d., Antislavery Collection, BPL; ECS to Elizabeth Smith Miller, 21 Nov. 1852, in Stanton and Blatch, *Elizabeth Cady Stanton* 2:46; Lydia Maria Child to Theodore Tilton, 21 July 1861, in Meltzer and Holland, *Lydia Maria Child: Selected Letters*, 389.

23. Frank Luther Mott, *A History of American Magazines*, 4 vols. (Cambridge: Harvard Univ. Press, 1938), 2:371–72.

24. *Independent*, 15 Nov. 1860.

25. Ibid., 25 April, 9 May 1861.

26. *Independent*, 13 June 1861, reprinted in *Standard*, 22 June 1861; *Independent*, 20 June 1861.

27. Stowe's letter was dated "Andover, July 21, 1861" (*Independent*, 1 Aug. 1861).

28. Ibid., 17 Oct. 1861; Henry Richards, *English Anti-Slavery and the American War: A Letter to Mrs. Harriet B. Stowe* (London: Richard Barrett, [1862]), 6. Among the newspapers that reprinted all or parts of Stowe's letter to Lord Shaftesbury without editorial comment were the London *Morning Post*, 6 Sept. 1861; London *Record*, 30 Aug. 1861; *John Bull*, 7 Sept. 1861; *Liverpool Mail*, 14 Sept. 1861. The following newspapers did not mention Stowe's letter: London *Morning Star*, London *Daily News*, London *Observer*, Manchester *Guardian*, Manchester *Daily Examiner and Times*.

29. *Saturday Review*, 14 Sept. 1861.

30. *Spectator*, 21 Sept. 1861; London *Sun*, 29 Aug. 1861.

31. London *Times*, 13 Sept. 1861. According to the *Spectator*, 10 Jan. 1863: "We could not have believed for a moment, a year ago, that the *Times* and *Saturday Review* would both in the same week devote their ablest pens to an apology, not merely for Slavery itself, but for the Christian character of that institution."

32. Leeds *Mercury*, 10 Sept. 1861.

33. *Economist*, 14 Sept. 1861.

34. *Freeman*, 28 Aug. 1861; *Nonconformist*, 4, 11 Sept. 1861; *Punch*, 14 Sept. 1861. The "bullying, bragging style" of American diplomacy to which the *Freeman* referred would become an issue again. In November 1861 Confederate diplomats en route to Europe aboard the English merchant ship *Trent* were captured and taken to Boston. President Lincoln released the diplomats after the British government protested this violation of their neutrality. The president's action averted an international crisis but brought him criticism at home.

35. *Independent*, 17 Oct. 1861; *Standard*, 24 Aug. 1861.

36. Lydia Maria Child to Sarah Shaw, 11 Aug. 1861, in Meltzer and Holland, *Lydia Maria Child: Selected Letters*, 390–91.

37. HBS to the Duchess of Argyll, 31 July 1862, Harriet Beecher Stowe Collection (no. 6318-c), UVA; *Independent*, 5 Sept. 1861. John Bright's pro-Northern speeches were reprinted by the London *Times*, 6 Dec. 1861, 17 June 1862, etc.

38. *Independent*, 31 July, 7, 28 Aug., 4 Sept. 1862.

39. Ibid., 12 Sept. 1861, reprinted in *Liberator*, 20 Sept. 1861.

40. HBS to James T. Fields, 13 Nov. 1862, James T. Fields Collection, HL.

41. HBS to Calvin Ellis Stowe, 16 Nov. 1862, Katharine S. Day Collection, SDL; HBS to James T. Fields, 19 Nov. 1862, James T. Fields Collection, HL.

42. Neither Stowe nor Lincoln left an account of their meeting. Stowe's daughter Hatty, who was not present at the historic meeting, attributed to Lincoln the line about the "little woman who made this great war." See Fields, *Authors and Friends*, 180–81; Charles Edward Stowe and Lyman Beecher Stowe, *Harriet Beecher Stowe: The Story of Her Life* (Boston: Houghton, Mifflin, 1911), 202–4; Stowe, *Saints, Sinners, and Beechers*, 205–6: Wilson, *Crusader in Crinoline*, 484–85; HBS to the Duchess of Argyll, 31 July 1862, Harriet Beecher Stowe Collection (no. 6318-c), UVA; HBS to Charles Sumner, 13 Dec. 1862, Sumner Collection, HH; HBS to James T. Fields, 27 Nov. 1862, James T. Fields Collection, HL.

43. Stowe's "Reply" was printed as a pamphlet in England by S. Low, Son and by Chiswick Press.

44. HBS, "A Reply to 'The Affectionate and Christian Address of Many Thousands of Women of Great Britain and Ireland to Their Sisters the Women of the United States,'" *Atlantic Monthly* 11 (Jan. 1863): 123–25, 127–30.

45. Ibid., 130.

46. Ibid., 131, 133.

47. John Bright to HBS, 9 March 1863, Stowe Collection, CHS; Archbishop Richard Whately to HBS, Jan. 1863, in Stowe, *Life of Harriet Beecher Stowe*, 391–93. Whately's letter was excerpted in some English newspapers including the London *Sun*, 19 Jan. 1863.

48. London *Morning Post*, 17 Jan. 1863; *John Bull*, 17 Jan. 1863; *Saturday Review*, 10 Jan. 1863; *Athenaeum*, 17 Jan. 1863; London *Sun*, 19 Jan. 1863.

49. *Punch*, 17 Jan. 1863; HBS to Annie Fields, 10 Feb. 1863, James T. Fields Collection, HL.

50. Mary Ellison, *Support for Secession: Lancashire and the American Civil War* (Chicago: Univ. of Chicago Press, 1972), 56–94.

51. Manchester *Guardian*, 9 Jan. 1863; Birmingham *Daily Gazette*, 14 Jan. 1863; Liverpool *Mail*, 17 Jan. 1863.

52. London *Record*, 14 Jan. 1863; London *Daily News*, 9 Jan. 1863; *Spectator*, 10 Jan. 1863.

53. *Freeman*, 14 Jan. 1863; *Nonconformist*, 14 Jan. 1863; London *Dial*, 10 Jan. 1863, reprinted in *Standard*, 31 Jan. 1863, and *Liberator*, 30 Jan. 1863; *Morning Star*, n.d., reprinted in *Standard*, 31 Jan. 1863. The *Morning Star*, John Bright's organ, devoted seven columns of its 8 Jan. 1863 edition to reprinting the text of Stowe's "Reply."

54. "Civis Anglicus," *Voice from the Motherland Answering Mrs. H. Beecher Stowe's Appeal* (London: Trübner and Co., 1863), 8–9, 45.

55. "Rejoinder to Mrs. Stowe's Reply to the Address of the Women of England," *Atlantic Monthly* 11 (April 1863): 527–28. British abolitionist Eliza Wigham published a book entitled *The Anti-slavery Cause in America and Its Martyrs* (London: A. W. Bennett, 1863; rept. Westport, Conn.: Negro Univ. Press, 1970). In her preface, dated July 1863, Wigham quoted Stowe regarding the "tragedy" of slavery and the "frightful reality of scenes daily and hourly acting in the United States." Wigham also warned Britain against "any action, social or political, which may tend to ally her with a Confederacy having for its corner-stone American Slavery."

56. Hernon, "British Sympathies in the American Civil War," 356–67; Ellison, *Support for Secession*, 56–94. See also Peter Stansky, *Gladstone: A Progress in Politics* (Boston: Little, Brown, 1979), 98.

57. Crook, *The North, the South, and the Powers*, 237–38.

58. J. E. B. Munson, "A Book Forming a Foreign Policy: *Uncle Tom* in England," *Civil War Times Illustrated* 21 (Jan. 1983): 40.

59. The "Reply" was mentioned by the New York *Tribune*, 20 Jan. 1863; reviews of it appeared in the *Liberator*, 30 Jan., 13 Feb., 20 March 1863, and the *Standard*, 3, 31 Jan. 1863.

60. Nathaniel Hawthorne to HBS, 4 March 1863, Stowe Collection, CHS; Charles Sumner to HBS, Christmas [1862], Sumner Collection, CHS. Later in 1863 Stowe was very critical of Hawthorne because he dedicated a book to his old friend Franklin Pierce. In a letter to her publisher, Stowe described the former president as an "arch traitor" because of his stance on slavery (HBS to James T. Fields, 9 Nov. 1863, James T. Fields Collection, HL).

61. Stowe, *Saints, Sinners, and Beechers*, 207.

62. FAK, *Record of a Girlhood*, 3 vols. (London: Richard Bentley and Son, 1878), 2:5–8; Constance Wright, *Fanny Kemble and the Lovely Land* (New York: Dodd, Mead, 1972), 17; FAK, *Journal of a Residence on a Georgian Plantation in 1838–1839*, ed. John A. Scott (New York: Alfred A. Knopf, 1961), x–xv (Scott's analysis is hereafter cited as Scott, "Introduction");

Allan Nevins, ed., *The Diary of Phillip Hone, 1828–1851* (New York: Arno Press and the New York *Times,* 1970), 77–78.

Wendell Phillips apparently never forgot his youthful infatuation with Fanny Kemble. In the 1880s, one year before he died, Phillips recalled how he and others "literally sold whatever they could lay their hands on" to obtain tickets (James Brewer Stewart, *Wendell Phillips: Liberty's Hero* [Baton Rouge: Louisiana State Univ. Press, 1986], 37–38).

63. Scott, "Introduction," xviii.

64. Ibid., xviii–xxii; FAK, *Records of a Later Life,* 3 vols. (London: Richard Bentley and Son, 1882), 1:26–27; Wright, *Fanny Kemble,* 150. According to the 1850 United States census, only eleven American families owned more than five hundred slaves (J. G. Randall and David Donald, *The Civil War and Reconstruction,* 2d ed. [Boston: D. C. Heath, 1961], 67).

65. FAK, *Later Life* 1:49; Scott, "Introduction," xxxi–xxxiv; Wright, *Fanny Kemble,* 53–54.

66. FAK, *Journal,* 2 vols. (London: John Murray, 1835), 1:66, 172; Scott, "Introduction," xxxi.

67. Scott, "Introduction," xxxv–xlii.

68. FAK, *Journal, 1838–39,* 11.

69. Ibid., 53; FAK, *Later Life* 2:22.

70. FAK, *Journal, 1838–39,* 67–68.

71. Ibid., 98–100, 194.

72. Ibid., 99, 137–40, 240.

73. Ibid., 153, 292, 317, 343–44.

74. FAK, *Later Life* 2:40–42; Scott, "Introduction," xliii–xliv.

75. FAK, *Later Life* 2:216, 237.

76. Wright, *Fanny Kemble,* 95–97.

77. Lytton Strachey and Roger Fulford, eds., *The Greville Memoirs, 1814–1860,* 8 vols. (London: Macmillan, 1938), 5:61; Wright, *Fanny Kemble,* 111–13, 132–33, 136. See also J. C. Furnas, *Fanny Kemble: Leading Lady of the Nineteenth Century Stage* (New York: Dial Press, 1982), 340–48. The separation and divorce were very painful for Kemble. Writing was apparently therapeutic, for in 1847 she published a book called *A Year of Consolation,* 2 vols. (London: Edward Moxon, 1847).

78. Nevins, *Diary of Phillip Hone,* 862–63; FAK, *Later Life* 3:140, 373, 422.

79. FAK, *Later Life* 1:260.

80. FAK, *Journal, 1838–39,* 369; Wright, *Fanny Kemble,* 148–51; FAK, *Further Records, 1848–1883: A Series of Letters,* 2 vols. (London: Richard Bentley and Son, 1890), 2:247, 279; *Standard,* 11 May 1861.

81. FAK, *Further Records* 2:228–31; Wright, *Fanny Kemble,* 157–58, 162, 182–83; Fanny Kemble Wister, "Sarah Butler Wister's Civil War Diary," *Pennsylvania Magazine of History and Biography* 102 (July 1978): 305. Sarah Wister's son Owen became a novelist and wrote, among other books, *The Virginian.* Fan Butler moved to Georgia where she helped her father run the family plantations. After his death from malaria in 1867, she tried unsuccessfully to make the operation profitable; eventually she married an English

clergyman and moved to England. See Frances Butler Leigh, *Ten Years on a Georgia Plantation since the War* (London: Richard Bentley & Son, 1883). Today Butler Island is a bird sanctuary.

82. FAK, *Later Life* 2:42–43; Wright, *Fanny Kemble*, 161–62; Scott, "Introduction," xlvii–xlix.

83. FAK, *Journal, 1838–39*, title, dedication, and preface pages, appendixes; Margaret Armstrong, *Fanny Kemble: A Passionate Victorian* (New York: Macmillan, 1938), 345; Scott, "Introduction," li. Fanny Kemble destroyed most of her correspondence relating to the Civil War years. No doubt the publicity surrounding the *Journal* was a source of embarrassment for her daughters, who had suffered so much public scandal already. Though Kemble wrote a dozen volumes of autobiography in her lifetime, she had little to say about the *Journal's* publication. Because the files of her London publisher, Longman and Company, were destroyed by German bombing in World War II, there is no extant record of the number of copies sold in Britain.

84. See Elizabeth Fox-Genovese's foreword to *Fanny Kemble: Journal of a Young Actress*, ed. Monica Gough (New York: Columbia Univ. Press, 1990), x–xi. See also John A. Scott, "On the Authenticity of Fanny Kemble's *Journal of a Residence on a Georgian Plantation in 1838–39*," *Journal of Negro History* 46 (Oct. 1961): 240–42.

85. Medora Field Pekerson, *White Columns in Georgia* (New York: Rinehard, 1952), 127; Margaret Davis Cate, *Our Todays and Yesterdays* (Brunswick, Ga.: Blover Books, 1930; rept. Spartanburg, S.C.: Reprint Co., 1972), 146; John Bright, *Speeches of John Bright on the American Question*, ed. Frank Moore (Boston: Little, Brown, 1865); Fanny Kemble Wister, ed., *Fanny, the American Kemble: Her Journal and Unpublished Letters* (Tallahassee, Fla.: South Pass Press, 1972), 209–10.

86. Mildred Lombard, "Contemporary Opinions of Mrs. Kemble's *Journal of a Residence on a Georgian Plantation*," *Georgia Historical Quarterly* 14 (Dec. 1930): 335–36.

87. Dorothie Bobbé, *Fanny Kemble* (New York: Minton, Blach, 1931), 273; *Standard*, 5 March 1864.

88. Charlotte Forten, *The Journal of Charlotte L. Forten*, ed. Ray Allen Billington (New York: W. W. Norton, 1981), 221 ("Sunday, September 6, 1863"). Charlotte Forten was the granddaughter of a wealthy ship-making magnate. In 1878 she married Francis James Grimké, nephew of Sarah and Angelina Grimké, a mulatto son of their brother Henry.

89. *Saturday Review*, 13 June 1863; *British Quarterly Review* 38 (July 1863): 244–45; *Athenaeum*, 6 June 1863; *Spectator*, 30 May 1863.

90. Scott, "Introduction," l–liii; *The Views of Judge Woodward and Bishop Hopkins on Negro Slavery at the South, Illustrated from the Journal of a Residence on a Georgian Plantation by Mrs. Frances Anne Kemble* (Philadelphia: n.p., 1863). The narrative of Pierce Butler's slave sale was also published. Its author was the young New York *Tribune* reporter who covered the auction in 1859: Mortimer Thomson, *What Became of the Slaves on a Georgia Plantation?: A*

Sequel to Mrs. Kemble's Journal (New York: n.p., 1863); the *Standard*, 12 Dec. 1863, reported the Union League as the publisher.

91. ECS, "The Future of the Republic," [after July 1863], Stanton Collection, LC; Lydia Maria Child to Oliver Johnson, [before 22 Aug. 1863], in Meltzer and Holland, *Lydia Maria Child: Selected Letters*, 435.

92. *Independent*, 16, 30 July 1863; *Standard*, 4 July, 19 Sept. 1863; see also *Liberator*, 15 Jan. 1864.

93. *Littell's Living Age* 78 (4 July 1863): 25–27; *North American Review* 97 (Oct. 1867): 582; *Harper's New Monthly Magazine* 27 (Aug. 1863): 416–17; *Atlantic Monthly* 12 (Aug. 1863): 260–63. See also *Frank Leslie's Illustrated Newspaper*, 9 May, 27 June 1863.

94. Wright, *Fanny Kemble*, 171. Nor has Kemble been forgotten since the war. Her *Journal, 1838–39*, has been reprinted several times and has been quoted extensively by historians in studying slavery. See Kenneth M. Stampp, *The Peculiar Institution: Slavery in the Antebellum South* (New York: Alfred A. Knopf, 1956), and Eugene D. Genovese, *Roll, Jordan, Roll: The World the Slaves Made* (New York: Vintage Books, 1974), among others.

95. Crook, *The North, the South, and the Powers*, 170.

96. ECS, "The Future of the Republic," [after July 1863], Stanton Collection, LC.

Chapter 5

1. Ellen Wright to Lucy McKim, 15 Aug. 1862, Garrison Family Papers, SSC. Ellen Wright, daughter of Martha Wright and niece of Lucretia Mott, married William Lloyd Garrison, Jr., on 14 Sept. 1864 (Walter M. Merrill, ed., *The Letters of William Lloyd Garrison*, 6 vols. [Cambridge: Belknap Press, 1979], 5:190). Lucy McKim and Wendell Phillips Garrison were married 6 Dec. 1865. Early in 1862 McKim had accompanied her father to Port Royal, S.C.; Miller McKim was heading a relief effort to help the newly freed slaves there. Lucy, a trained musician, collected slave songs, some of which she published in 1862; *Slave Songs of the United States*, which she coedited in 1867, became the standard book on slave music (James, *Notable American Women* 2:23–24).

2. Gibbons, *Life of Abby Hopper Gibbons* 1:324, 338; McPherson, *Struggle for Equality*, 171.

3. Mary Elizabeth Massey, *Bonnet Brigades* (New York: Alfred A. Knopf, 1966), 271; *Thirteenth Annual Report of the Rochester Ladies Anti-Slavery Society* (Rochester, N.Y.: Democrat Steam Printing House, 1864), Garrison Family Papers, SSC; *Fourteenth Annual Report of the Rochester Ladies Anti-Slavery Society* (Rochester, N.Y.: William Falls Book and Job Printer, 1865), HL; Lydia Maria Child to Lydia B. Child, 11 Feb. 1865, in Meltzer and Holland, *Lydia Maria Child: Selected Letters*, 451.

4. Birney, *The Grimké Sisters*, 285; Lumpkin, *The Emancipation of Angelina Grimké*, 216–17; Lerner, *The Grimké Sisters*, 356; McPherson, *The Struggle for*

Equality, 211–12, 230–31; Hallowell, *James and Lucretia Mott,* 407–8; Shafer, "Sojourner Truth," 38–39.

5. Deborah Pickman Clifford, *Mine Eyes Have Seen the Glory: A Biography of Julia Ward Howe* (Boston: Little, Brown, 1979), 40, 60, 66, 118–19; Laura E. Richards and Maud Howe Elliott, *Julia Ward Howe, 1819–1910,* 2 vols. (Boston: Houghton, Mifflin, 1916), 1:137–44; Louise Tharp Hall, *Three Saints and a Sinner: Julia Ward Howe, Louisa, Annie, and Sam Ward* (Boston: Little, Brown, 1956), 233–35.

6. Julia Ward Howe, "Recollections of the Antislavery Struggle," *Cosmopolitan* 7 (1889): 279–86; Julia Ward Howe, *Reminiscences, 1819–1899* (Boston: Houghton, Mifflin, 1899), 252–53; Clifford, *Mine Eyes Have Seen the Glory,* 113–14, 130–34, 136–37. See also Jeffrey Rossbach, *Ambivalent Conspirators: John Brown, the Secret Six, and a Theory of Slavery Violence* (Philadelphia: Univ. of Pennsylvania Press, 1982).

7. Howe, *Reminiscences,* 271–72.

8. Ibid., 274–75.

9. Julia Ward Howe to Annie Mailliard, 3 April 1865, Howe Papers, HH; Howe, *Reminiscences,* 276; Clifford, *Mine Eyes Have Seen the Glory,* 146–47; Tharp, *Three Saints and a Sinner,* 246.

10. Julia Ward Howe, "Battle Hymn of the Republic," *Atlantic Monthly* 9 (Feb. 1862): 10; Clifford, *Mine Eyes Have Seen the Glory,* 144–47. See also Edward D. Snyder, "The Biblical Background of the Battle Hymn," *New England Quarterly* 24 (June 1951): 231–38.

11. Howe, "Battle Hymn"; *Standard,* 1 Feb. 1862; Richards and Elliott, *Julia Ward Howe* 1:191–92.

12. ECS, "Letter to the People of the North," read at the New York State Anti-Slavery Convention in Albany, printed in *Liberator,* 21 Feb. 1862; SBA, "Speech re: the Civil War and Slaves," 1862?, Anthony Collection, SLR.

13. "Mrs. Lydia Maria Child to the President of the United States," *Liberator,* 29 Aug. 1862; *Standard,* 6 Sept. 1862; SBA, "Fourth of July Address, Framingham, Massachusetts," 1862, Anthony Collection, SLR.

14. T. Harry Williams, *Abraham Lincoln: Selected Speeches, Messages, and Letters* (Chicago: Holt, Rinehart and Winston, 1957), 246–47; SBA, "Speech re: the Civil War and Slaves," 1862?, Anthony Collection, SLR; "Letter from Mrs. Child to a Member of Congress," from the Washington *National Republican,* reprinted in *Standard,* 9 Aug. 1862.

15. *Liberator,* 23 May 1862; James, *Notable American Women* 1:399–401.

16. Cutler wrote detailed accounts of her Illinois lectures to Garrison, who published them in the *Liberator,* 23, 30 May, 13 June, 4 July 1862; Peoria *Transcript,* n.d., reprinted in *Liberator,* 13 June 1862; Jacksonville *Sentinel,* 13 June 1862.

17. *Liberator,* 14 March, 6 June 1862; James, *Notable American Women* 2:2–4.

18. Lydia Maria Child to Anne Loring, 11 Feb. 1862, Child Collection, SLR; *Liberator,* 23 May 1862.

19. Mary Grew to Helen Benson Garrison, 20 June 1862, Maria Weston

Chapman to Anne Greene Chapman, 21 July (?) 1862, Antislavery Collection, BPL; McPherson, *Struggle for Equality*, 111–12.

20. McPherson, *Struggle for Equality*, 96, 111, 117–18.

21. Maria Weston Chapman to Abby Hopper Gibbons, 5 Jan. 1863, in Gibbons, *Life of Abby Hopper Gibbons* 1:384; Philadelphia Female Anti-Slavery Society Minute Books, 8 Jan. 1863, Pennsylvania Abolition Societies Collections, PHS; William Lloyd Garrison to Fanny Garrison, 25 Sept. 1862, in Merrill, *The Letters of William Lloyd Garrison* 5:115; *Liberator*, 26 Sept. 1862; *Standard*, 27 Sept. 1862; *Independent*, 25 Sept. 1862.

22. Amy Post to Isaac Post, 13 Jan. 1863, Post Family Papers, RUL; Lydia Maria Child to Sarah Shaw, 30 Oct. 1862, in Meltzer and Holland, *Lydia Maria Child: Selected Letters*, 419. See also Fanny Garrison to AED, 12 Oct. 1862, Dickinson Collection, LC.

23. Ellen Wright to Laura Stratton, 7 Jan. 1863, Garrison Family Papers, SSC. See also Stephen S. Foster to George Thompson, 16 March 1862, Abigail Kelley Foster Collection, AAS.

24. Henry B. Stanton to SBA in Harper, *Life and Work of Susan B. Anthony* 1:226; Griffith, *In Her Own Right*, 108.

25. ECS, *Eighty Years and More*, 235–36.

26. *Congressional Globe*, 37th Cong., 2d sess., 104, 1678, 2327; London *Times*, 29 April, 10 June 1862.

27. McPherson, *Struggle for Equality*, 123; Hartford *Connecticut Courant*, 4, 11 April 1863; WNLL, *Proceedings of the Meeting of the Loyal Women of the Republic, Held in New York, May 14, 1863* (New York: Phair, 1863), 55–78.

28. Lerner, "The Political Activities of Antislavery Women," 126; Mary P. Ryan, *Women in Public: Between Banners and Ballots, 1825–1880* (New Haven: Yale Univ. Press, 1990), 152.

29. *Liberator*, 17 April, 1 May 1863; *Independent*, 16 April 1863; *Standard*, 2 May 1863; *New York Tribune*, 24 April 1863, Manchester *Guardian*, 9 May 1863; *HWS* 2:51–53. Two scholarly interpretations of republican motherhood are Kerber, *Women of the Republic*, and Mary Beth Norton, *Liberty's Daughters: The Revolutionary Experience of American Women, 1750–1800* (Boston: Little, Brown, 1980).

30. WNLL, *Proceedings*, 4; *HWS* 2:53. The Woman's National Loyal League was occasionally referred to as the National Woman's Loyal League or as the Woman's Loyal National League. To avoid confusion, I have used the title Woman's National Loyal League throughout since that is the title Stanton and Anthony used in the *History of Woman Suffrage*.

31. WNLL, *Proceedings*, 4, 18. For newspaper coverage of the league's founding convention, see *Liberator*, 29 May 1863; *Standard*, 23 May 1863; *New York Tribune*, 16 May 1863. See also *HWS* 2:50–78, 875–99; WNLL, *Proceedings*, 82–86.

32. WNLL, *Proceedings*, 10, 16, 30, 35.

33. Ibid., 7, 10–14.

34. Ibid., 15, 31.

35. Ibid., 20–24.

36. Ibid., 24–25, 27, 30.

37. Ibid., 32–35, 48.

38. Lori D. Ginzberg, "'Moral Suasion Is Moral Balderdash': Women, Politics, and Social Activism in the 1850s," *Journal of American History* 73 (Dec. 1986): 601–22.

39. Maria Weston Chapman to ECS, [2 July 1863], Stanton Collection, LC; Helen Benson Garrison to Sally Holley, 15 Feb. 1863, Helen Benson Garrison Papers, HH; Maria Weston Chapman to Anne Greene Chapman, 21 June 1862 and 1863?, Helen Garrison to Mr. May, 20 Nov. 1862, Antislavery Collection, BPL; Maria Weston Chapman to Elizabeth Chapman Laugel, 17 Jan. [1864], quoted in Jane H. Pease and William H. Pease, *Bound with Them in Chains: A Biographical History of the Antislavery Movement* (Westport, Conn.: Greenwood Press, 1972), 55–56.

Helen Benson Garrison was the wife of William Lloyd Garrison. Never a dynamic personality, she preferred to leave lecturing and confrontation to her husband while she participated in fund-raising activities on behalf of the abolitionists (Lutz, *Crusade for Freedom*, 59–60).

40. *Standard*, 5 Oct. 1861, 4 Jan. 1862.

41. Lydia Maria Child to Samuel May, [after 25 Jan.] 1862, Child Collection, SLR; Child to William Lloyd Garrison, 27 Dec. 1863, Antislavery Collection, BPL; Child to ECS, 24 May 1863, Stanton Collection, LC; Child to ECS, 28 Sept. 1863, Stanton Collection, VCL.

42. Lucretia Mott to Wendell Phillips, 17 April 1866, Mott Collection, HH.

43. Griffith, *In Her Own Right*, 76–77.

44. WNLL, *Proceedings*, 57–68.

45. William Lloyd Garrison to Helen Benson Garrison, 14 May 1863, in Merrill, *The Letters of William Lloyd Garrison* 5:153–54.

46. Lumpkin, *The Emancipation of Angelina Grimké*, 216–19; Hays, *Morning Star*, 177–78; WNLL, *Proceedings*, 75–76. During the war Angelina Weld wrote "A Declaration of War on Slavery," according to her contemporary and biographer "one of the most powerful things she ever wrote"; unfortunately, no copy exists (Birney, *The Grimké Sisters*, 285; see also Lerner, *The Grimké Sisters*, 355).

47. ECS to Elizabeth Smith Miller, 1 Sept. 1863, in Stanton and Blatch, *Elizabeth Cady Stanton* 2:95–96; SBA to Mrs. Drake, 18 Sept. 1863, Anthony Collection, VCL; WNLL form letter in Anthony's hand, 20 June 1863, Anthony Collection, LC. The new league officers were: "Mrs. Elizabeth Cady Stanton, President; Mrs. Col. A. B. Eaton, Mrs. Edward Bates, Mrs. Mary S. Hall, Vice Presidents; Susan B. Anthony, Secretary; S. E. Draper, Corresponding Secretary; Mrs. H. F. Conrad, Treasurer; Miss Mattie Griffith, Miss R. K. Shepherd, Mrs. B. Peters, Mrs. E. S. Lozier, M.D., Mrs. Mary A. Halsted, Mrs. Laura M. Ward, M.D., and Mrs. Mary F. Gilbert, Executive Committee" (WNLL, *Proceedings*, 79).

48. *Liberator*, 2, 16 Oct., 6 Nov. 1863; ECS to Fanny and Frank Garrison, 25 May 1863, Antislavery Collection, BPL.

49. *HWS* 2:50; *Standard,* 20 June 1863; McPherson, *Struggle for Equality,* 125.

50. Harper, *Life and Work of Susan B. Anthony* 1:234.

51. SBA to Samuel May, 21 Sept. 1863, SBA to "My dear Friend," 1 July 1863, SBA to Edmund G. Galin, 14 Dec. 1863, Anthony Collection, VCL; Ellen Wright to Martha Wright, 21 May 1863, Martha Wright to Ellen Wright, 22 June 1863, Garrison Family Papers, SSC.

52. *Standard,* 19 Sept., 10 Oct., 21 Nov. 1863. The contributions totaled about $3,000.

53. SBA to Samuel May, 1 July 1863, Anthony Collection, VCL; Mrs. Draper to Gerrit Smith, 21 Oct. 1863, Gerrit Smith to ECS, 23 Oct. 1863, Stanton Collection, LC; Ralph Volney Harlow, *Gerrit Smith, Philanthropist and Reformer* (New York: Henry Holt, 1939), 436; *Liberator,* 10 July 1863, 1 April 1864; *Standard,* 12 Dec. 1863; *Independent,* 6 Aug. 1863, 7 April 1864.

54. ECS, "What Can Women Do for the War?" New York, [after 1 Jan. 1863], Stanton Collection, LC.

55. Ibid.

56. Lydia Maria Child to Abraham Lincoln, *Liberator,* 29 Aug. 1862; SBA, "Speech re: the Civil War and Slaves," 1862?, SLR; SBA, "Speech during the Wadsworth Campaign," 1862, Anthony Collection, LC.

57. SBA, "Speech during the Wadsworth Campaign," 1862, Anthony Collection, LC; Lydia Maria Child to William Haskins, 30 April 1863, Child Collection, SLR; ECS, "Address before the Woman's Loyal League," 1863, Stanton Collection, LC.

58. ECS, "Address before the Woman's Loyal League," 1863, Stanton Collection, LC; ECS, "To the Women of the Republic," *Standard,* 2 May 1863.

59. SBA, "Speech re: the Civil War and Slaves," 1862?, Anthony Collection, SLR; Sarah Grimké to William Lloyd Garrison, 30 Nov. 1863, Antislavery Collection, BPL.

60. WNLL, *Proceedings,* 51–53. This address was reprinted in *Liberator,* 2 Oct. 1863, and Chicago *Tribune,* 30 May 1863.

61. Lydia Maria Child to William Haskins, 30 April 1863, Child Collection, SLR.

62. SBA, "Fourth of July Oration," Framingham, Mass., 1862, Anthony Collection, SLR; ECS, "To the Women of the Republic," *Standard,* 1 May 1863.

63. ECS, "What Can Women Do for the War," New York, [after 1 Jan. 1863], and "The Future of the Republic," [after July 1863], Stanton Collection, LC.

64. *Standard,* 21 Nov. 1863, 9, 16 Jan., 13 Feb. 1864; New York *World,* 21 Nov. 1863; New York *Times,* 22 Nov. 1863; New York *Tribune,* 19, 21 Nov. 1863; Ellen Wright to William Lloyd Garrison, Jr., 29 April 1863, Garrison Family Papers, SSC; *HWS* 2:45–46.

65. Mott, *A History of American Magazines* 2:536; *Liberator,* 16 Oct. 1863; *Independent,* 7 April 1864.

66. New York *World*, 16 May, 25 July 1863; Springfield, Mass., *Republican*, n.d., reprinted in *Standard*, 2 Jan. 1864, and *Liberator*, 8 Jan. 1864; London *Times*, 15 May 1863. See also New York *Herald*, 15–16 May 1863.

67. New York *Tribune*, 16 May 1863, 13 April 1864; New York *Times*, 24 May 1863; *HWS* 2:50–51. Anthony had written to Horace Greeley, editor of the *Tribune*, seeking his support for the league (see SBA to William Lloyd Garrison, [1863 or 1864?], Anthony Collection, VCL).

68. ECS, "What Can Women Do for the War," New York, [after 1 Jan. 1863], Stanton Collection, LC.

69. *Standard*, 26 Dec. 1863, 9 Jan., 27 Feb. 1864. For a discussion of women's prewar petitioning as a force galvanizing their political participation, see Lerner, "The Political Activities of Antislavery Women," 125.

70. Ibid.

71. Nancy A. Hewitt, *Women's Activism and Social Change: Rochester, New York, 1822–1872* (Ithaca, N.Y.: Cornell Univ. Press, 1984), 196–97.

72. "A New Year and New Hopes," *Godey's Lady's Book* 66 (Jan. 1863): 92; "The Bereaved Mother," *Lady's Friend* 1 (July 1864): 517; "The Dead Soldier's Ring," *Arthur's Home Magazine* 21 (Jan. 1863): 13; "Woman the Soldier's Friend," *Ladies' Repository* 24 (May 1864): 305; "Editorial Chit-Chat: Women and the Sanitary Commission," *Peterson's Magazine* 43 (May 1863): 398–99; Kathleen L. Endres, "The Women's Press in the Civil War: A Portrait of Patriotism, Propaganda, and Prodding," *Civil War History* 30 (March 1984): 31–53. The women's journals that eventually endorsed emancipation were *Arthur's Home Magazine*, the Methodist-Episcopal *Ladies Repository*, the Universalist *Ladies' Repository*, and *Sibyl*; the latter two were edited by women.

73. Gibbons, *Life of Abby Hopper Gibbons* 1:248–49, 2:43–44.

74. ECS to Nancy Smith, 20 July 1863, in Stanton and Blatch, *Elizabeth Cady Stanton* 2:94–95; Harper, *Life and Work of Susan B. Anthony* 1:230–31.

75. *Liberator*, 31 July 1863; New York *World*, 25 July 1863.

76. *HWS* 2:26–39; Hannah Tracy Cutler's autobiography in *Woman's Journal*, 10 Oct. 1896; Charles Sumner to Josephine Griffing, 11 April 1862, Griffing Collection, CUB; *Standard*, 8 Aug. 1863.

77. *Liberator*, 16 Oct. 1863; *Standard*, 28 Nov. 1863; Chicago *Tribune*, 11, 26 Feb. 1864.

78. American Anti-Slavery Society, *Proceedings . . . at Its Third Decade*, 41, 65, 72, 124–30.

79. Ibid., 73–74, 82–84.

80. *Liberator*, 1, 15 Jan. 1864; *Standard*, 16 Jan. 1864.

81. *Liberator*, 11 March 1864; McPherson, *Struggle for Equality*, 126; Margaret Hope Bacon, *I Speak for My Slave Sister: The Life of Abby Kelley Foster* (New York: Thomas Y. Crowell, 1974), 194.

82. WNLL to Senator Charles Sumner, 4 Feb. 1864, Sumner Collection, HH. This letter, expressing the sentiments of Stanton and Anthony, was written by Charlotte Wilbour, corresponding secretary of the league. See also SBA to Sumner, 1 March 1864, ibid.

83. *Congressional Globe*, 38th Cong., 1 sess., 536; *Liberator*, 1 April 1864;

Independent, 18 Feb. 1864; New York *Tribune,* 10 Feb. 1864; New York *Times,* 10 Feb. 1864; New York *Herald,* 10 Feb. 1864; Philadelphia *Daily News,* 10 Feb. 1864; *HWS* 2:78–80; David Donald, *Charles Sumner and the Rights of Man* (New York: Alfred A. Knopf, 1970), 148–49.

84. *Congressional Globe,* 38th Cong., 1 sess., 536; Donald, *Charles Sumner,* 148.

85. *Congressional Globe,* 38th Cong., 1 sess., 536; *HWS* 2:79; *Liberator,* 29 Jan. 1864; Chicago *Tribune,* 15 Feb. 1864. Sumner may have rounded his numbers; the New York *Times,* 10 Feb. 1864, reported the total as 100,698.

86. Hewitt, *Women's Activism and Social Change,* 196–97. The Philadelphia Female Anti-Slavery Minute Books for 10 Sept., 8 Oct., 12 Nov., 10 Dec. 1863 and 11 Feb. 1864 include brief notations regarding WNLL activities (Pennsylvania Abolition Societies Collection, PHS).

87. *Standard,* 26 Dec. 1863; Concord, N.H., *Independent Democrat,* n.d., reprinted in *Standard,* 9 Jan. 1864.

88. *Liberator,* 29 Jan. 1864; Susan B. Anthony, "Woman's Half-Century of Evolution," *North American Review* 175 (Dec. 1902): 807.

Chapter 6

1. Lydia Maria Child to Charles Sumner, 3 Oct. 1862, and Child to Lucy Searle, 11 Oct. 1861, in Meltzer and Holland, *Lydia Maria Child: Selected Letters,* 396, 416–17. See also Fanny Garrison to AED, 12 Oct. 1862, and Lillie Chace to AED, 30 March 1863, Dickinson Collection, LC; Hallowell, *James and Lucretia Mott,* 405–6.

2. William Lloyd Garrison to Oliver Johnson, 17 June 1864, Antislavery Collection, BPL. In his "10 percent plan," Lincoln proposed to readmit any former Confederate state in which 10 percent of the voters had taken a loyalty oath.

3. *Liberator,* 5 Feb. 1864; McPherson, *Struggle for Equality,* 260–61, see also 268–69.

4. Ibid.

5. T. Harry Williams, *Lincoln and the Radicals* (Madison: Univ. of Wisconsin Press, 1941), 311–12; McPherson, *Struggle for Equality,* 262–65.

6. "Undersigned" to AED, 16 Dec. 1863, Dickinson Collection, LC.

7. *Independent,* 21 Jan. 1861; Young, "Anna Elizabeth Dickinson," 155–59.

8. New York *Tribune,* 18 Jan. 1864; *Independent,* 21 Jan. 1864; *Liberator,* 29 Jan. 1864; *Standard,* 30 Jan. 1864; *HWS* 2:47–48.

9. *Standard,* 30 Jan. 1864; Young, "Anna Elizabeth Dickinson," 163.

10. Washington *Daily National Republican,* 18 Jan. 1864, Washington *Daily Morning Chronicle,* 17 Jan. 1864, Dickinson Scrapbooks, LC; *Liberator,* 29 Jan. 1864; Young, "Anna Elizabeth Dickinson," 164–65.

11. Charles Dudley Warner to AED, 19 Jan. 1864, Dickinson Collection, LC; Washington *Daily Morning Chronicle,* n.d., *Missouri Democrat,* 18 Jan. 1864, Cincinnati *Gazette,* 18 Jan. 1864, Chicago *Tribune,* 29 Feb. 1864,

Dickinson Scrapbooks, LC; *Standard*, 23 Jan. 1864; *Frank Leslie's Illustrated Newspaper*, 6 Feb. 1864.

12. Pennsylvania State Senate and House to AED, 28 Jan. 1864, Ohio General Assembly to AED, 8, 25 Feb. 1864, New York Assembly to AED, 9, 10, 15 March 1864, Philadelphia Academy of Music invitation, 18 Jan. 1864, Dickinson Collection, LC; New York *World*, n.d., Dickinson Scrapbooks, LC; Philadelphia *Evening Bulletin*, 28 Jan. 1864; New York *Tribune*, 3 Feb. 1864; Boston *Evening Transcript*, 12 Feb. 1864; *Standard*, 30 Jan., 6 Feb. 1864.

13. S.C. Pomeroy to AED, 2 Nov. 1863, Feb. 1864, Dickinson Collection, LC; Young, "Anna Elizabeth Dickinson," 179–85.

14. Whitelaw Reid to AED, 3 April 1864, Dickinson Collection, LC.

15. New York *Times*, 20 April 1864; New York *Tribune*, 20 April 1864; New York *World*, 20 April 1864.

16. Boston *Daily Courier*, 28 April 1864.

17. Young, "Anna Elizabeth Dickinson and the Civil War," 73.

18. William Lloyd Garrison to Helen Garrison, 13 June 1864, Antislavery Collection, BPL.

19. T. Allston Brown, *History of the American Stage* (New York: Burt Franklin, 1969), 383; George C. D. Odell, *Annals of the New York Stage*, 15 vols. (New York: Columbia Univ. Press, 1931; rept. New York: AMS Press, 1970), 7:230, 279, 495.

20. New York *Times*, 7 April 1864; New York *Herald*, 6 April 1864; New York *World*, 5, 6 April 1864. See also Odell, *Annals of the New York Stage* 7:605. Thomas H. Seymour was the Democratic candidate for governor of Connecticut whom AED helped to defeat. Clement L. Vallandigham, an Ohio congressman, was the nation's most outspoken Copperhead.

21. Undated clipping, Dickinson Scrapbooks, LC; *Liberator*, 15 April 1864.

22. New York *World*, 4 April 1864.

23. New York *Herald*, 21 May 1863; *Frank Leslie's Illustrated Newspaper*, 6 June 1863, 18 March 1865; New York *World*, 4 April 1864; Massey, *Bonnet Brigades*, 158–59; Harold Earl Hammond, ed., *Diary of a Union Lady, 1861–1865* (New York: Funk & Wagnalls, 1962), 349; Dickinson Scrapbooks, LC.

24. *Liberator*, 18 March 1864; Thomas, *The Liberator*, 423–27.

25. SBA to AED, 1 July 1864, Dickinson Collection, LC.

26. ECS to Jessie Benton Frémont, 4 May 1864, in Stanton and Blatch, *Elizabeth Cady Stanton* 2:97–99; William Frank Zornow, *Lincoln and the Party Divided* (Norman: Univ. of Oklahoma Press, 1954), 77; Allan Nevins, *Frémont: Pathmarker of the West* (New York: D. Appleton-Century, 1939), 574.

27. Griffith, *In Her Own Right*, 105–15.

28. ECS to Wendell Phillips, 6 June [1864; misdated 1863], 3 July [1864], Stanton Collection, HH; ECS to Caroline Dall, [1864], Dall Collection, MHS.

29. WNLL broadside, *Anniversary of the Woman's Loyal National League* (n.d.), Dickinson Collection, LC; Jessie Frémont to ECS, 4 May 1864, Stanton Collection, VCL.

30. Caroline Dall to ECS, 1 May 1864, printed in *Liberator,* 6 May 1864, and *Standard,* 7 May 1864.

31. ECS to Caroline Dall, 7 May 1864, printed in *Liberator,* 3 June 1864, and *Standard,* 11 June 1864.

32. Ibid.

33. Ibid.; SBA to Charles Sumner, 14 April 1864, Anthony Collection, HH.

34. Wendell Phillips to ECS, April 1864, Stanton Collection, SLR; ECS to Wendell Phillips, 26 April [1864], Stanton Collection, HH.

35. ECS to William Lloyd Garrison, 22 April 1864, William Lloyd Garrison to Oliver Johnson, 28 April, 5 May 1864, Antislavery Collection, BPL.

36. HWS 2:80–87.

37. Ibid., 2:84, 86–87.

38. Ibid., 2:82–87; WNLL broadside, *Anniversary of the Woman's Loyal National League,* Dickinson Collection, LC; New York *Herald,* 13 May 1864; New York *Tribune,* 12–13 May 1864; see also *Standard,* 28 May 1864; *Independent,* 19 May 1864.

39. HWS 2:85.

40. Wellman, "Women and Radical Reform in Antebellum Upstate New York," 121–24.

41. A large body of manuscript material regarding WNLL activities can be found among the papers of league officers such as Stanton and Anthony. Scattered copies of petition forms and letters on league letterhead written by Anthony and others reached states from Maine to California. See, for example, WNLL form letter in Anthony's hand, 20 June 1863, Maine Historical Society, Portland, and Anthony to R. W. Lyman, 14 Dec. 1863, California Historical Society, San Francisco.

42. HWS 2:86.

43. Ibid., 2:85.

44. William Lloyd Garrison to Helen Garrison, 13 May 1864, Antislavery Collection, BPL; New York *Tribune,* 13 May 1864; McPherson, *Struggle for Equality,* 265; ECS to SBA, 22 Aug. 1864, in Stanton and Blatch, *Elizabeth Cady Stanton* 2:100.

45. Williams, *Lincoln and the Radicals,* 314; McPherson, *Struggle for Equality,* 269–70; SBA to ECS, 12 June 1864, Stanton Collection, LC.

46. Wood Gray, *The Hidden Civil War: The Story of the Copperheads* (New York: Viking Press, 1942), 178; ECS to SBA, 22 Aug. 1864, in Stanton and Blatch, *Elizabeth Cady Stanton* 2:100; ECS to Wendell Phillips, 13 Aug.? [1864], Stanton Collection, HH.

47. *Standard,* 20 Aug. 1864; Gerrit Smith wrote a similar letter to Elizabeth Cady Stanton, 6 June 1864, printed in *Liberator,* 17 June 1864. The Wade-Davis bill would have required a majority of the voters in a Confederate state to take a loyalty oath in order for the state to be readmitted to the Union.

48. *Standard,* 20 Aug. 1864.

49. HBS, "Abraham Lincoln: From *The Watchman and Reflector,*" *Littell's Living Age* 80 (6 Feb. 1864): 282–84; also reprinted, Herbert Mitgang, ed.,

Lincoln As They Saw Him (New York: Holt, Rinehart, 1956), 373–79. Stowe expounded on this theme in a book published after the war entitled *Men of Our Times or Leading Patriots of the Day* (Hartford: Hartford Publishing Co., 1868), 12, 72–73. See also Oates, *With Malice toward None*, 422–23.

50. Maria Weston Chapman to Elizabeth Chapman Laugel, 23 Feb. 1864, Josephine Griffing to William Lloyd Garrison, 24 March 1864, Mary Grew to Samuel May, Jr., 31 March 1864, Elizabeth Buffum Chace to Garrison, 5 May 1864, Antislavery Collection, BPL; Sarah Pugh to Caroline Dall, 13 May 1864, Dall Collection, MHS.

51. Jane Grey Swisshelm, *Half a Century* (Chicago: Jansen, McClurg, 1880; rept. New York: New York Source Book Press, 1970), 236–37; Justin G. Turner and Linda Levitt Turner, *Mary Todd Lincoln: Her Life and Letters* (New York: Alfred A. Knopf, 1972), 145–46; Jean H. Baker, *Mary Todd Lincoln: A Biography* (New York: W. W. Norton, 1987), 231.

52. McPherson, *Struggle for Equality*, 272–75.

53. Lydia Maria Child to John Greenleaf Whittier, 19 June 1864, in John Albree, ed., *Whittier Correspondence from the Oak Knoll Collections, 1830–92* (Salem, Mass.: Essex Book and Print Club, 1911; rept. Ann Arbor, Mich.: Univ. Microfilms, 1976), 147; Child to Friend Whittier, 3 July 1864, Child Collection, LC.

54. Lucy Stone to SBA, 12 July 1864, Blackwell Family Collection, LC; McPherson, *Struggle for Equality*, 270.

55. Zornow, *Lincoln and the Party Divided*, 85; Wendell Phillips to ECS, 22 Aug. 1864, Stanton Collection, LC.

56. Gray, *The Hidden Civil War*, 183–84; Lydia Maria Child to Anna Loring, 11 Oct. 1864, Child Collection, SLR.

57. *Liberator*, 23 Sept. 1864; Lydia Maria Child to Friend Wallcut, 26 Aug. 1864, Antislavery Collection, BPL.

58. McPherson, *Struggle for Equality*, 281.

59. Ibid., 282–85.

60. ECS to SBA, 25 Sept. 1864, in Stanton and Blatch, *Elizabeth Cady Stanton* 2:100–101; Wendell Phillips to ECS, 27 Sept. [1864], Stanton Collection, LC.

61. Young, "Anna Elizabeth Dickinson," 215; William Lloyd Garrison to Helen Garrison, 6 June 1864, Antislavery Collection, BPL; SBA to AED, 1 July 1864, Dickinson Collection, LC. Dickinson's attitude toward Frémont is implied in Theodore Tilton's letter to her, 13 July 1864, ibid.

62. Whitelaw Reid to AED, 6 June 1864, Theodore Tilton to AED, 30 June, 13 July, 3 Sept. 1864, Benjamin Prescott to AED, 13 March, 4 April 1864, Dickinson Collection, LC.

63. Dickinson complained of the "systematic lying of the Administration papers, in regard to my position" in a letter to Illinois journalist Logan U. Reavis, 29 Aug. 1864, Reavis Collection, CHS. Her 3 Sept. letter, "The Duty of the Hour," was first printed in the *Independent*, 8 Sept. 1864, and later in the *Liberator*, 16 Sept. 1864.

64. Ibid.

65. Theodore Tilton to AED, 5 Sept. [1864], Whitelaw Reid to AED, 11 Sept. 1864, Oliver Johnson to AED, 22 Sept. 1864, Lillie Chace to AED, 19 Sept. 1864, Dickinson Collection, LC.

66. Young, "Anna Elizabeth Dickinson," 221–22; Hartford *Connecticut Courant*, 22, 29 Oct. 1864; *Boston Evening Transcript*, 25–26 Oct. 1864.

67. New York *Herald*, 30 Oct. 1864; New York *Tribune*, 31 Oct. 1864; Philadelphia *Daily News*, 3 Nov. 1864; undated clipping, Dickinson Scrapbooks, LC.

68. Ibid.

69. Philadelphia *Daily News*, 3 Nov. 1864; Philadelphia *Press*, 3 Nov. 1864, Dickinson Scrapbooks, LC.

70. Arthur M. Schlesinger and others, eds., *History of American Presidential Elections, 1789–1968*, 4 vols. (New York: McGraw-Hill, 1971), 2:1244.

71. Lydia Maria Child to Eliza Scudder, 1864, in Whittier, *Letters of Lydia Maria Child*, 183–84; Hays, *Morning Star*, 183; Gerrit Smith to ECS, 19 Nov. 1864, Stanton Collection, LC.

72. Stanton and Blatch, *Elizabeth Cady Stanton* 2:355. Stanton discussed her meeting with the president in a letter to Wendell Phillips, 6 May 1863 (Stanton Collection, HH), telling Phillips that she was concerned about women employees in the Treasury Department and alluding to the first Loyal League Convention, which was to take place in a few days. Whether she discussed the WNLL with President Lincoln is not known.

73. Wendell Phillips to ECS, 20 Nov. 1864, Stanton Collection, LC.

74. SBA to Charles Sumner, 1 March 1864, Sumner Collection, HH; WNLL broadside, *Office of the Women's Loyal National League, Room No. 20, Cooper Institute, New York, May 12, 1864*, signed by Anthony, CUL.

75. WNLL broadside, *Office of the Women's Loyal National League*, CUL.

76. *Liberator*, 22 April 1864; *Standard*, 4 June 1864.

77. Donald, *Charles Sumner and the Rights of Man*, 149–52.

78. ECS to Charles Sumner, 23 June [1864] and [June 1864], Sumner Collection, HH; *Congressional Globe*, 38th Cong., 1 sess., 536, 581, 1107, 1247, 1607, 1635, 1840, 1887, 2170, 2621, 2651, 2751, 2777, 2920, 2962, 3001, 3086, 3156, 3188, 3218, 3285, 3412; Harper, *Life and Work of Susan B. Anthony* 1:238; "Mrs. Stanton's Seventieth Birthday," *New Era* 1 (Nov. 1885), Stanton Collection, LC.

When Loyal League members sent the initial 100,000 signatures to Charles Sumner, they expressed the desire that these petitions "be preserved as part of our National History" (WNLL to Sumner, Feb. 1864, Sumner Collection, HH). More than 300,000 signatures have survived; see Records of the U.S. Senate (RG 46), 38th Cong., Petitions Referred to the Select Committee on Slavery and Freedmen, NA.

79. McPherson, *Struggle for Equality*, 126.

80. According to the 1860 census, the white population of men and women over the age of twenty in the states of California, Connecticut, Delaware, Illinois, Indiana, Iowa, Kansas, Maine, Massachusetts, Michigan, Minnesota, New Hampshire, New Jersey, New York, Ohio, Oregon, Pennsylvania, Rhode

Island, Vermont, and Wisconsin was 9,558,531 (U.S. Census Office, 8th Census, 1860, *Population of the United States in 1860; Compiled from the Original Returns* [Washington, D.C.: GPO, 1864], 592–93). Adults over the age of eighteen could sign league petitions.

81. ECS to SBA, 8 Dec. 1864, in Stanton and Blatch, *Elizabeth Cady Stanton* 2:102–3.

82. New York *Tribune*, 31 Oct. 1864; see also New York *Herald*, 30 Oct. 1864.

83. Wright, *Fanny Kemble and the Lovely Land*, 172; 15 April 1865 entry, Julia Ward Howe Diary, HH; Lydia Maria Child to Sarah Shaw, [after 15 April] 1864, in Meltzer and Holland, *Lydia Maria Child: Selected Letters*, 453.

Chapter 7

1. DuBois, *Feminism and Suffrage*, 57–60.

2. Ibid., 77; Flexner, *Century of Struggle*, 145; ECS to Wendell Phillips, 25 May 1865, in Stanton and Blatch, *Elizabeth Cady Stanton* 2:104–5; Stewart, *Wendell Phillips*, 282–83; Griffith, *In Her Own Right*, 125.

3. Susan Anthony's attitude about wartime woman's rights conventions is implied in her letter to Wendell Phillips, 29 April 1861, Anthony Collection, HH. Griffith, *In Her Own Right*, 109–10; ECS to Charles Sumner, 3 April [1866], Stanton Collection, HH.

4. Stanton's letter, dated 2 Jan. 1866, was published in the *Standard* on 6 Jan.

5. ECS, *Eighty Years and More*, 242–43; DuBois, *Feminism and Suffrage*, 60–61.

6. *Standard*, 10 Feb. 1866; "Petition of Elizabeth Cady Stanton and other women," 29 Jan. 1866, Records of the U.S. House of Representatives (RG 233), 39th Cong., Committee on the Judiciary, NA.

According to Susan Anthony, a duplicate petition was presented to the House of Representatives (SBA to Caroline Dall, 30 Jan. 1866, Dall Collection, MHS). In a letter to Wendell Phillips, 28 Jan. 1866, Anthony wrote about the "skill [with which New York congressman James] Brooks managed to get it before the House" (Anthony Collection, HH). See also *Congressional Globe*, 39th Cong., 1 sess., 380; HWS 2:95–97.

7. SBA to Caroline Dall, 30 Jan. 1866, Dall Collection, MHS; DuBois, *Feminism and Suffrage*, 61.

8. ECS, "Speech to Electors of the 8th Congressional District," 10 Oct. 1866, Stanton Collection, LC; Griffith, *In Her Own Right*, 125–26. For newspaper reactions to Stanton's 1866 campaign, see *Standard*, 20 Oct. 1866.

9. Griffith, *In Her Own Right*, 126–27; Flexner, *Century of Struggle*, 146–47.

10. Flexner, *Century of Struggle*, 151–52; Griffith, *In Her Own Right*, 137–38.

11. DuBois, *Feminism and Suffrage*, 73, 190, 193.

12. Ibid., 163–64, 195–96.

13. Flexner, *Century of Struggle*, 149–51; Griffith, *In Her Own Right*, 132–33.

14. Flexner, *Century of Struggle*, 142; DuBois, *Feminism and Suffrage*, 52. See also Hays, *Morning Star*, 175; Barry, *Susan B. Anthony*, 158.

15. *HWS* 1:747.

16. AED to Abby Kelley Foster, 21 Oct. 1862, Abigail Kelley Foster Collection, AAS.

17. *Independent*, 3, 24 March 1864, 12 Jan. 1865; New York *World*, 3, 5 Dec. 1863. See also *Liberator*, 22 April 1864.

18. *HWS* 2:88; Harriot Stanton Blatch, *Challenging Years: The Memoirs of Harriot Stanton Blatch* (New York: G. P. Putnam's Sons, 1940), 17; Yee, "Black Women Abolitionists," 347; Griffith, *In Her Own Right*, 119, 124.

19. Ann Firor Scott, *The Southern Lady: From Pedestal to Politics, 1830–1930* (Chicago: Univ. of Chicago Press, 1974), 182; Aileen Kraditor, *Ideas of the Woman Suffrage Movement* (New York: Columbia Univ. Press, 1965), 165.

20. Ginzberg, "'Moral Suasion Is Moral Balderdash,'" 622.

21. DuBois, *Feminism and Suffrage*, 164, 182–84; ECS to Ann Greene Phillips, 1 May [1866?], Stanton Collection, HH. See also Eric Foner, *Reconstruction: America's Unfinished Revolution, 1863–1877* (New York: Harper and Row, 1988), 255–56.

22. Richards and Elliott, *Julia Ward Howe* 1:360; Clifford, *Mine Eyes Have Seen the Glory*, 170–71, 176.

23. Mary A. Livermore, *The Story of My Life* (Hartford: A. D. Worthington, 1899), 479.

24. *Standard*, 28 Jan. 1865; New York *Tribune*, 31 Oct. 1864; Philadelphia *Press*, 3 Nov. 1864, Dickinson Scrapbooks, LC.

25. Tarbell, "The American Woman," 809; Livermore, *The Story of My Life*, 490.

26. Massey, *Bonnet Brigades*, 353. Dickinson's postwar life was filled with both success and tragedy. Although the press often linked her romantically with Whitelaw Reid, she never married. Not surprisingly, she tried her hand at the theater after the war, both performing and writing plays, but she was successful at neither. She made a brief political comeback in 1888 campaigning on behalf of the Republican National Committee and lambasting Grover Cleveland. Sadly, she became deeply depressed as the public lost interest in her, and after she had locked herself in a room for three days, her sister had her committed to the state hospital for the insane. Infuriated by this action, Dickinson won an early release, but her attempts to win financial redress from her incarcerators were unsuccessful. She died in 1932 (James, *Notable American Women* 1:475–76).

27. Kelley, *Private Woman, Public Stage*, 333; Jeanne Boydston, Mary Kelley, and Anne Margolis, *The Limits of Sisterhood: The Beecher Sisters on Women's Rights and Woman's Sphere* (Chapel Hill: Univ. of North Carolina Press, 1988), 258–79.

28. ECS, *Eighty Years and More*, 240.

29. Ibid., 259–82; Griffith, *In Her Own Right*, 161–62.

30. Harper, *Life and Work of Susan B. Anthony* 2:665; Griffith, *In Her Own Right*, 161–63, 196. Stanton's likeness was used in an advertisement for "Fairy Soap" manufactured by the N. K. Fairbank Company. A reprint of one ad, dated 10 June 1899, may be found in Andrew Sinclair, *The Better Half: The Emancipation of American Woman* (New York: Harper and Row, 1965).

Ellen DuBois has argued that Stanton and Anthony altered their tactics from "agitation" to "organizing," from radicalism to a more temperate appeal, after they ceased to be associated with Garrisonian abolitionism (*Feminism and Suffrage*, 182–84). Stanton's and Anthony's WNLL activities indicate they learned to temper their radicalism long before the split with Garrison. Their printed broadsides and speeches were painstakingly worded and designed to encourage female political participation based on women's traditional role as moral and religious teachers of the family.

Essay on Sources

This essay is not intended as a comprehensive list of books and articles about antislavery and nineteenth-century feminism, nor even a complete discussion of every source consulted in writing this book. Rather, it is a list of the major sources that shaped my thinking about antislavery, women's sphere, and women's political efforts.

Manuscript Collections

The "mammoth petition" of the Woman's National Loyal League is preserved in the records of Senator Charles Sumner's committee. See Records of the U.S. Senate (RG 46), 38th Cong., Petitions Referred to the Select Committee on Slavery and Freedmen. The petitions are folded or rolled into bundles, many bearing their original red tape. Most of the petitions have a cover sheet listing signature totals by state and gender. Until conservation work on these fragile bundles is completed, researchers are not allowed to unroll them.

Very little manuscript material has survived concerning activities of the league in Illinois, the state with the greatest number of signatures. Civil War manuscripts housed at the Chicago Historical Society burned in the Great Fire of 1871. Scattered manuscripts concerning the Loyal League may be found at the California Historical Society and the Maine Historical Society.

The Library of Congress is a major repository for abolition manuscripts, including collections of the papers of Susan Anthony, the Blackwell family, Lydia Maria Child, Anna Dickinson, and Elizabeth Cady Stanton. Most of Stanton's wartime speeches are included in this Library of Congress collection. Anna Dickinson's scrapbooks contain hundreds of newspaper clippings representing her Civil War activities. The Anthony, Dickinson, and Stanton collections are vast and can be obtained on microfilm.

The Boston Public Library has an immense Antislavery Collection, probably the largest single collection in this country, including the papers of Susan Anthony, Elizabeth Buffum Chace, Maria Weston Chapman, Lydia Maria Child, Abby Kelley Foster, Frances D. Gage, Helen Benson and William Lloyd Garrison, Mary Grew, Josephine Griffing, Sarah Grimké, Oliver Johnson, Lucretia Mott, Lydia Mott, Elizabeth Pease Nichol, Sarah Remond, and Anne, Caroline, and Deborah Weston. Of particular note are the collections of William Lloyd Garrison and the Weston sisters, central figures in the Boston Female Anti-Slavery Society. Papers of Boston's sister society, the Philadelphia Female Anti-Slavery Society, are located in the Pennsylvania Abolition Societies Collection of the Historical Society of Pennsylvania.

The Houghton Library at Harvard holds the rich collection of Charles Sumner papers, as well as correspondence of Wendell and Ann Greene Phillips. These three figures all exchanged important and revealing letters with Elizabeth Cady Stanton and Susan B. Anthony regarding the activities of the Woman's National Loyal League. The Houghton also houses the letters and diary of Julia Ward Howe.

The renowned collections of the Schlesinger Library, Radcliffe College, include manuscript letters of Susan Anthony, the Blackwell family, Maria Weston Chapman, Lydia Maria Child, Abby Kelley Foster, William Lloyd Garrison, Julia Ward Howe, Elizabeth Cady Stanton, Lucy Stone, and Harriet Beecher Stowe. The Anthony papers include several of her wartime speeches.

The Sophia Smith Collection, Smith College, houses the magnificent Garrison family collection, including letters of William Lloyd and Helen Benson Garrison, Ellen Wright Garrison, Martha Coffin Wright, and Lucy McKim Garrison. This extended family played a pivotal role in defining both the prewar abolition movement and the Woman's National Loyal League.

The Vassar College Library collections include letters of Susan Anthony and Elizabeth Cady Stanton about the Loyal League and an important speech of Stanton's defining her role during the secession crisis.

Several repositories permitted me to use their important collections of Harriet Beecher Stowe letters: the Stowe-Day Library, Hartford; the Clifton Waller Barrett Library, Manuscripts Division, Special Collections, University of Virginia Library; the Chicago Historical Society; and the Henry E. Huntington Library, San Marino, California. The Huntington Library also has letters of Susan Anthony, Jessie Frémont, Julia Ward Howe, and Fanny Kemble.

The American Antiquarian Society houses the most important collection of Abby Kelley Foster papers, including letters of her husband Stephen Symonds Foster. The Massachusetts Historical Society is the repository for Caroline Healey Dall's letters, including her correspondence with Anna Dickinson, Susan Anthony, and Elizabeth Cady Stanton. Most of Josephine Griffing's manuscripts are now in the Butler Library of Columbia University. The papers of Amy and Isaac Post, who spearheaded the Woman's National Loyal League in Rochester, New York, are owned by the University of Rochester, and the Cornell University Library has a valuable collection of antislavery pamphlets.

Newspapers and Periodicals

Of inestimable value in researching the activities of American abolitionists, male and female, are the antislavery weeklies: the *Liberator*, published in

Boston, and the *National Anti-Slavery Standard*, published in New York. Not only did these papers print regular features about abolitionist activities, but they frequently reprinted articles from regional newspapers both favorable and unfavorable to the abolitionists. Also important is the New York–based *Independent*, edited during the war by Henry Ward Beecher. Harriet Beecher Stowe wrote a column for this newspaper early in the war. The disposition of the Woman's National Loyal League "mammoth petition" can be charted through the pages of the *Congressional Globe*. The rival postwar suffrage journals, *Revolution* and *Woman's Journal*, provide insights into the evolution of feminist divisions after the war.

Among American newspapers, I found material about the activities of women abolitionists in the Boston *Daily Advertiser*, Boston *Daily Courier*, Boston *Evening Transcript*, Chicago *Evening Post*, Chicago *Tribune*, Hartford *Connecticut Courant*, Hartford *Daily Times*, *Illinois State Journal*, New York *Herald*, New York *Times*, New York *Tribune*, New York *World*, Philadelphia *Daily News*, and Philadelphia *Evening Bulletin*.

American journals of opinion were a useful source, including *Atlantic Monthly*, *Harper's New Monthly Magazine*, *Littell's Living Age*, and *North American Review*. The women's periodical press was noteworthy both in its coverage of Anna Dickinson's activities and in its lack of coverage of the Woman's National Loyal League. See *Arthur's Home Magazine*, *Demorest's New York Illustrated News*, *Frank Leslie's Illustrated Newspaper*, *Godey's Lady's Book*, *Lady's Friend*, *Ladies' Repository*, and *Peterson's Magazine*.

Among British newspapers, I examined the following for reviews of the work of Harriet Beecher Stowe and Fanny Kemble: Leeds *Mercury*, London *Daily News*, London *Morning Post*, London *Morning Star and Dial*, London *Observer*, London *Record*, London *Times*, Manchester *Daily Examiner and Times*, and Manchester *Guardian*. I also looked for reviews in these journals of opinion: *Athenaeum*, *British Quarterly Review*, *Economist*, *Freeman*, *Frazer's Magazine*, *Nonconformist*, *Saturday Review*, and *Spectator*.

Published Documents

The best starting place for any topic relating to nineteenth-century feminism is the mammoth *History of Woman Suffrage*, 3 vols. (2d ed., Rochester, N.Y.: Charles Mann, 1889), edited by Elizabeth Cady Stanton, Susan B. Anthony, and Matilda Joslyn Gage. The Woman's National Loyal League published the *Proceedings of the Meeting of the Loyal Women of the Republic Held in New York, May 14, 1863* (New York: Phair, 1863), though sadly it did not publish the proceedings of its anniversary meeting in May 1864. The American Anti-Slavery Society published annual reports ending with the twenty-eighth report for the year ending 1 May 1861. Many volumes have been reprinted, as has the *Proceedings of the American Anti-Slavery Society at Its Third Decade* (New York: American Anti-Slavery Society, 1864; rept. New York: Arno Press and the New York *Times*, 1969).

Published Memoirs and Correspondence

The abolitionists never underestimated the importance of their work. They saved much of their correspondence, and many also published memoirs. Among the most useful are Elizabeth Cady Stanton's *Eighty Years and More: Reminiscences of Elizabeth Cady Stanton* (New York: European Publishing Company, 1898); Susan Anthony's "Woman's Half-Century of Evolution," *North American Review* 175 (Dec. 1902); "Recollections of the Antislavery Struggle," by Julia Ward Howe, *Cosmopolitan* 7 (1889), along with Howe's *Reminiscences, 1819–1899* (Boston: Houghton, Mifflin, 1899). In *Sunny Memories of Foreign Lands*, 2 vols. (Boston: Phillips, Sampson, 1854), Harriet Beecher Stowe recounted her triumphal European tour in 1853. Fanny Kemble published many autobiographical volumes, including *Record of a Girlhood*, 3 vols. (London: Richard Bentley and Son, 1878) and *Record of a Later Life*, 3 vols. (London: Richard Bentley and Son, 1882). Mary Livermore published two popular volumes of autobiography that cast light on her own experiences and those of Anna Dickinson: *My Story of the War: A Woman's Narrative of Four Years Personal Experience* (Hartford: A. D. Worthington, 1890) and *The Story of My Life* (Hartford: A. D. Worthington, 1899). Samuel J. May's *Some Recollections of Our Antislavery Conflict* (Boston: Fields, Osgood, 1869) contains valuable insights about the activities of female abolitionists.

Volumes of correspondence and memoirs edited by children or friends of reformers are of tremendous value to modern researchers, especially since some of the manuscripts are no longer extant. See Theodore Stanton and Harriot Stanton Blatch, *Elizabeth Cady Stanton As Revealed in Her Letters, Diary, and Reminiscences*, 2 vols. (New York: Harper and Brothers, 1922); John Greenleaf Whittier, ed., *Letters of Lydia Maria Child* (Boston: Houghton, Mifflin, 1884); Laura E. Richards and Maud Howe Elliott, *Julia Ward Howe, 1819–1910*, 2 vols. (Boston: Houghton, Mifflin, 1916); Anna Davis Hallowell, ed., *James and Lucretia Mott: Life and Letters* (Boston: Houghton, Mifflin, 1884); Wendell Phillips Garrison, *William Lloyd Garrison, 1805–1879: The Story of His Life Told by His Children*, 4 vols. (New York: Century Company, 1885). A volume of Wendell Phillips's speeches was published during the war. See *Speeches, Lectures, and Letters* (Boston: Walker, Wise, 1864).

Elizabeth Buffum Chace, Sallie Holley, and Abby Hopper Gibbons were important figures of the prewar antislavery movement who left extensive collections of letters. See Lillie Buffum Chace Wyman and Arthur Crawford Wyman, *Elizabeth Buffum Chace, 1806–1899: Her Life and Its Environment*, 2 vols. (Boston: W. B. Clarke, 1914); John White Chadwick, ed., *A Life for Liberty: Anti-Slavery and Other Letters of Sallie Holley* (New York: G. P. Putnam's Sons, 1899; rept. New York: Negro Univ. Press, 1969); Sarah Hopper Emerson, ed., *Life of Abby Hopper Gibbons, Told Chiefly through Her Correspondence*, 2 vols. (New York: G. P. Putnam's Sons, 1897). John Jay Chapman included an article about his famous grandmother Maria Weston Chapman in his *Memories and Milestones* (New York: Moffat, Yard, 1915).

Harriet Beecher Stowe's descendants were very active in publishing volumes about their family's most famous member. See Charles Edward Stowe, *A Life of Harriet Beecher Stowe Compiled from Her Letters and Journals* (Boston: Houghton, Mifflin, 1891); Charles Edward Stowe and Lyman Beecher Stowe, *Harriet Beecher Stowe: The Story of Her Life* (Boston: Houghton, Mifflin, 1911); Lyman Beecher Stowe, *Saints, Sinners, and Beechers* (New York: Blue Ribbon Books, 1937). Also important are the volumes published by Stowe's friend Annie Fields, the wife of her publisher; see *Authors and Friends* (Boston: Houghton, Mifflin, 1898) and Fields, ed., *Life and Letters of Harriet Beecher Stowe* (Boston: Houghton, Mifflin, 1897).

Among modern editions of letters, *Elizabeth Cady Stanton, Susan B. Anthony: Correspondence, Writings, Speeches*, ed. Ellen Carol DuBois (New York: Schocken Books, 1981) is brief but useful. William Lloyd Garrison's massive collected correspondence has been edited by Walter M. Merrill and Louis Ruchames, *The Letters of William Lloyd Garrison*, 6 vols. (Cambridge: Belknap Press, 1979). Lydia Maria Child was among the most prolific abolitionist correspondents. A microfilm edition of her papers was edited by Patricia G. Holland and Milton Meltzer under the title *The Collected Correspondence of Lydia Maria Child, 1817–1880* (Millwood, N.Y.: Kraus Thomson, 1979); a one-volume letterpress edition was published several years later: Milton Meltzer and Patricia G. Holland, eds., *Lydia Maria Child: Selected Letters, 1817–1880* (Amherst: Univ. of Massachusetts Press, 1982).

Secondary Literature

On the prewar antislavery movement, two good general histories are Ronald G. Walters, *The Antislavery Appeal: Abolition after 1830* (Baltimore: Johns Hopkins Univ. Press, 1976), and James Brewer Stewart, *Holy Warriors: The Abolitionists and American Slavery* (New York: Hill and Wang, 1976). Among the more specialized studies, see Aileen S. Kraditor's outstanding analysis of Garrisonian philosophy in *Means and Ends in American Abolitionism: Garrison and His Critics on Strategy and Tactics, 1834–1850* (New York: Pantheon Books, 1969). Lewis Perry and Michael Fellman edited an insightful volume of essays, *Antislavery Reconsidered: New Perspectives on the Abolitionists* (Baton Rouge: Louisiana State Univ. Press, 1979). On black abolitionists, see Benjamin Quarles, *Black Abolitionists* (New York: Oxford Univ. Press, 1969). On abolitionists and the Republican party, see Eric Foner, *Free Soil, Free Labor, Free Men: The Ideology of the Republican Party before the Civil War* (New York: Oxford Univ. Press, 1970).

The best place to start in studying the general history of women's reform is Keith E. Melder, *Beginnings of Sisterhood: The American Woman's Rights Movement, 1800–1850* (New York: Schocken Books, 1977). On female volunteerism, see Lori D. Ginzberg, *Women and the Work of Benevolence: Morality, Politics, and Class in the Nineteenth-Century United States* (New Haven: Yale Univ. Press, 1990). On women's social and political activism, see Mary P.

Ryan, *Women in Public: Between Banners and Ballots, 1825–1880* (Baltimore: Johns Hopkins Univ. Press, 1990). For local studies, see Mary P. Ryan, *Cradle of the Middle Class: The Family in Oneida County, New York, 1790–1865* (New York: Cambridge Univ. Press, 1981), and Nancy A. Hewitt, *Women's Activism and Social Change: Rochester, New York, 1822–1872* (Ithaca, N.Y.: Cornell Univ. Press, 1984). For legal and property reform, see Peggy A. Rabkin, *Fathers to Daughters: The Legal Foundations of Female Emancipation* (Westport, Conn.: Greenwood Press, 1980), and Norma Basch, *In the Eyes of the Law: Women, Marriage, and Property in Nineteenth-Century New York* (Ithaca, N.Y.: Cornell Univ. Press, 1982). On political activism, see Ellen Carol DuBois, *Feminism and Suffrage: The Emergence of an Independent Women's Movement in America, 1848–1869* (Ithaca, N.Y.: Cornell Univ. Press, 1978); Eleanor Flexner, *Century of Struggle: The Woman's Rights Movement in the United States* (New York: Atheneum, 1974); and Lori D. Ginzberg, "'Moral Suasion Is Moral Balderdash'; Women, Politics, and Social Activism in the 1850s," *Journal of American History* 73 (Dec. 1986). On health and sexuality, see William Leach, *True Love and Perfect Union: The Feminist Reform of Sex and Society* (New York: Basic Books, 1980).

General studies of women's prewar abolition work include Alma Lutz, *Crusade for Freedom: Women of the Antislavery Movement* (Boston: Beacon Press, 1968); Blanche Glassman Hersh, *The Slavery of Sex: Feminist-Abolitionists in America* (Urbana: Univ. of Illinois Press, 1978); and Gerda Lerner, "The Political Activities of Antislavery Women," in *The Majority Finds Its Past: Placing Women in History* (New York: Oxford Univ. Press, 1979). For the role of black women, see Shirley Jo-ann Yee, "Black Women Abolitionists: A Study of Gender and Race in the American Antislavery Movement, 1828–1860" (Ph.D. diss., Ohio State Univ., 1989). For local studies, see Hewitt on Rochester and Judith Wellman, "Women and Radical Reform in Antebellum Upstate New York: A Profile of Grassroots Female Abolitionists," in Mabel E. Deutrich and Virginia C. Purdy, eds., *Clio Was a Woman: Studies in the History of American Women* (Washington, D.C.: Howard Univ. Press, 1980). See also Ira V. Brown, "Cradle of Feminism: The Philadelphia Female Anti-Slavery Society, 1830–1840," *Pennsylvania Magazine of History and Biography* 102 (April 1978).

For biographies of important feminist abolitionists, see Elisabeth Griffith, *In Her Own Right: The Life of Elizabeth Cady Stanton* (New York: Oxford Univ. Press, 1984). A recent biography of Susan B. Anthony is Kathleen Barry, *Susan B. Anthony: A Biography of a Singular Feminist* (New York: New York Univ. Press, 1988). Also useful is the two-volume biography written by Anthony's friend Ida H. Harper, *Life and Work of Susan B. Anthony* (Indianapolis: Bowen-Merrill, 1899). There is only one biography of Anna Dickinson, Giraud Chester, *Embattled Maiden: The Life of Anna Dickinson* (New York: G. P. Putnam's Sons, 1951). Because Chester's book lacks formal documentation, the best source for Dickinson's career remains James Harvey Young's dissertation, "Anna Elizabeth Dickinson and the Civil War" (Ph.D. diss., Univ. of Illinois at Urbana-Champaign, 1941), and his article, "Anna Elizabeth Dickinson and the Civil War: For and Against Lincoln," *Mississippi Valley Historical Review* 31 (June 1944).

For the Grimké sisters, see Gerda Lerner, *The Grimké Sisters from South Carolina: Pioneers for Woman's Rights and Abolition* (New York: Schocken Books, 1975) and Katharine Du Pre Lumpkin, *The Emancipation of Angelina Grimké* (Chapel Hill: Univ. of North Carolina Press, 1974). On Lydia Maria Child, see Helen G. Baer, *The Heart Is Like Heaven: The Life of Lydia Maria Child* (Philadelphia: Univ. of Pennsylvania Press, 1964). Jean Fagan Yellin's recent book *Women & Sisters: The Antislavery Feminists in American Culture* (New Haven: Yale Univ. Press, 1989) includes an analysis of Angelina Grimké, Lydia Maria Child, Sojourner Truth, and Harriet Jacobs. See also Yellin's introduction to Harriet A. Jacobs's *Incidents in the Life of a Slave Girl Written by Herself* (Cambridge: Harvard Univ. Press, 1987). Elizabeth Fox-Genovese analyzed Jacobs's book in the epilogue of *Within the Plantation Household: Black and White Women of the Old South* (Chapel Hill: Univ. of North Carolina Press, 1988).

The best biography of Julia Ward Howe is Deborah Pickman Clifford, *Mine Eyes Have Seen the Glory: A Biography of Julia Ward Howe* (Boston: Little, Brown, 1979). On Lucretia Mott, see Margaret Hope Bacon, *Valiant Friend: The Life of Lucretia Mott* (New York: Walker, 1980). Maria Weston Chapman has never been the subject of biographical study, although Catherine Clinton's essay "Maria Weston Chapman, 1806–1885" offers valuable insights; see G. J. Barker-Benfield and Catherine Clinton, *Portraits of American Women from Settlement to the Present* (New York: St. Martin's Press, 1991). There is a chapter on Chapman in Jane H. Pease and William H. Pease, *Bound with Them in Chains: A Biographical History of the Antislavery Movement* (Westport, Conn.: Greenwood Press, 1972).

The best source about Fanny Kemble is John A. Scott's introduction to her *Journal of a Residence on a Georgian Plantation in 1838–1839* (New York: Alfred A. Knopf, 1961). Also useful is Constance Wright's biography *Fanny Kemble and the Lovely Land* (New York: Dodd, Mead, 1972). Elizabeth Fox-Genovese's introduction to Kemble's 1835 journal, *Fanny Kemble: Journal of a Young Actress*, ed. Monica Gough (New York: Columbia Univ. Press, 1990), includes important comments about the polemical nature of Kemble's writing.

On Wendell and Ann Phillips, see Irving H. Bartlett, *Wendell and Ann Phillips: The Community of Reform, 1840–1880* (New York: W. W. Norton, 1979). Joel Bernard's article "Authority, Autonomy, and Radical Commitment: Stephen and Abby Kelley Foster," *Proceedings of the American Antiquarian Society* 90 (1980), is useful. Lucy Stone's biographer is Elinor Rice Hays, *Morning Star: A Biography of Lucy Stone, 1818–1893* (New York: Harcourt, Brace, and World, 1961). An excellent biography of Charles Sumner is David Donald's *Charles Sumner and the Rights of Man* (New York: Alfred A. Knopf, 1970). On Garrison, see John L. Thomas, *The Liberator: William Lloyd Garrison* (Boston: Little, Brown, 1963).

There are the hundreds of books on Harriet Beecher Stowe. Forrest Wilson's Pulitzer Prize–winning 1941 biography is still useful, *Crusader in*

Crinoline: The Life of Harriet Beecher Stowe (New York: J. B. Lippincott, 1941).
Two modern interpretations of her life and work are Mary Kelley, *Private
Woman, Public Stage: Literary Domesticity in Nineteenth-Century America* (New
York: Oxford Univ. Press, 1984), and Jeanne Boydston, Mary Kelley, and
Anne Margolis, *The Limits of Sisterhood: The Beecher Sisters on Women's Rights
and Woman's Sphere* (Chapel Hill: Univ. of North Carolina Press, 1988).
Recent interpretations of *Uncle Tom's Cabin* include Thomas F. Gossett's
Uncle Tom's Cabin and American Culture (Dallas: Southern Methodist Univ.
Press, 1985) and Eric J. Sundquist, ed., *New Essays on Uncle Tom's Cabin*
(New York: Cambridge Univ. Press, 1986). See also Jane Tompkins, *Sensa-
tional Designs: The Cultural Work of American Fiction, 1790–1860* (New York:
Oxford Univ. Press, 1985).

The role of Northern women in the Civil War has not been thoroughly
researched. Mary Elizabeth Massey's *Bonnet Brigades* (New York: Alfred A.
Knopf, 1966) covers both Northern and Southern women and provides valu-
able background about wage-earning women, deprivation, and family life.
Catherine Clinton has a chapter on the Civil War in *The Other Civil War:
American Women in the Nineteenth Century* (New York: Hill and Wang, 1984).
For a general source on the Northern home front during the war, see Phillip
Shaw Paludan, *"A People's Contest": The Union and Civil War, 1861–1865*
(New York: Harper and Row, 1988). A good discussion of women's periodicals
can be found in Kathleen L. Endres's "The Women's Press in the Civil War: A
Portrait of Patriotism, Propaganda and Prodding," *Civil War History* 30 (March
1984).

On women's benevolent activities, L. P. Brockett and Mary C. Vaughan,
Woman's Work in the Civil War: A Record of Heroism, Patriotism, and Patience
(Chicago: Zeigler, McCurdy, 1867) provides valuable insights about soldier's
aid societies. There is a chapter on Civil War volunteerism in Ginzberg,
Women and the Work of Benevolence. On nurses, see Ann Douglas Wood, "The
War within a War: Women Nurses in the Union Army," *Civil War History* 18
(Sept. 1972); William Quentin Maxwell, *Lincoln's Fifth Wheel: A Political
History of the United States Sanitary Commission* (New York: Longmans, Green,
1956); Agatha Young, *The Women and the Crisis: Women of the North in the Civil
War* (New York: McDowell, Obolensky, 1959); Sylvia G. L. Dannett, ed.,
Noble Women of the North (New York: Thomas Yoseloff, 1959); Marjorie Latta
Greenbie, *Lincoln's Daughters of Mercy* (New York: G. P. Putnam's Sons,
1944); Nina Brown Baker, *Cyclone in Calico: Mary Ann Bickerdyke* (Boston:
Little, Brown, 1952); and Ishbel Ross, *Angel of the Battlefield: Clara Barton*
(New York: Harper and Row, 1956).

The best source on women's wartime activism is the monumental *History of
Woman Suffrage*, volume 2. James M. McPherson's *The Struggle for Equality:
Abolitionists and the Negro in the Civil War and Reconstruction* (Princeton, N.J.:
Princeton Univ. Press, 1972) is an excellent source for the activities of both
male and female abolitionists. See also Ida M. Tarbell, "The American
Woman: How She Met the Experience of War," *American Magazine* 69 (April
1910).

Index